The Lost Works of William Carlos Williams

The Volumes of Collected Poetry as Lyrical Sequences

Robert J. Cirasa

Madison • Teaneck
Fairleigh Dickinson University Press
London: Associated University Presses

Associated University Presses
440 Forsgate Drive
Cranbury, NJ 08512

Associated University Presses
25 Sicilian Avenue
London WC1A 2QH, England

Associated University Presses
P.O. Box 338, Port Credit
Mississauga, Ontario
Canada L5G 4L8

The paper used in this publication meets the requirements
of the American National Standard for Permanence of Paper
for Printed Library Materials Z39.48-1984.

Library of Congress Cataloging-in-Publication Data

Cirasa, Robert J., 1950–
    The lost works of William Carlos Williams : the volumes of
collected poetry as lyrical sequences / Robert J. Cirasa.
    p. cm.
    Includes bibliographical references and index.
    ISBN 0-8386-3576-8 (alk. paper)
    1. Williams, William Carlos, 1883–1963 Criticism and
interpretation. 2. Cycles (Literature) I. Williams, William
Carlos, 1883–1963. II. Title.
PS3545.I544Z5827   1995
811'.52—dc20   94-41572
                                                CIP

PRINTED IN THE UNITED STATES OF AMERICA

The Lost Works of
William Carlos Williams

To Nancy High Cirasa

Contents

Preface

"The main effort, for now many years, has been a critical effort," wrote Matthew Arnold in his 1864 essay "The Function of Criticism at the Present Time" (9). Had he substituted "theoretical" for "critical," he might easily have been prophesying the state of affairs in literary studies more than a century later here in our own moment, when even "practical" critics (at least of the scholarly sort) routinely spend more time sorting through recondite semantic and epistemological issues than in observing anything directly about their purported literary subjects. The impetus for such a pervasive theoretical orientation, of course, has been the impact of the various poststructuralist reading strategies (deconstruction, reader-response, new historicism, and others, including much new Marxism) that have been conceived or inspired by a host of philosophers, psychotherapists, anthropologists, ideologues, and savants of all sorts (except literary, for the most part). Infatuated with the abstract *principles* of making linguistic meaning and with the deconstructive or at least subversive power of their own operations, these strategies collectively tend to supplant the general human and aesthetic synergy of a literary work with either the narrow and partisan social arguments—or "discourse"—of gender, race, sexuality, and class or with the solipsistic "pleasure" of profoundly entropic metaphysical exegesis. Thus it is that texts have become pretexts and criticism has become theory.[1]

Much of this has always struck me as a belated and neurotic response to the epistemological revolutions of relativity and quantum physics (especially the uncertainty principle) achieved during the earlier part of this century. Certainly, the notion that the observer (or reader) of any reality (or literary work) participates in or "creates" that reality with the act of observation is rather old news among scientists. Yet they have not resigned themselves to cognitive solipsism or ideological partisanship as a substitute for universally valid (however impermanent or circumstantial) descriptions of reality. Collectively, they have fashioned pragmatic and common understandings of space, time, matter, energy, and of information itself—all of it shown to have fixable if not absolute values

9

according to the careful constraints of any well designed act of observation, be it an empirical experiment or a theoretical calculation. Their reality, in short, works in predictable and reproducible ways, even as it denies the very possibility of perfect knowledge.

Of course, science does not pretend that this predictability and reproducibility are entirely aspects of reality's external objectivity. As the perpetually revisionist record of scientific inquiry demonstrates, these features of scientific knowledge are artifacts of the powers of observation unique to any human moment. Certain intellectual developments (of all sorts: theoretical, technological, social, imaginative, etc.) and even certain simply serendipitous events were necessary, for instance, before atomic radiation could "become" a human reality. And obviously, such collective phenomenology involves the elusive and complicated but (at least for science) always synthesizing dynamics of human community itself—that same entity the students of "discourse" take as the basis for their more factious and political interests. My purpose, however, is not to analyze the unique epistemological dynamics of scientific meaning, but to recognize its extraordinarily robust epistemological spirit, avoiding as it does the paralysis or relativism into which some of its own precepts could so easily tempt it and into which literary scholarship has so woefully fallen.

To be less abstract about the matter—if we are to live and to live as a human community, however narrowly or broadly defined, we in the study of literature (students of theory itself may follow what path they please) need to acquire the same robust spirit—to cease brooding nihilistically over all the paradoxical mechanisms of meaning and to resume making and exchanging actual, living meaning. In large part, this means subsuming our obsessively theoretical concerns within the—yes—within the implicitly "biased" responses to literary works that mark the best practical criticism, for it is in those responses that we creatively possess—and then re-possess again and again—literary works and the human experiences they (along with us) shape or define. We must, in other words, dare to behave as truly living humanity—people, alive at a particular time, in a particular place, and with a particular identity—reciprocally bringing to bear upon literature all the peculiar accidents of our existence and shaping something equally accidental and unique for sharing with one another.

Obviously, I mean nothing really very new or extraordinary in all this (although Stanley Fish and Hans Robert Jauss have relatively recently fashioned these rather self-evident notions of communal meaning and tradition into, of course, theories of "interpretive communities" and "reception-history"). And I am anxious to avoid the common appropriation practiced by so many theorists, who, for example, in deconstructing a piece of literature will seize upon every instance of ambiguity or irony as proof of entropy itself and of the sheer impossibility of meaning—as though irony and ambiguity were not compatible with systems of coherence and had not in fact been perfectly functional concepts in all the coherence-based literary approaches of the millennia before our own century! I pretend no such neonomianism. In fact I am not arguing for some competing theory at all. I am arguing for a course of literary action (really a resumption of literary action) in which students—lovers—of the *aesthetic* construct we define as literature set metaphysics aside and devote themselves to relishing and celebrating the determinate beauties they perceive in the works they read, however illusory theorists consider those beauties to be.

The most obvious paradigm for this course of action is the perennial production of Shakespeare. For the past four hundred years, directors, performers, and audiences from one generation to the next and across populations of all sorts have found beauties worth celebrating in Shakespeare's plays, even as they have routinely reconceived them in the likeness of their own historical moment—their unique emotional, social, political, etc. circumstances. Obviously, such is the nature of dramatic literature: whenever a play is performed, even the most trivial of production details can occasion a reinterpretation, and directors have always understood their very purpose as the creative—and again, perpetual—renewal and repossession of the play book. Yet the intrinsic aesthetic properties of the Shakespearean text, defined as they are by the moments of their own creation as well as by subsequent interpretations, have always exerted their own force upon directorial inventions, and it is testimony to the superiority of Shakespearean literature that from age to age it still resembles its original self (however absurd it sounds to say such a thing) even as it comes to resemble ever different and greater ranges of human sensibility and experience.

Notwithstanding the special advantage of dramatic literature in this regard, I believe that all literature by definition demands that we reciprocally and perpetually recognize its aesthetic facts. And beyond dizzying ourselves with the proliferative possibilities of literary meaning in general, we must *perform* or creatively *reconstruct* (rather than deconstruct) particular works of literature, one at a time. This is what I, at least, have set out to do in the following study, and I have done so chiefly in response not to the theoretical concerns I have outlined above nor to the recent anti-theory polemic of the so-called new pragmatism, but rather to the pioneering and exemplary work of the great critic and poet, M. L. Rosenthal.

Recognizing the lyrical dynamics of literature as the most complete aesthetic expression of its living human meaning and affirming the accomplishments of individual works of literature as the necessary origin and end of all worthwhile thinking about theory, Rosenthal has over the last forty years founded an entirely new critical approach (rather than theory)—what he calls "evaluative" criticism but what I might easily call "reconstructive" or "performance" criticism: criticism so sensitive to its subject's living literary character (that is, to all the aesthetic and communally defined language values that inhere in the literary product at a given human moment) and so powerfully eloquent in its own expressive possession of them that it truly becomes nothing less than a creative performance of the work. This, I believe, is the kind of critical empowerment and salutary relationship with literature we must seek as critics. And it requires a very robust spirit indeed in these very theoretical times. I hope more will take it on.

R.J.C.

September 1994

Acknowledgments

Above all, I thank M. L. Rosenthal, whose greater insight and constant guidance have been indispensable. I am also grateful to Peggy Fox of New Directions for her generous and gracious assistance and to James Laughlin for access to New Directions archives and for permission to quote from his unpublished letter to me (Copyright © 1994 by James Laughlin). Acknowledgment is also made to New Directions Publishing Corporation and to Carcanet Press Limited for permission to quote from the following copyrighted works of William Carlos Williams: *The Autobiography of William Carlos Williams* (Copyright 1948, 1951 by William Carlos Williams); *Collected Poems: Volume I, 1909–1939* (Copyright 1938 by New Directions Publishing Corporation, Copyright 1951 by Wiliam Carlos Williams, Copyright © 1982, 1986 by William Eric Williams and Paul H. Williams); *Collected Poems: Volume II, 1939–1962* (Copyright 1944, 1953, Copyright © 1962, by William Carlos Williams, Copyright © 1988 by William Eric Williams and Paul H. Williams); *I Wanted To Write a Poem* (Copyright © 1958 by William Carlos Williams); *Imaginations* (Copyright © 1970 by Florence H. Williams); *Selected Essays* (Copyright 1954 by William Carlos Williams); *Selected Letters of William Carlos Williams (Copyright 1957 by William Carlos Williams); previously unpublished material by William Carlos Williams and Florence H. Williams (Copyright © 1968, 1981, 1989, 1994 by William Eric Williams and Paul H. Williams), used by permission of New Directions Publishing Corporation, agents. Acknowledgment is given as well to New Directions Publishing Corporation and Faber & Faber Limited for permission to quote from the following works by Ezra Pound: Literary Essays* (Copyright 1918, 1920, 1935 by Ezra Pound); and his poetry and prose contributions to periodicals (Copyright © 1991 by the Trustees of the Ezra Pound Literary Property Trust). And acknowledgments are made to W. W. Norton & Company, Incorporated, for permission to quote from *William Carlos Williams and James Laughlin: Selected Letters,* edited by Hugh Witemeyer (Copyright © 1989 James Laughlin, Copyright © 1989 Estate of William Carlos Williams); to Oxford University

Press for permission to quote from *The Modern Poetic Sequence* by M. L. Rosenthal and Sally Gall (Copyright © 1983 Oxford University Press, Incorporated); to Michael Burke for permission to quote "Heaven's First Law" by Kenneth Burke; to Janet Winters for permission to quote from "Poetry of Feeling" by Yvor Winters; to Viking Penguin, a division of Penguin Books USA Incorporated, for permission to quote from "Things Oters Never Notice" by Marianne Moore (Copyright 1928, 1956 Marianne Moore) from *The Complete Prose of Marianne Moore* by Patricia C. Willis, editor; to Adam Yarmolinsky for permission to quote from Babette Deutsch's essay "Heirs of the Imagists"; to Putnam Publishing Group for permission to quote from *Our Singing Strength* by Alfred Kreymborg (Copyright 1929 Coward-McCann).

I also wish to thank a number of people and libraries helpful to my research for this work: A. Walton Litz and Christopher MacGowan; Robert Bertholf of the Poetry and Rare Books Collection at SUNY Buffalo; the Beinecke Rare Book Room and Manuscript Library, Yale University; the Houghton Library, Harvard University; Cathy Henderson of the Harry Ransom Humanities Research Center, the University of Texas at Austin; Bett Miller of the Mandeville Department of Special Collections, Central University Library, University of California, San Diego; and Robert Hull of the Alderman Library, University of Virginia.

The Lost Works of
William Carlos Williams

Introduction
"To Gain 'Profundity'"

During the nearly sixty years of his life as a poet, William Carlos Williams stopped to put volumes of collected poetry together three times: in 1934 he published the partially comprehensive *Collected Poems 1921–1931;* in 1938, *The Complete Collected Poems 1906–1938;* and in the early fifties he issued the two companion volumes entitled *The Collected Later Poems* (1950) and *The Collected Earlier Poems* (1951). Outside of *Paterson,* it is these four collections that most embody Williams's ambition to go beyond the limits of his shorter lyrics. In each of them he gathered work from over broad periods of his career—work arising from sometimes widely different lyrical impulses and stages of poetic development—and attempted to assemble it all into a single coherent work of major proportions. For the most part, the basic elements—that is, the constituent sections—of these large-scale structures were the tacit lyrical sequences that had constituted Williams's individual volumes of verse. But he also added new groupings and made changes to the old as he sought to link them all into a *series* of lyrical sequences that would give something like a unified lyrical definition to the great bulk of his poetic record.

The obvious model for this sort of undertaking was, of course, Pound's *Cantos,* and no doubt Williams took at least some inspiration from his old friend's steadily accumulating magnum opus. But he also had his own more instinctive motivation for recasting his poetry on a grand and unified scale. Reflecting upon the genesis of *Paterson,* for instance, Williams would say that "the longer I lived in my place, among the details of my life, [the more] I realized that these isolated observations and experiences needed pulling together to gain 'profundity'" (*Autobiography* 391). And indeed, Williams probably felt the need for that "profundity" more than do most poets, for up until the first books of *Paterson* appeared in 1947, when he was sixty-three and had been publishing books for thirty-seven years, he had been constantly criticized for not using his admirable imagistic skills to help him create work of greater depth and scope.

Even an intelligent critic and sympathetic friend like Kenneth Burke could in the Imagist days of 1922 compliment the Williams of *Sour Grapes* as merely "the master of the glimpse . . . the minute fixating of a mood, an horizon, a contrast" (197). As good as they were, Burke believed such miniature effects to be so ultimately detached from any larger governing context as to render the very principle of organization meaningless: "to add organization to his poetry would have no more meaning than to insist that his lines begin in alphabetical rotation" (197). By the time *Collected Poems 1921–1931* appeared in 1934, Babette Deutsch could in her review invoke what by then had become an inveterate critical formula: "The reliance on the eye, the singling out of the brief moment, however intense, is a limitation upon his work. There is keenness here, there is energy, there is not the exaltation that comes of a myth-making power" (16). And from, at the time, an otherwise friendly Yvor Winters, *The Complete Collected Poems of William Carlos Williams 1906–1938* would provoke: "it offers merely sharp impressions of objects observed, either in isolation, or in accidental sequence, or forced by a purely rhetorical violence, as in 'Romance Moderne,' into a formal and emotional unit" (105).

Not all of Williams's critics were so censorious of him in this matter, however. In assessing his prose works of the twenties, Ezra Pound could freely concede that

> very well, he does not "conclude"; his work has been "often formless," "incoherent," opaque, obscure, obfuscated, confused, truncated, etc.
>
> I am not going to say: "form" is a non-literary component shoved onto literature by Aristotle or by some non-literatus who told Aristotle about it. . . . But it can do us no harm to stop an hour or so and consider the number of very important chunks of world-literature in which form, major form, is remarkable mainly for its absence. . . .
>
> The component of these great works and *the* indispensable component is texture; which Dr. Williams indubitably has in the best, and in increasingly frequent, passages of his writing. (*Dr Williams' Position* 400–401)

Pound was not entirely dismissing a structural evaluation of Williams's work, but he was trying to place it in proper perspective to the affective substance—the "texture"—of that work and of Williams's agenda in general. "Williams," Pound went on to say, "has written: 'All I do is to try to understand something in its natural colours and shapes.' There cd. be no better effort underlying any literary process" (396). The real problem, Pound insisted, was that the fresh examination of subject which so distinguished Williams at his best entailed a perhaps too radical jolt to intellectual complacency: "We are still so generally obsessed by monism and monotheistical backwash, and ideas of orthodoxy that we . . . can hardly observe a dissociation of ideas without thinking a censure is somehow therein implied" (399). Pound had done something more than complain, and Williams was deeply appreciative. Soon after "Dr Williams' Position" appeared, he wrote Pound: "Nothing will ever be said of better understanding regarding my work. . . . Without question you have hit most of the trends that I am following" (*Selected Letters* 108).

In fact, Pound had quite accurately restated the positions on poetic structure that Williams himself had declared ten years earlier in his 1918 "Prologue" to *Kora in Hell. Kora* was a flagrant assault upon traditional principles of coherent major form, and Williams anticipated in the "Prologue" that the book would draw the kind of criticism he had once received from another eminent (if less supportive) friend, Wallace Stevens:

> Stevens' letter applies really to my book of poems, *Al Que Quiere* . . . but the criticism he makes of that holds good for each of the improvisations if not for the oeuvre as a whole. . . . "What bothers me most about the poems themselves is their casual character. . . . Personally I have a distaste for miscellany. It is one of the reasons why I do not bother about a book myself." (*Imaginations* 14–15)

Fortunately, Williams was able to defuse Stevens's complaint by prefacing it with his own analysis of aesthetic coherence:

> The imagination goes from one thing to another. Given many things of nearly totally divergent natures, but possessing one-thousandth part of a quality in common, provided that be new, distinguished, these things belong in an imaginative category and not in a gross natural array. To me this is the gist of the whole matter. It is easy to fall under the spell of a certain mode, especially if it be remote of origin, leaving thus certain of its members essential to a reconstruction of its significance permanently lost in an impenetrable mist of time. But the thing that stands eternally in the way of really good writing is always one: the virtual impossibility of lifting to the imagination those things which lie under the direct scrutiny of the senses, close to the nose. . . . Thus the so-called natural or scientific array becomes fixed, the walking devil of modern life. He who even nicks the solidity of this apparition does a piece of work superior to that of Hercules when he cleaned the Augean stables. (14)

However clear his mission was to him, it took Williams nearly thirty years before he would create in *Paterson* a work which would manifestly realize his aspirations. Yet those thirty years were surely more than a simple postponement of those ambitions. His eleven-year sabbatical (1923–34) from publishing volumes of verse in favor of avant-garde fiction and what Kenneth Burke called "subjective history" was, for instance, very much a search in these superficially more continuous prose forms for a new "array" to supplant the "natural or scientific array" which had so insidiously obfuscated the senses of modern man. And a few contemporaries did in fact recognize the structural initiatives that the prose experiments represented. Waldo Frank, to Williams's delight, had "recognized the technical difficulty [in making the Columbus chapter of *In the American Grain* end with the discovery of America] and wrote me a letter praising the ending" (*I Wanted to Write a Poem* 42); he was "the first who has valued the Columbus chapter highly or in fact paid any attention to the design in the book at all" (quoted by Paul Mariani in *A New World Naked* 799). And Pound too would note that "if one read it often enough the element of form emerges in *The Great American Novel,* not probably governing the whole, but in the shaping of at least some of the chapters" ("Dr Williams' Position" 403).

With *Homage to Sextus Propertius,* the *Hugh Selwyn Mauberley* sequences, and even some early Cantos already behind him, Pound was naturally alert to struggles with major form. But most critics resorted to the standard complaint about Williams's "scope." Unhappy with his rigorous use of the "particulars" of historical documents in *In the American Grain,* Gorham Munson admonished him that "not by descent into actualized and fragmentary resources but by ascent into our unrealized potentials does greatness in literature come." He then urged him to take heed if he ever wished his work to ascend "from the category of minor to the category of major in aim, scope and power" (135). Ironically, it was criticism of exactly this sort which had prompted the ambitious prose experiment in *Spring and All*; the interspersed theoretical prose in that volume provided nothing less than a prepared critical apparatus for its own evaluation. But again, the tactic had provoked only more negative criticism. His old "friend" Alfred Kreymborg, for instance, was downright vehement, charging that "his adolescent persistence in courting fame, of explaining himself in the midst of his writing, of quoting what Ezra says about him is stupidly redundant" (510).

Thus, although Williams's prose experiments with extended structure in the twenties were no doubt valuable, they were worse than useless as bids for greater critical recognition. In fact, they nearly annihilated the already narrow (though very select) audience he had secured with his early poetry. By 1933, he complained to Pound that, despite having "the best agent in New York fairly comb the city for me," he could not find a publisher for

> a volume of verse which I have been in the process of making for the past ten years, that is the best collection of verse in America today . . . while, at the same time, every Sunday literary supplement has pages of book titles representing the poetry of my contemporaries. (*Selected Letters* 138)

At the age of fifty, then, Williams was to all intents and purposes going to have to make his poetic debut all over again. Obviously, his continuing obscurity rankled; but it also spurred him on even more to make a really big public splash with his next appearance.

Thus, when Carl Rakosi's Objectivist Press agreed later that year to publish the book, Williams recruited the prestigious Wallace Stevens for an introduction. He also reenlisted the editorial assistance of Louis Zukofsky, who had edited "The Descent of Winter" for him in 1928.[1] When the collection finally appeared the next year, Williams would express his satisfaction with it to Zukofsky in almost mystically holistic terms:

> The whole book has a definite shape now, to me, seems to come up to the attention as a whole—appears to be a creation. That is the test of a book: Is it a book at all or just so many pages of printed matter. More and more one realizes that the creation of a book is a sudden miracle which happens, just like that, at the moment it is assembled— or it doesn't happen. (quoted in *New World Naked* 340)

Clearly, *Collected Poems 1921–1931* was more than just a typical volume of a poet's recent work. For one thing, it collected—and arranged in a distinctly nonchronological order—not just the periodical publications of the past decade but poems from *Spring and All* and earlier work dating as far back as 1913. It rescued poems from irrecoverable consignment to the realm of "the glimpse"—from the oblivion of fugitive periodicals and from Williams's own miserably unsuccessful earlier publications—and placed them on the more significant structural ground of a genuinely new *book*. In other words, Williams was trying to recast his work in a significantly structuring way, and in doing so, he created a coherent and compelling complex of lyrical sequences that might well be called a super-sequence.

Similar considerations attended the publication of *The Complete Collected Poems of William Carlos Williams 1906–1938*. James Laughlin, Williams's new publisher, encouraged him in that project with high hopes that the gathered corpus of Williams's work would be impressive enough to win the Pulitzer Prize (*New World Naked* 408). And though the volume was more faithful to the original chronology of the poems, there were still significant additions and re-arrangements (especially in an entirely new grouping nondescriptly entitled "Longer Poems") that established a superbly articulated large-scale lyrical coherence for an even greater span of Williams's poetic record.

Remarkably powerful as unique works in themselves, both of these first two volumes of collected poetry deserve to be recognized as major, even defining works in the Williams canon, surpassed in lyrical scope and structure only by *Paterson*. Yet they have always been in effect lost works, uncredited in their own time and then entirely superseded in the early fifties.

Ironically, the two volumes that would finally serve (at least until 1986) as the definitive collections of Williams's poetry never equaled the achievement of their predecessors. By the time *The Collected Later Poems* (1950) and *The Collected Earlier Poems* (1951) appeared, Williams had all but completed *Paterson* itself and was, one would think, presumably concerned more than ever with the principles of large-scale lyrical structure. But the untoward circumstances of his life and career—most notably his 1951 stroke and the distracting allure of commercial success for his fiction and autobiography—apparently prevented Williams from fully dedicating himself to the preparation of those volumes. Marred by outright production blunders (including numerous omissions) and possibly even by Williams's own abdication of responsibility for their basic arrangement to his friend and typist Kitty Hoagland, these works never really achieve a fully lyrical coherence. They observe (and promote) instead a generally thematic perspective for Williams's work—sometimes to a tendentious extent. It is an unfortunate and inadvertent outcome that stands in striking contrast to the very exacting judgment Williams himself passed in his concurrent 1951 review of Carl Sandburg's *Collected Poems:*

> In this massive book covering a period close to forty years the poems show no development of the thought, in the technical handling of the material. . . . a horde walks steadily, unhurriedly through its pages, following without affection one behind the other.

It is a monstrous kind of show. . . . There is only a pressing forward (without understanding), pressing forward, an unrelenting drive, ox-like. . . . Fatigue is the outstanding phenomenon. . . . It is the very formlessness of the material . . . the drift of aimless life through the six hundred and seventy-six pages that is the form. . . . The *Collected Poems* make a dunelike mass; no matter where you dig into them it is sand. (*Selected Essays* 278–79)

Williams was, of course, indicting Sandburg for a personal failure to advance or even to change his art. But he was couching his judgment in terms of the overall affect which that failure had created in *Collected Poems*—in terms of the unrelenting "fatigue" of over six hundred tedious pages. And by the same token he was apparently promoting something more than simple variety as the antidote; he was apparently demanding some sort of structural articulation, a "pressing forward" *with* understanding. Such implicit criteria may not have been entirely fair to Sandburg or his book, but they tellingly reflect Williams's own long-standing desire to make a better account of his own poetic life. They also further suggest the special significance of determining Williams's relative success in realizing that desire.

Thus, the present study seeks to apply to Williams's collected volumes the proposal by M. L. Rosenthal and Sally Gall in their landmark study of *The Modern Poetic Sequence: The Genius of Modern Poetry* that we see

the whole, complex mass of modern poetry in a unified purview. That purview is of the struggle of our poetry, almost independently of the poets' will, to realize itself through the emergence of the lyrical sequence and thereby triumph over all tendencies to render it obsolete, precious, and palatable only in tiny doses. (*The Modern Poetic Sequence* ix)

The essential terms and considerations for such an undertaking have, of course, been established in detail by Rosenthal and Gall themselves (see pages 3–18 of *The Modern Poetic Sequence*), but it will be useful if we condense them here as follows:

The modern lyrical sequence . . . is a grouping of mainly lyric poems and passages, rarely uniform in pattern, which tend to interact as an organic whole. It usually includes narrative and dramatic elements, and ratiocinative ones as well, but its structure is finally lyrical. . . . The balance of affects—radiant tonal centers of specific qualities, and intensities, of emotionally and sensuously charged awareness—. . . provides the germ of how a sequence works. It precisely indicates the

nature of lyrical structure, which is based on dynamics: the succession
and interaction of units of affect. . . . The relevant questions are simple: What are the successive affects, and what poetic resources have
been used to create them? is there a cumulative, psychologically sat-
isfying curve of movement? is there sufficient variety to make for a
rich and complex experience? (9, 15)

Such considerations form the heart of what Rosenthal and Gall call
the "evaluative, or dynamic, criticism" that grows out of "direct
engagement and sufficient empathy with literary works" (ix). Expressed in its simplest form as a critical protocol for the examination of extended poetic structure, it is an approach to literature
that provides this present study with a relatively simple but highly
responsive procedure:

we open ourselves to the way a work enters upon its journey and
moves from beginning to end: quite simply, from its initial self-
presentation through its unfoldings and shifts of direction or subjective
emphasis to whatever volatile equilibrium it seems to reach." (ix)

It is along these lines, then, that each of Williams's four volumes
of collected poetry is evaluated in the succeeding chapters for its
accomplishment as a coherent super-sequence linking together the
individual sequences of Williams's originally separate volumes.[2] Of
course, such an evaluation means paying particular attention to
the changes those collections make in the original poem-by-poem
arrangements—and therefore in the lyrical dynamics—of the originally separate volumes incorporated by the collections. But more
primarily it means examining the new and overall lyrical dynamics
that each of the collections establishes (or fails to establish) for
itself as it recovers, revises, and aligns the parts of Williams's
poetic record within a composite whole. There is, in other words,
more attention paid here to the large-scale, lyrically based development of each collection than to the simple textual variations among
the various books or than even to the original lyrical character
and structure of the originally separate volumes subsumed by the
collections. We begin, therefore, with a rather direct attention to
the book Williams once called "the best collection of verse in
America"—*Collected Poems 1921–1931*.

Part I
Collected Poems 1921–1931

1

A New Textual Order, New Lyrical Focus

·*Collected Poems 1921–1931* is certainly not a scholarly, chronologically ordered edition. For one thing, as we have already noted, it
presents poems from well over more than the single decade its title
indicates. Moreover, its organization departs extensively from that
in previous publications of the same material. The book consists
of six sections originally printed in a different time order. The first
and last are entirely new arrangements of previously published
individual poems; the second, third, and fourth sections are equally
new versions of previously published sequences; and the fifth section is a single poem, included in an earlier volume with the poems
of the second section.[1] Listed out all together, the sections are:
"Poems" (1922–32: twenty-nine poems); "Della Primavera Transportata Al Morale" (first published in 1930: eight poems, alter-
nately entitled simply "Primavera"); "Spring and All" (1923:
twelve poems); "The Descent of Winter" (1927–28: nine poems,
untitled except as dated entries); "The Flower" (1930: a single
poem); and "(Prior to 1921)" (1913–23: eight poems).

Not only are the sections arranged without regard to their
chronological order, but the poems within them are so arranged as
well. Also, the poems are often shifted from their original groupings. The poems of "Descent of Winter" (the fourth section), for
instance, were drawn from the *opening* portion of a journal Williams kept during 1927–28, while those of "Primavera" (the second
section) were drawn from the *later* portions. In fact, only the final
section is dated at all, and the collection as a whole deliberately
avoids indicating the time or order of original composition.

The lyrical structure of each given sequence, however, clarifies
itself readily. Thus, "All the Fancy Things," which opens the first
sequence, "Poems," focuses very quickly upon the key affects and
themes underlying this sequence. It presents an old Puerto Rican
woman's discontent with her life on the American mainland—
which she thinks of as the aimless and implicitly Philistine world

of "up here"—and her nostalgia for the finer aesthetic world of her island youth:

> music and painting and all that
> That's all they thought of
> in Puerto Rico in the old Spanish
> days when she was a girl
>
> So that now
> she doesn't know what to do
> with herself alone
> and growing old up here—[2]

Against this nostalgia is poised an affectionate caution, quite filial in its character, about the hazards of obsessive retrospection:

> Green is green
> but the tag ends
> of older things, *ma chère*
>
> must withstand rebuffs
> from that which returns
> to the beginnings—

Thus, within this dilemma of temperaments, there is established a clear association between the tropical latitudes of the old woman's youth and her notion of the ethereal realms of fine art. As the succeeding poems of the sequence unfold and the old woman's discontent becomes further bound up with her geographic displacement, the association is increasingly generalized and opposed to a special, uplifting perception of beauty in the temperate, northern world. In the next two poems, for instance, this mixture of an unhappy senescence with issues of aesthetic perception develops into something more like a cultural malaise than a family problem of what-to-do-with-mama. "Hemmed-In Males" repeats in gruffer, more masculine and public terms the same unhappy difficulties of old age, enfeeblement, and dislocation, and then "Brilliant Sad Sun" returns to the privately familial and literally aesthetic tensions of "All the Fancy Things," this time raising the pitch of the speaker's (presumably a son's) frustration at not being able to dispel the old woman's depressive obsession with the irrecoverable world of her youth:

> Look!
> from a glass pitcher she serves
> clear water to the white chickens.

> What are your memories
> beside that purity?
> The empty pitcher dangling

The obvious reciprocity among the first three poems projects enough shared feeling in them to constitute something like an opening chord for the initial sequence. Indeed it is so distinct that it resonates rather powerfully throughout the remaining twenty-six pieces making up "Poems." In the immediately succeeding "Young Sycamore," for example, the insistent notation of growth in a thriving sycamore sapling seems a clear extension of the son's exasperation at his mother's depressive self-absorption:

> I must tell you
> this young tree
> whose round and firm trunk
> between the wet
>
> pavement and the gutter
> (where water
> is trickling) rises
> bodily

Even the tree's distinctly northern character appears to be in deliberate opposition to the tropical world so bemoaned by the old woman.[3] In musical terms, "Young Sycamore" is the single strong note of northern beauty that answers the chord of northern malaise struck in the opening three poems.

At this point in the sequence, the music is more discordant than harmonious. There is an opposition of affects: the one (the mother's) inconsolable and self-absorbed, the other (the son's) frustrated yet intensely excited by the physical beauties of the immediate world. To all intents and purposes, the sensibility associated with the former affect is left behind in the opening three poems. It is the sensibility associated with the latter affect that assumes the opening lyrical tensions and that becomes the central one of the sequence as it seeks to answer the old woman's opening sadness with a convincingly uplifting aesthetic sense of present experience. By the time the literal interpersonal situation between mother and son reappears—not until "Birds and Flowers," the penultimate poem in the sequence—a great lyrical and phenomenological distance has been traversed.

"Birds and Flowers" is as effusive and happy as its title suggests. In contrast to "Young Sycamore," there is brilliant presence of color and sweetness of atmosphere, not just forceful growth. Note for instance the difference in these lines:

> into the air with
> one undulant
> thrust half its height—
> and then
>
> dividing and waning
> sending out
> young branches on
> all sides—
>
>   (from "Young Sycamore)
>
> Nothing is lost! the white
> shellwhite
> glassy, linenwhite, crystalwhite
> crocuses with orange centers
> the purple crocus with
> an orange center, the yellow
> crocus with a yellow center—
>
>   (from "Birds and Flowers")

A basic celebration of the life force is present in both passages, but it is softer and seems more truly joyous in the second one. There is a geometric language in "Young Sycamore" ("half its height," "dividing, waning," "all sides," and even "one") that strips everything to mathematical considerations of force and direction; the figure of the sycamore is more a schematic than an image. The lines from "Birds and Flowers," on the other hand, abound with an excited repetition of color words and a refreshing synesthesia ("shellwhite / glassy, linenwhite, crystalwhite"); the crocuses are more to be enjoyed than analyzed.

So too are the lines themselves. The conspicuous balance in the placement of identical rhymes creates in the lines from "Birds and Flowers" a leisurely, retrorse sense of movement, while the lines from "Young Sycamore" are dominated by enjambed, initially stressed, and rhymeless lines which literally rush themselves. We sense, in other words, that the rather strident counternote in "Young Sycamore" to the old woman's funk has mellowed during the course of poetic events.

This change is equally apparent in the relationship between mother and son. Compare the son's annoyed reproach of the mother in "Brilliant Sad Sun" with his more solicitous overture in "Birds and Flowers":

and raw Winter's done
to a turn—Restaurant: Spring!
Ah, Madam, what good are your thoughts

romantic but true

(from "Brilliant Sad Sun")

What have I done
to drive you away? It is
winter, true enough, but

this day I love you.
This day
there is no time at all

(from "Birds and Flowers")

The first passage is loaded with supercilious touches: a flippant trope disposes of the old woman's depression as though it were a pancake; a patronizing "Ah, Madam" adds mock formality to the address; and a special emphasis is given to the disparagement of the third line, separated as it is by a stanza break from the mitigating line that follows. Such touches contrast sharply with the tender ones of the latter passage: with the nearly dolorous question posed to the woman; with the enamored repetition of "This day"; with the special emphasis given to the concessionary "true enough" by two strong caesuras.

Finally, in the suspended apostrophe of "Full Moon," the very last poem of the sequence, there is a note of hopeful yearning that reformulates in more positive terms the more desperate longing of the opening poem's intractable depression:

Blessed moon
noon
of night

that through the dark
bids love
stay—

The distance between these poles, however, is more than a matter of simple lyrical contrast. Some twenty-seven poems intervene between "Young Sycamore" and "Birds and Flowers," and each in its own way contributes something indispensable to the lyrical and phenomenological progress of the sequence. The final affect in "Full Moon" doesn't just inversely (and remotely) complement that of the opening poem; whatever contentment the final poem embodies is dictated by the exact and incremental affective development of *all* the poems that precede it. And, again, despite their lack of explicit subgroupings with suggestive headings, the middle poems of "Poems" do manage to focus themselves with the same effectiveness as did the opening four poems that we have already mentioned. In summary, the lyrical dynamics for the balance of the sequence (and then for the balance of the volume) are roughly as follows.[4]

After the rather strident "Young Sycamore," the lyrical intensity drops in the fifth through ninth poems ("It is a Living Coral," "To," "This Florida, 1924," "The Sun Bathers," and "The Cod Head"). The aesthetically based malaise and vigor which were so clearly distinguished and couterpoised in the opening poems now assume a more fluid, unstable relationship within an even broader cultural context. We move literally through the hodgepodge of a museum, and there are startling shifts in literal reference and complicated lyrical probings as the sequence struggles to render beautiful even the most disagreeable climatic and cultural particulars of the northern world. Then in "The Cod Head" there is a strongly tranquil pause that halts the confusion. The image of a severed cod's head loses all its factual repugnance in a soothing display of marine light and color.

The tenth poem ("Struggle of Wings"), however, returns us to the more complicated state of the immediately preceding poems, only raised to a higher pitch. A zany mania mixes with momentary brooding as the speaker translates the lyrical difficulties of the sequence thus far into the terms of an explicitly aesthetic issue. Despite its affective volatility, however, "Struggle of Wings" does establish a certain measure of intellectual clarity for the sequence, and the succeeding five portraits and landscapes complement that clarity with increasingly confident projections of the northern aestheticism which the sequence seeks. A skywalking Indian construction worker in "Down-town" and a brisk snowscape in "Winter" restate the original themes of cultural displacement and seasonal distress in boldly positive and delightful terms. That sheer delight in turn prepares for the intensity of perception in the next three poems ("The Waitress," "The Bull," and "In the 'Sconset Bus"). A sexually intriguing but unattainable waitress, a "godlike" but "captive" bull, and a Cleopatra-like woman on an ordinary bus—each increases the sense of transporting beauty to an almost religious rapture.

In "Poem," the sixteenth and title piece of the sequence, this ecstatic state discovers its more commonplace expression: a quiet wonder at the perfect grace of an acrobatic housecat. And exactly at this point of lyrical and quantitative equipoise (the poem is very nearly at dead center of the section), the sequence reformulates its opening themes and affects. The seventeenth through nineteenth poems transmute the tropical nostalgia of the opening poems into a more complicated tropical enchantment. Exotic notes mix with the mundane in a sustained episode of aesthetic splendor that gradually works its way from the nearly magical rescue out of the anxious interior of "The Jungle" to the thrilling, almost predatory yet domesticated beauty of "The Lily" and finally to the lavish, incantational floral designs of "On Gay Wallpaper." Similarly, the three succeeding poems transmute the earlier northern malaise into an intensely animated northern realm. A druidic awe inhabits the primeval forest of "The Source"; a stark brilliance vivifies the hotel interior of "Nantucket"; and a near hurricane invigorates the common northern March of "The Winds."

After this set of rather exhilarating poems, the sequence settles into something like a happy anticlimax. The twenty-third through twenty-seventh poems return to the specific, personal world of the opening poems but with a generally happier disposition. There is a quiet contentment in the humble achievements of glasswork and one's own poetry in "Lines on Receiving the Dial's Award"; a modest but wholehearted preference for the common beauty of roadside flora in "The Red Lily"; a spartan transcendentalism in the austere accommodations of "The Attic Which Is Desire"; an easy kindliness in the springtime housecall of "Interests of 1926"; and, finally, the most innocent of pleasures in the plum stealing of "This Is Just to Say." With this last poem, the sequence has finally and convincingly struck something like that which the son had only obliquely urged upon the old woman in the opening poems—a sustaining delight in the immediate moment and things of the world.

That delight is, of course, firmly emplaced within the context of the lyrical and aesthetic developments of the preceding poems, and it in turn seems naturally to spawn the finale in three parts that is the twenty-eighth poem, "Birds and Flowers." The first part restates the initial estrangement between mother and son—a sunny disposition and a bitter rebuff. The second part more fully explores this lyrical predicament. There is a greater sadness at the state of affairs, yet there is also a more pronouncedly affectionate resolve to overcome them. Finally, there is in the third part the glorious explosion of color and passionate belief in beauty that serves as a reprise of the entire sequence's lyrical accomplishment.

The sequence might well end at this point, but it instead concludes on the brief "Full Moon," an afterbeat of hopeful yearning. The poem both answers the intractable depression of the opening set and clearly signals that the sanguine lyrical impulse of the sequence has someplace to go. And indeed it does. There follow in the volume three sequences which apply the aesthetic and lyrical dispositions evolved in "Poems" to, respectively, the primarily natural world of beauty in its nascent state ("Primavera"); the manufactured and inhabited world of man ("Spring and All"); and finally, the interior world of a single sensibility ("The Descent of Winter").

Each of these environments proves to be increasingly difficult for those dispositions. The buoyant and familiar state which closes "Poems" and opens "Primavera," for instance, succeeds in developing by the end of the latter sequence into the very stylized elegance of "The Botticellian Trees"—but only after some very disconcerting bluntness in the next-to-last "Death." And that elegance itself then turns vaguely cynical at the start of "Spring and All" and yields at the end to the cultural despair and anger of "To Elsie." Finally, "The Descent of Winter" inherits that despair and anger as a claustrophobic brooding, from which there is recovery only in the precarious, fatigued, and hard-won aesthetic minimalism of its closing entries.

There is, in short, greater adversity in the three middle sequences, and the single summative poem that follows quite accurately reflects that condition. Resembling in title and function the earlier "Birds and Flowers," there is in "The Flower" a much more restrained assessment of the preceding achievements. Instead of effusive optimism, the later poem expresses a sober realism turning on the uncomfortable reappraisal of a poet reviewing his native environs and coming to grips with both the failures of his artistic life and the impurity of his artistic motives. Yet its affirmation of an indomitable beauty is virtually identical to the earlier poem's. So we sense not defeat here but maturity of perspective, especially as the poem grows into a generous spirit with a precise and exquisite restatement of the old woman's Puerto Rican youth:

> into the past, to Porto Rico
> when my mother was a child bathing in a small
>
> river and splashing water up on
> the yucca leaves to see them roll back pearls.

Devoid of all contention, the poem focuses, finally, only on the indivisible fact of beauty, northern or southern, past or present.

It is a very credible conclusion to the entire volume. Yet rather than closure, the sympathetic spirit of "The Flower" invokes the even broader and gentler retrospection of the sixth section and fifth sequence, "(Prior to 1921)." Chronology suddenly emerges as a defining feature of the volume's organization, although powerfully subordinated as it is to the lyrical developments of the volume thus far, that chronology involves a profound literary revisionism rather than a simple accuracy of the textual record. That is, the final sequence emphasizes properties in the older work that especially anticipate or speak to the more recent work in the book's earlier sequences. And as the eight poems of the sequence begin to address in a decidedly less artful way the basic lyrical issues of the volume, they reveal themselves as plainly journeyman preparations for the later labors of the preceding sequences. More important, however, there emerges in these poems an endearing naiveté that governs the momentary triumphs and the more persistent failures of these early efforts. So that this final sequence completes the sympathetic closing impulse of "The Flower" and provides a lyrical corollary to all the difficulties of the previous sequences—a retrospective wisdom and affection that precisely counteract the easy and disabling nostalgia of the old woman in "All the Fancy Things."

But all of this is summary, and as such it is intrinsically suspect; the real coherence of each sequence and of the entire volume lies in the very immediate continuity from one individual poem to the next and from one individual sequence to the next. That is, no matter how clear an affective course we chart for the volume as a whole, the individual poems and sequences themselves generally discover different literal referents for their lyrical burdens. If it is to be truly clear why one affective state reasonably follows another—if the archetectonics of the sequences are to be really convincing—even the very rudimentary phenomenological connections among the poems must be somehow noted. For this reason, the preeminent analysis of coherence in the lyrical sequence is inescapably descriptive and comprehensive. As Professors Rosenthal and Gall have put it,

> we are not allowed to forget that, although an overview is a grand thing for helping to relate poems to one another, it will not be worth much unless it results from engagement with one poem at a time. And not to grow too metaphysical, we must also say that immersion in any poem of substance will for the moment change the proportions of the whole sequence and make everything center on the chosen center. This is a crucial consideration in getting in touch with a sequence; the object is never to *schematize* its movement, but rather to experience it. (34)

"To experience it"—the objective is even more important for works that, like *Collected Poems 1921–1931* and its successors, only tacitly assume a lyrically based coherence. Lacking such explicitly unifying devices as a single subject matter or numbered sections, these works require greater attention to the subtler connections which the individual poems and sequences cumulatively establish among themselves. Thus, it is desirable to examine the poems of at least this first of Williams's "collecteds" ad seriatim.

2

The Opening Sequence of "Poems"

At the very beginning of the "Poems" group, then, we are invited by the generic title itself to make our way one poem at a time, with no guidance save that which the poems themselves provide. And the first line of the first poem ("All the Fancy Things") places us squarely within an aesthetic realm—"music and painting and all that"—while the succeeding lines introduce the worlds of memory, nostalgia, and bitter human loss:

> music and painting and all that
> That's all they thought of
> in Puerto Rico in the old Spanish
> days when she was a girl
>
> So that now
> she doesn't know what to do
> with herself alone
> and growing old up here—
>
> Green is green
> but the tag ends
> of older things, *ma chère*
>
> must withstand rebuffs
> from that which returns
> to the beginnings—
>
> Or what? a
> clean air, high up, unoffended
> by gross odors

This opening poem introduces the lyrical motifs of the "Poems" sequence—and ultimately of the entire book. It does so not because it is particularly intense or effective as an isolated poem, but because it so quickly and exactly provides a frame of complex emotional reference *and* an occasion for further resolution. At first the language seems casual enough in its colloquial immediacy, which catches, precisely but lightly, an old woman's unhappiness and manner of speech. But real, serious problems are nonetheless clearly introduced: old age, idleness, and displacement. Moreover, these objective problems are fraught with a sense of irreconcilable loss and nagging dilemma, especially in the pining first line and then in the irrepressible return of that pining in the last two lines.

At the same time, there are also more positive elements at play here in the third and fourth stanzas. With its affectionate French and circumspect (if confusing) euphemisms, the speaker's gentle warning of the hazards that attend age and retrospection adds notes of compassion to those of artistic sensitivity, misery, and identity-confusion introduced earlier. But it hardly solves the old woman's problem; it simply creates a pathos that impels an interest in the lyrical state of affairs forward. Thus, the following poem, "Hemmed in Males," appears to align itself with the residual pressure of these unresolved difficulties. The gallows humor of some barroom euphemisms for the same displacement, decline, and idleness of old age translates the old woman's pining into a gruffer idiom and a more masculine tone. The episode also expands the frame of reference from the personal difficulties of the previous poem to something very much like folklore:

> The saloon is gone up the creek
> with the black sand round its
> mouth, it went floating like
>
> a backhouse on the Mississippi in
> flood time but it went up
> the creek into Limbo from whence
>
> only empty bottles ever return
> and that's where George is
> He's gone upstream to ask 'em
>
> to let him in at the hole
> in the wall where the W.C.T.U
> sits knitting elastic stockings
>
> for varicose veins. Poor George
> he's got a job now as janitor
> in Lincoln School but the saloon

Clearly, there is a good deal of an old man's wryness here, beginning with the acronymic pun of the poem's title (HIM), and the tale does somewhat leaven the pathos of "All the Fancy Things." But the opening image of "the creek / with the black sand round its / mouth" nonetheless manages to suggest something of a frighteningly abysmal presence, and the poem, finally, does sympathetically confirm the woman's earlier despair as it gives way to the speaker's dismal anticipation of his own imminent senescence:

> a bat. Poor George, they've cut
> out his pituatary gland and his
> vas deferens is in the spitoon—
>
> You can laugh at him without his
> organs but that's the way with
> a river when it wants to
>
> drown you, it sucks you in and
> you feel the old saloon sinking
> under you and you say good-by
>
> just as George did, good-by poetry
> the black sand's got me, the old
> days are over, there's no place
>
> any more for me to go now
> except home—

Similarly, the third poem, "Brilliant Sad Sun," gathers up the lyrical and literal situations that precede it and effects enough of a closure to make the opening group of poems something of a cynosure for the entire sequence. As in "All the Fancy Things," a speaker admonishes an older woman for her overweening nostalgia, and once again, as in "Hemmed in Males," there is a conspicuous male identification with public houses. But the wryly morbid mood of the second poem is replaced here with a cheerful delight in a restaurant, and the previously mild admonishment of the first poem is cast here in much bolder terms:

LEE'S
LUNCH

Spaghetti   Oysters
a Specialty   Clams

> and raw Winter's done
> to a turn—Restaurant: Spring!
> Ah, Madam, what good are your thoughts
>
> romantic but true
> beside this gayety of the sun
> and that huge appetite?

The net effect is to balance the darker response of "Hemmed in Males" with a more positive outlook and to strengthen the tension between the male speaker's original optimism and the old woman's depression. Calling the immediately thrilling vividness of a serving girl to her attention, for instance, the speaker succeeds in evoking from the old woman only the bittersweet memory of another young lady from her own distant past, and the poem finally closes with a note of sad defeat:

> Look!
> from a glass pitcher she serves
> clear water to the white chickens.
>
> What are your memories
> beside that purity?
> The empty pitcher dangling
>
> from her grip
> her coarse voice croaks
> *Bon jor'*
>
> And Patti, on her first concert tour
> sang at your house in Mayagues
> and your brother was there
>
> What beauty
> beside your sadness—and
> what sorrow

Thus, thrown back upon its original difficulties, the sequence has now evolved a very distinct and persistent tension. It is a tension that the ensuing poems cannot avoid addressing in one way or another. "Young Sycamore," for instance, opens with a single urgent line—"I must tell you"—that appears to resume the explicit attempt at a solution for the problem of the old woman's depression. The poem then just as urgently turns into a breathlessly imagistic attempt to render some exhilarating, vegetative paradigm for the growth and dispersion which ultimately underwrites even the forces of death and decline that so besiege the old woman:

> I must tell you
> this young tree
> whose round and firm trunk
> between the wet
>
> pavement and the gutter
> (where water
> is trickling) rises
> bodily
>
> into the air with
> one undulant
> thrust half its height—
> and then
>
> dividing and waning
> sending out
> young branches on
> all sides—
>
> hung with cocoons
> it thins
> till nothing is left of it
> but two
>
> eccentric knotted
> twigs
> bending forward
> hornlike at the top

The poem is beautifully done. Precise in image and thrusting in rhythm, it quietly employs the key motif left hanging at the end of "All the Fancy Things" ("a / clean air, high up"). It also manages to invigorate the normally painful details of age ("it thins," "eccentric knotted," "bending forward") with a real sense of dynamic growth; there is even a hint of sexual vigor in the "horn" figure of the last line.

It is all an invigorating ascent, and it strikes a defining counternote to the problematic malaise elucidated in the preceding three poems. Yet that counternote is very clearly a reference and not a resolution for the central lyrical tension of the sequence. For one thing, it is, as has been earlier noted, far too strident a poem to suggest anything but a contention of opposing positions. And for another, its triumphant manner is all too momentary, for the succeeding poem, "It Is a Living Coral," plummets with a single line that, along with the title, redefines in more chilling terms what the elderly more usually become:

> a trouble

The startle effectively dissipates the implicit tendentiousness of the previous poem, and it signals as well the precarious nature of the lyrical countermeasures that follow in this and the next three poems. The new poem also initiates a general fluctuation in its literal frame of reference as it passes through the montage of a museum (or, as Litz and MacGowan suggest, the public art displays of the Capitol) in search of a broad cultural notion of the antique and archaic. At first, there follows of succession of classically oriented details: a Latin tag; the personfied figures of Armed Liberty, Mars, Minerva; the classical architectural principles of arch and dome. They all assume an obsolete, ponderous inutility. But despite their archaism, these very same features still evidence the traces of an underlying classical attention to a delicate and sublime natural beauty:

> sculpture straddled by
> a dome
>
> eight million pounds
> in weight
>
> iron plates constructed
> to expand
>
> and contract with
> variations
>
> of temperature
> the folding
>
> and unfolding of a lily.

Such features quietly promise the sort of sublime involvement with living beauty that the sequence offers as an alternative to the old woman's discontented absorption with the past in "All the Fancy Things." But at this point, that involvement is much too muted and its context too remote from genuine human misery to be really effective as an antidote. Thus, the poem's panorama expands to a more familiar domain (our own colonial heritage), and details from various works of American art are translated into the slightly more affecting coziness of something like loose personal memories, privately meaningful names, and familiar raillery:

> this scaleless
>
> jumble is superb
>
> and accurate in its
> expression
>
> of the thing they
> would destroy—
>
> Baptism of Poca-
> hontas
>
> with a little card
> hanging
>
> under it to tell
> the persons
>
> in the picture.
>
> It climbs
>
> it runs, it is Geo.
> Shoup
>
> of Idaho it wears
> a beard
>
> it fetches naked
> Indian
>
> women from a river
> Trumbull
>
> Varnum Henderson
> Frances
>
> Willard's corset is
> absurd—

Banks White Columbus
stretched

in bed men felling trees

Ironically, however, the increasingly personal tone seems to prompt
an equally personal sense of time and mortality, and the poem
closes with a suddenly transfigured, ghoulish marine image:

The Hon. Michael
C. Kerr

onetime Speaker of
the House

of Representatives
Perry

in a rowboat on Lake
Erie

changing ships the
dead

among the wreckage
sickly green

In the aftermath of this sudden horror follows a cleverly titled
poem—"To"—which fixes the Davy Jones motif within the perspective of a small boy busy about his play. There is a momentary
tension as the syntactical connection of the poems and their similar
stanza forms at first threaten something insidious for the child:

among the wreckage
sickly green

TO

a child (a boy) bouncing
a ball (a blue ball)—

But then the new poem quickly and impishly parodies the eerie
descent that has preceded it with a charming descent of the
boy's own:

> He bounces it (a toy racket
> in his hand) and runs
>
> and catches it (with his
> left hand) six floors
>
> straight down—
> which is the old back yard

The atheletic delight here serves, very lightly and briefly, to reintroduce the element of innocent joy that was ultimately the target of the old woman's opening nostalgia for her own lost childhood in "All the Fancy Things." Perhaps more significantly, "To" releases that affect as a separate one, out from the oppressive context of that nostalgia; the image is very much one of a playful contemporary tenement child ("six floors // straight down"), not a memory of a lost tropical childhood. But by the same token, the image is ultimately inadequate to the larger challenge posed by the old woman's longing. The acrobatic boy, thoroughly divorced from any meaningful *adult* context, remains a merely impish, not sustaining, figure. There is refreshment here, but not redemption.

"This Florida: 1924" seems to confirm that distinction by returning us to a more fatigued state. Recalling the tropical yearnings of "All the Fancy Things," the opening here at once suggests something like both the profound despair of Eliot's "ragged claws" wish and the simple escapism of a winter-bound northerner's longing for tropical relief:

> of which I am the sand—
> one of the sands—in which
> the turtle eggs are baking—
>
> The people are running away
> toward me, Hibiscus,
> where I lie, sad,
>
> by the stern
> slaying palm trees—
> (They're so much better

The ambiguity persists in the poem's conflation of tropical curiosities, enigmatic statements of sadness, a threatening natural violence, and, finally, even a paradoxical confusion of the northern and southern perspectives:

> at a distance than they are
> up close. Cocoanuts
> aren't they?
>
> or Royal palms?
> They are so tall the wind
> rips them to shreds)
>
> —this frightened
> frantic pilgrimage has left
> my bungalows up here
>
> lonely as the Lido in April
> "Florida the Flowery!"
> Well,

Finally, the confusion proves itself to be the mild delirium of a speaker's daydream as his wish to join the flight of tourists grates against the realities of his detention:

> it's a kind of borrowed
> pleasure after all (as at the movies)
> to see them
>
> tearing off to escape it
> this winter
> this winter that I feel
>
> So—
> already ten o'clock?
> *Vorwärts!*

"Vorwärts!"—the single word of resignation breaks the reverie and snaps the attention back to more pressing matters. And by virtue of a single pun ("rime"), the poem incorporates into its dilemma of fatigue the equally real difficulties of poetic composition:

> e-e i-i o-o u-u a-a
> Shall I write it in iambs
> Cottages in a row
>
> all radioed and showerbathed?
> But I am sick of rime—
> The whole damned town

is riming up one street
and down another, yet there is
the rime of her white teeth

the rime of glasses
at my plate, the ripple rime
the rime her fingers make—

And we thought to escape rime
by imitation of the senseless
unarrangement of wild things—

The redefinition of the poem's burden in these explicitly aesthetic
terms has a potent impact. What began as a tired and disjointed
daydream suddenly becomes a consolidated tour de force of the
tropical imagination, and the color orange leaps to vibrant life over
six full stanzas:

the stupidest rime of all—
Rather, Hibiscus,
let me examine

those varying shades
of orange, clear as an electric
bulb on fire

or powdery with sediment—
matt, the shades and textures
of a Cubist picture

the charm
of fish by Hartley; orange
of ale and lilies

orange of topaz, orange of red hair
orange of Çuraçoa
orange of the Tiber

turbid, orange of the bottom
rocks in Maine rivers
orange of mushrooms

of Cepes that Marshal loved
to cook in copper
pans, orange of the sun—

Finally, the poem breaks off at the very crest of this ecstatic extravaganza, and an impish alphabetic pun ("pees") returns us to the aesthetic *issue* that the roster of vowels had earlier introduced. Now, however, working off the vigor of the preceding stanzas, vision itself seems newly focused, and even a routine urine analysis yields a lighthearted mood and an at least interesting luminescence:

> I shall do my pees, instead—
> boiling them in test tubes
> holding them to the light
>
> dropping in the acid—
> Peggy has a little albumen
> in hers—

Clearly, the speaker has achieved some sort of imaginative conquest over the sources of his—and by extension, the old woman's—initial discontent. Instead of tedium, this routine lab task is alive with an invigorating curiosity, a curiosity that in its concentration is greater than the rather dispersed curiosity about the palm trees in the poem's opening tropical fantasy. And the amiable thinking out loud in the last stanza especially contrasts with the near delirium of the opening daydream. But again, as with the other poems since "Young Sycamore," any real sense of victory is oblique at best, and the next poem in the sequence attempts to restate the enlivening aesthetic reorientation in much more striking terms.

Like "This Florida: 1924," the title of "The Sun Bathers" suggests something of a tropical quality; and like the ending of the preceding poem, the opening quatrain of the newer one deploys a very sharply defined and lucid visual field. Only here that field presents an image more factually disagreeable than Peggy's innocuous albumen:

> A tramp thawing out
> on a doorstep
> against an east wall
> Nov. 1, 1933:

The jolt of the precision dating also assaults us with a telescoped passage of ten years since the 1924 of the previous poem, and the discouraging evidence of human decline has once again encroached upon the frail aesthetic refreshment of the previous winter-bound speaker's closing vision. And in the larger terms of the overall sequence, the derelict's very appearance further complicates the personal difficulties of loss and decline with a broader cultural symptom. But despite the rather disturbing literal evidence of degeneration, there still remains to the scene a discernably aesthetic evaluation that transforms the features of this destitute young bum into the components of a splendidly beautiful day:

> a young man begrimed
> and in an old
> army coat
> wriggling and scratching
>
> while a fat negress
> in a yellow-house window
> nearby
> leans out and yawns
>
> into the fine weather

Even in the midst of the cold northern Depression, there could be a lazy pleasure with the "fine weather" of the aesthetic imagination. It is a conviction that "The Cod Head," as its own cold North Atlantic title suggests, neatly endorses. Resuming the seaside motif of "This Florida: 1924," the opening two stanzas restate the squalor of "The Sun Bathers" in more properly marinal terms, ones which can more easily assemble themselves into a purely aesthetic design:

> Miscellaneous weed
> strands, stems, debris—
> firmament
>
> to fishes—
> where the yellow feet
> of gulls dabble

There are no disagreeable social or political facts behind this sea clutter, and the "dabble" of the gull's feeding signals as well a lazy pleasure with the scene that is more thoroughly innocent than was the pleasure of "The Sun Bathers."

This particular refinement of the earlier affect persists throughout "The Cod Head" as it brings the salutary lyrical impulse of the preceding five poems to a momentary repose. Especially in the poem's final movement, there is an aqueous motion which softens our examination of the sea's uglier secrets. Even an objectively repulsive decapitation becomes involved with the gestures of solace:

> amorphous waver-
> ing rocks—three fathom
> the vitreous
>
> body through which—
> small scudding fish deep
> down—and
>
> now a lulling lift
> and fall—
> red stars—a severed cod-
>
> head between two
> green stones—lifting
> falling

The algae-covered rocks almost seem pillows, and the rocking rhythms a lullaby. Yet nowhere is there a hint of metaphor. There is only an imagination highly alert to nature's truest maternal embrace.

There is in "The Cod Head," then, a sense of real progress in the evolution of a sustaining aesthetic perception of experience. And indeed, the succeeding poem seems almost a schematic advancement of that progress from the sea to the planet's other firmament, the air. Celestial images like the moon and stars that were mirrored in the waters of "The Cod Head" now dominate as primary phenomena, and they raise the sequence to a crisper state. From a nearly viscous portrait of a severed cod head, we enter the more blustery "Struggle of Wings":

> Roundclouds occluding patches of the
> sky rival steam bluntly towering,
> slowspinning billows which rival
> the resting snow, which rivals the sun
>
> beaten out upon it, flashing
> to a struggle (of wings) which
> fills the still air—still
> but cold—yet burning . . .

It is an exhilarating and strenuous ascent, full of striving relative clauses and buoyant participial phrases, and it renews the assault upon the cold-numbing northern climate that had been *the* environmental culprit of the old woman's complaint in "All the Fancy Things." In fact, beginning with the speaker's initial reproofs of the old woman's lack of imagination, it has been the literal struggle of the sequence to demonstrate an imaginative capacity that can convincingly create sustaining beauty out of the harshest northern materials—out of even winter itself. And there is in "Struggle of Wings" a glimmer of success, as the winter landscape momentarily assumes a lover's passionate countenance:

> It is the snow risen upon itself, it is
> winter pressed breast to breast
> with its own whiteness, transparent
> yet visible:

There is, however, something *too* breathless about this pristine vision, arising as it does out of the poem's earlier turbulence, and with a commensurate suddenness, the rapturous moment yields to a skeptical reexamination of the entire struggle and landscape. The headlong energy of the opening slows into the observation of a comically suspicious survey:

> Together, with their pigeon's heads whose
> stupid eyes deceive no one—
> they hold up between them something
> which wants to fall to the ground . . .

> And there's the river with thin ice upon it
> fanning out half over the black
> water, the free middlewater racing under its
> ripples that move crosswise on the stream

> But the wings and bodies of the pigeonlike
> creatures keep fluttering, turning together
> hiding that which is between them. It seems
> to rest not in their claws but upon their breasts—

By the middle of the poem, the entire episode breaks out into broad, biting satire, as the birds farcically reveal their true identity to be a metamorphosis of a travestied "Poesy":

> It is a baby!
> Now it is very clear (*) they're keeping the child

(naked in the air) warm and safe between them.
The eyes of the birds are fixed in

a bestial ecstasy. They strive together panting.
It is an antithesis of logic, very
theoretical. To his face the baby claps
the bearded face of Socrates . . .

Ho, ho! he's dropped it. It was a mask.
Now indeed the encounter throws aside all dissim-
ulation. The false birdheads drop back, arms
spring from the wingedges, all the parts

of two women become distinct, the anatomy
familiar and complete to the smallest detail:
A meaning plainly antipoetical . . . and
   . . . all there is is won
                    (.   .   .   .   .

It is Poesy, born of a man and two women

The antics here recapture some of the poem's opening energy
level, but they also clearly deflate the latent romantic pretensions
of the earlier skyscape. The effect helps prepare for a reorientation
in the succeeding lines toward the darker sides of human emotion.
"Poesy" is reclothed in the garb of something strongly suggestive
of a furtive assignation, an infidelity, which painfully vacillates between the pleasure of its own moment and the insomnia of a later
guilt. It is all, however, redeemed by an unimpeachable and powerful precision of rendering, measured by a reassuring refrain:

It is Poesy, born of a man and two women
Exit No. 4, the string from the windowshade
has a noose at the bottom, a noose? or
a ring—bound with a white cord, knotted
around the circumference in a design—
              And all there is is won

And it is Inness on the meadows and fruit is
yellow ripening in windows every minute
growing brighter in the bulblight by the
cabbages and spuds—
              And all there is is won

What are black 4 a.m.'s after all but black
4 a.m.'s like anything else: a tree

a fork, a leaf, a pane of glass—?
And all there is is won

A relic of old decency, a "very personal friend"
And all there is is won

This is "Poesy" out of the ether and into the world. It has not vanquished the corruptions of that world, nor has it resolved its discontents and recriminations, but it balances all these things with the uplifting beauty of vivid if minor details from concrete experience—the design of a windowshade "noose," the hue of fruit in the bulblight, the black 4 a.m.'s. The refrain might best be read "And *all* there *is,* is won." With at least this measure of assurance, the poem can return more credibly to its earlier burlesque of grander aesthetic notions:

(Envoi

Pic, your crows feed at your windowsill
asso, try and get near mine . . .
And all there is is won
(.   .   .   .   .   .

The mild buffonery of these lines is truly functional; bound up as it is with the more pensive refrain, it redefines the earlier mockery of the poem as something more than facile high-spiritedness. The *entire* poem, including its high jinks, becomes involved with the very serious, aesthetically minded disposition of the middle part. And it is the resonance of this association that saves from pure whimsicality the brightly confident aesthetic injunction that closes the poem:

Out of such drab trash as this
by a metamorphosis
bright as wallpaper or crayon
or where the sun casts ray on ray on
flowers in a dish, you shall weave
for Poesy a gaudy sleeve
a scarf, a cap and find him gloves
whiter than the backs of doves

.   .   .

Clothe him
richly, those who loathe him
will besmirch him fast enough.

A surcease to sombre stuff—
black's black, black's one thing
but he's not a blackbird. Bring
something else for him to wear.
See! he's young he has black hair!
Very well then, a red vest . . .

The tumbling phrases of the third and fourth lines repeat the opening motions of clouds and sunlight in the less grandiose, more commonplace terms dictated by the aesthetic position that the poem has evolved. And the winter motifs of the first stanza's last two lines subtly address the continuing challenge to the northern imagination posed by the old woman's opening complaint in "All the Fancy Things." Then the final stanza repeats in a more elaborate way the initial reproof to that challenge, only now the reproof is not so easily deflected; it is simply compromised by another's preference in color.

The happy aesthetic imagination, then, is put forth here as a potent transformational force and a serious remedy to the depressed sensibility that is the implicit audience for the final lines. But it is above all the sheer exuberance of "Struggle of Wings" itself that establishes the lyrical credibility for that position. The poem's clowning and its rapid rhetorical shifts that establish a serious aesthetic purpose to that clowning—such things create a commanding sense of confidence. And the next three poems build that confidence into a more complicated and intense state.

"Down-town," for instance, begins by repeating the confident spirit with an attractive portrait of a daring young Indian welder working at skyscraper heights. What makes this image especially effective, though, is not its intrinsic freshness, but the subtly defining context of the poem's beginning. The very first line simulates something like a prose continuation of the implicit dialogue at the close of "A Struggle of Wings," especially in the way the succeeding poem implicitly continues the tutorial tone:

DOWN-TOWN

is a condition—

One might almost confuse the proposition with the more common proverb that unhappiness is "a state of mind." But then, as though having quickly exhausted the opening pseudointellectual note solely for the sake of a transition, the poem immediately and almost perversely muddles any trace of intellectual clarity with a confusing constructional analysis:

> is a condition—
> of bedrooms whose electricity
>
> is brickish or made into
> T beams—They dangle them[1]

The confusion, of course, encourages a slightly lewd double entendre in the passage, and in so doing, permits the introduction of a more refreshing, more sexual statement of the poem's position. So when the poem clarifies into the explicit scene of the skywalking construction worker, his male bravado seems a deliberate extension of the entire preceding context; he even more convincingly expresses the unpretentious imaginative vigor so confidently proclaimed at the end of "A Struggle":

> on wire cables to the tops
> of Woolworth buildings
>
> five and ten cents worth—
> There they have bolted them
>
> into place at masculine risk—
> Or a boy with a rose under
>
> the lintel of his cap
> standing to have his picture
>
> taken on the butt of a girder
> with the city a mile down—
>
> captured, lonely cock atop
> iron girders wears rosepetal
>
> smile—a thought of Indians
> on chestnut branches
>
> to end "walking on the air"

The final stanzas constitute a blissful note, and they deliberately recall in tone and actual phrasing the "clean air, high up, unoffended" of the old woman's desires in "All the Fancy Things." So that the northern motif which had in that earlier poem been identified with irredeemable displacement and decline has now been associated with the irrepressibly blithe disposition of this equally displaced modern young Indian; his imaginative flourishment in an alien, distinctively urban setting makes him the exact lyrical and imaginative antitype to the old woman. (Indeed, the ultimately revised title of the poem, "New England," seems to recognize formally this lyrical fact and to add extra irony to the geography of the poem.)

In these terms, the following poem, "Winter," is a similar but much bolder challenge to the old woman's initial complaint. It is a pure and unabashed portrait of a northern winter scene. The colors are sharp, the shapes finely etched. There are no apologies here for the cold, only a great relish for its brisk and exact features:

> Now the snow
> lies on the ground
> and more snow
> is descending upon it—
> Patches of red dirt
> hold together
> the old
> snow patches
>
> This is winter—
> rosettes of
> leather-green leaves
> by the old fence
> and bare trees
> marking the sky—
>
> This is winter
> winter, winter
> leather-green leaves
> spearshaped
> in the falling snow

The purity of this endorsement is as bracing as the vividness of its images, and it prepares the sequence for the more difficult enterprise of "The Waitress." An entranced study of an ordinary waitress, this next poem sets out to redeem a female idol of the imagination from the oppressive circumstances of an aesthetically insensible modern world. More completely drawn than the portrait of the Indian in "Down-town," the woman's figure also represents a far more complicated state of affairs. While, for instance, the waitress herself clearly recalls the cheerful French-speaking serving girl of "Brilliant Sad Sun," that earlier poem's clear distinction between buoyant youth and sour age is entirely gone. This waitress is no idyllic young maid but a kitchen laborer with ample evidence of her own sad entrapment and decline:

> No wit (and none needed) but
> the silence of her ways, gray eyes in
> a depth of black lashes—
> The eyes look and the look falls
>
> There is no way, no way. So close
> one may feel the warmth of the cheek and yet there is
> no way.
>
> The benefits of poverty are a roughened skin
> of the hands, the broken
> knuckles, the stained wrists.

"No wit . . . no way, no way"—the refrain is bleakness itself. And in the earlier "Brilliant Sad Sun," a kindred outlook had merely provoked a testy reproach of an old woman's self-absorbed indifference to the immediate beauty at hand. But here in "The Waitress," this woman is, at least for a moment, actually rescued from her condition by an admiring vision that subsumes all considerations of predicament within the irreducible visual beauty of her precisely rendered person and movements.

> Serious. Not as the others.
> All the rest are liars, all but you.
> Wait on us.
> Wait on us, the hair held back practically
> by a net, close behind the ears, at the sides of
> the head. But the eyes—
> but the mouth, lightly (quickly)
> touched with rouge.
>
> The black dress makes the hair dark, strangely
> enough, and the white dress makes it light.
>
> There is a mole under the jaw, low under
> the right ear—
>
> And what arms!
>
> The glassruby ring
> on the fourth finger of the left hand.

> —and the movements
> under the scant dress as the weight of the tray
> makes the hips shift forward slightly in lifting
> and beginning to walk—

There is something very much like adoration here, especially in the petitionary repetition of "Wait on us." Indeed, it seems not at all odd that as the poem expands the scene to include the broader arena of something like a Rotary dinner and we get snippets of parliamentary motions, the noise of hotel foot traffic, the details of a table setting—that these things incite a nearly religious exhilaration:

> O unlit candle with the soft white
> plume, Sunbeam Finest Safety Matches all together in
> a little box—
>
> And the reflections of both in
> the mirror and the reflection of the hand, writing
> writing—
> Speak to me of her!

Yet this beauty that has so invigorated the perception of this poem only evades rather than removes the ultimate burden of the entire sequence. The brand name of some matches, the electric brilliance of a neon sign—these things momentarily seize the attention with a concrete excitement that banishes all but their own pleasures; but the seizure ultimately gives way to a nagging awareness of transience and loss:

> Speak to me of her!
>
> —and nobody else and nothing else
> in the whole city, not an electric sign of shifting
> colors, fourfoot daisies and acanthus fronds going from
> red to orange, green to blue—forty feet across—
>
> Wait on us, wait
> on us with your momentary beauty to be enjoyed by
> none of us. Neither by you, certainly,
> nor by me.

Still, the conclusion of "The Waitress" marks a great advance for the sequence. The aching recitation of time's hazards is now at least attached (rather than simply opposed) to an equally powerful if not greater litany of faith—"Wait on us." And an epiphanic dimension has evolved for a lyrical position that had been previously affirmed as pretty much a matter of individual temperament or personal aesthetic preference. It is a dimension that "The Bull" then confirms with a symbolic majesty:

> It is in captivity—
> ringed, haltered, chained
> to a drag
> the bull is godlike
>
> .   .   .   .   .   .
>
> then stays
> with half-closed eyes,
> Olympian commentary on
> the bright passage of days.

There is no doubt of a divine presence now, and after its ephemeral modern appearance in "The Waitress," beauty now makes a more classically defined and imposing manifestation:

> —The round sun
> smooths his lacquer
> through
> the glossy pinetress
>
> his substance hard
> as ivory or glass—
> through which the wind
> yet plays—
>   Milkless.
>
> he nods
> the hair between his horns
> and eyes matted
> with hyacinthine curls

There is a concentration in the more firmly defined quatrains of "The Bull" that eludes the kinetic, irregular lines of "The Waitress." In fact, the overall effect of the former poem is to consolidate the inspiring sense of sustaining beauty that "The Waitress" only momentarily evolves. The beauty of the stately bull is more substantial, more permanent than that of the rushing waitress. And the hectic interior setting of "The Waitress" contrasts with the placid outdoors of "The Bull."

There is as well a generally more domineering masculine cast to "The Bull" that supports the precious quality of the very feminine beauty in "The Waitress." The slow delectation of the women's facial features in the one poem ("But the eyes— / but the mouth, lightly (quickly) / touched with rouge") seems to elicit in the other a corresponding male primping ("Milkless // he nods / the hair between his horns / and eyes matted / with hyacinthine curls"). Naturally, some of this reciprocity translates into an underlying sexual excitement between the poems, and it is with this extra impulse that the last of this immediate group of poems finally brings the sequence to its most sublime and convincing aesthetic epiphany.

Seamlessly picking up the tone, idiom, and motifs of the closing description in "The Bull," "In the 'Sconset Bus" translates the impressive aspect of the nearly supernatural animal into the intensely alluring cosmetic accessories of an ordinary lady bus passenger:

> Upon the fallen
> cheek
>
> a gauzy down—
> And on
>
> the nape
> —indecently
>
> a mat
> of yellow hair
>
> stuck with
> celluloid
>
> pins
> not quite
>
> matching it
> —that's
>
> two shades
> darker
>
> at the roots—
> Hanging

from the ears
the hooks

piercing the
flesh—

gold and semi-
precious

stones—
And in her

lap the dog
(Youth)

resting
his head on

the ample
shoulder his

bright
mouth agape

pants restlessly
backward

The preceding poem's apotheosized sexual overtones still resonate throughout here. There is something coy about the woman's mildly meretricious appearance—her "indecently" dyed hair, her "piercing" earings—that seems a direct response to the sexual display at the close of "The Bull": "he nods / the hair between his horns / and eyes matted / with hyacinthine curls." And the mythic potency of the bull seems to be answered by a voluptuousness in the woman passenger's description that clearly echoes Shakespeare's legendary Cleopatra upon her barge, while the supine dog appears a sybaritic Cupid to the bull's Minotaur.

Of course, the general sexual excitement recalls as well the more breathless examination of "The Waitress." Yet at the same time there is in the comically panting "dog / (Youth)" and in the plainly bathetic setting of the bus a clear diminishment, but not elimination, of the divinely ecstatic elements so strongly and seriously established in both that poem and "The Bull." It is as if the adorational intensity of "The Waitress" had been paradoxically reduced (and thereby made more profoundly credible) to the more common human admiration of "In the 'Sconset Bus" by virtue of the blatant mythical translation of "The Bull." And obversely, the pedestrian beauty of "In the 'Sconset Bus" is charged with an authentically heightened—even divine—reality. This is everyday aesthetic awareness of a truly special and transporting sort.

Together, in other words, these last three poems accomplish an aesthetic animation of the ordinary world (or at least a small part of it) that is way beyond what might be achieved through some simple and gratuitous imposition of an Olympian lexicon upon a modern subject. The poems cumulatively, credibly, *acquire* the exciting sense of a transfigured beauty. Yet at the same time, each poem is rigorously faithful to the mundane details of its own specific literal scene. "The Waitress" is irreducibly an infatuation with a real waitress; "The Bull" is an exalting glimpse of the divinity inherent in a real bull in a real pasture; and "In the 'Sconset Bus" is a sensual arousal over a real and slightly tawdry lady on a bus. But in their composite—in their networking of themes, motifs, and affects—they exalt their subjects.

It is just such networking that makes the very next poem so curiously effective. In its miniature scenario of a deft cat's careful passage over furniture and into a flowerpot, "Poem" would normally seem a merely charming if well done effect. But coming as it does after the profound aesthetic transfiguration of the previous few poems, the poem delivers a good deal more than charm:

> As the cat
> climbed over
> the top of
>
> the jamcloset
> first the right
> forefoot
>
> carefully
> then the hind
> stepped down
>
> into the pit of
> the empty
> flowerpot

In the mild illusion of the cat's actual disappearance into a finally "empty" pot, there is a nearly perfect complement to the very sudden appearance of the dog at the end of "In the 'Sconset Bus," and the connection suggests an almost marvelous process of metamorphosis and apparition.

Of course, magical or not, the image is not the most prominent feature of the poem. Instead, the suspension of phrasing from line to line and stanza to stanza conveys a stronger impression of motion than of vision, and the overall affect of the poem really has more to do with the cat's deliberate skill than with its sentimental charm. This fact becomes especially noticeable in connection to the poem's title—"Poem." Coming after so many poems with very distinctive (and functional) titles, this title would seem anomalistically bland, were it not for the fact that it is, after all, something of a title poem for the sequence. In this light, the impression of magic in the poem expresses itself more as a feature of the *poem's craft* than of the cat's tread per se.

The clever emphasis upon the poem's special effects helps return to the fore the general aesthetic objective of the entire sequence: the development of an imaginative faculty which can convincingly transform the mundane things of the world into the delightful occasions of beauty. The previous few poems, of course, have accomplished something of just this sort, and "Poem" is a sort of coda to that accomplishment as well as being the eponym for the entire sequence. So that here, at almost exactly its dead center, the sequence seems aesthetically equipped and lyrically strong enough to satisfy fully (not discredit) the demands of the old woman in "All the Fancy Things." And that is precisely what the next six poems do as they apply the evolved aesthetics and affects to the particular terms of the woman's original discontent.

"The Jungle," for instance, returns us strongly to the tropical motif of the woman's desires:

> It is not the still weight
> of the trees, the
> breathless interior of the wood,
> tangled with wrist-thick
>
> vines, the flies, reptiles
> the forever fearful monkeys
> screaming and running
> in the branches—

The tropics here, however, are clearly less hospitable than those of the old woman's longings; certainly they are not the rarefied "music and painting and all that / . . . they thought of in Puerto

Rico . . . / . . . when she was a girl." But then immediately, the poem can nonetheless locate within this claustrophic, menacing domain the more inviting aspect of a submissive young black girl:

                                        but
            a girl waiting
            shy, brown, soft-eyed—
            to guide you
                                Upstairs, sir.

The entire juxtaposition might normally be considered gratuitous, even racist and stereotyped. In the local terms of the sequence, however, the tropics are a meaningful continuation of the cat's imaginary descent into the subterranean "pit" of the flowerpot, and the girl is the logical restatement in these more distressing tropical terms of the little girl and her lost youth so poignantly recalled by the old woman in "All the Fancy Things." Such connections help establish the harshness of the tropical scene as an important lyrical redefinition of the old woman's original longings, a redefinition that is an extension of the imaginative accomplishment in the previous four poems.

The tropics, in other words, are no longer exclusively the realm of a nostalgic and irrecoverable ethereal beauty; instead, they assume some of the same oppressive distress originally associated with northern climes *and,* by the same token, they also assume the same imaginative deliverance from that distress that the sequence has so recently secured. In this sense, the meek "Negress" really does rescue the poem with her enchanting appearance, and what reprieve she offers is beyond any simply fatuous notion of primitivism. Her soothing beauty represents an authentic structural and lyrical imperative for the sequence.

The next few poems continue that imperative. Each in its way moves the sequence closer to an uplifting sense of aesthetic reconciliation between the tropical and the temperate, the exotic and the domestic. "The Jungle," for instance, achieves a remarkable sense of enchantment in its conflation of exotic tropical details with the basically routine greeting at the door to a common residence, and "The Lily" builds directly upon this in generating something like an exotic wildness for a thoroughly domesticated flower. "Upstairs, sir" had been the closing line of "The Jungle." "The Lily" brings the flora inside with the leap of a wild cat:

> The branching head of
> tiger-lilies through the window
> in the air—

The ordinary and the exotic are inextricable here. It is as if one's backyard really were a rare and busy paradise:

> A humming bird
> is still on whirring wings
> above the flowers—

> By spotted petals curling back
> and tongues that hang
> the air is seen—

And all the elements together are bound up in a ferocious sense of the exquisite. Even the unavoidable hint of predation at the end is inseparable from the precious beauty of the rare moment:

> It's raining—
> water's caught
> among the curled-back petals

> Caught and held
> and there's a fly—
> are blossoming

All of this is completely evident only in the context of the entire sequence, a context which the poem quite effectively annexes. Take, for instance, the opening image of the lily. In its projective geometry, it noticeably recalls the earlier "Young Sycamore." But where that poem had something too insistent, something strident about it, "The Lily" seems entirely relaxed. There is less striving enjambment, for example, and less explicit insistence upon the *effort* of upward ascent. Instead, the tiger lilies are instantly "through" the window: there is more the accomplished *fact* of beauty's growth and motion, a principle which the deceptively stationary humming bird illustrates equally perfectly. The aesthetics, in other words, is less tendentious, and the difference marks the lyrical growth of the sequence as well.

"On Gay Wallpaper" does something similar to "The Lily," but it inverts the components of this new imaginative order. Where the house had been an inconspicuous frame for a botanical paradise, now the house serves as the more prominent body itself of a floral splendor, and its wallpaper-skin becomes literal foilage:

> Mat roses and tridentate
> leaves of gold
> threes, threes and threes
>
> Three roses and three stems
> the basket floating
> standing in the horns of blue

The poem also reintroduces the supernatural dimension that had appeared so forcefully as an avatar in "The Bull." Now, that same element emerges with a distinctly astrological inflection:

> The green-blue ground
> is ruled with silver lines
> to say the sun is shining
>
> And on this moral sea
> of grass or dreams lie flowers
> or baskets of desires
>
> Heaven knows what they are
> between cerulean shapes
> laid regularly round

There is an exuberance here, however, that sets this off from the earlier, more staid manifestation of the divine in "The Bull." Majestic as he was, the mythically defined bull had been an ultimately ready-made, classical expression of a modern imagination augmenting its world. Now that imagination appears more excitedly attuned to the sublime in even the decorative minutae of its own time. And while "The Bull" ultimately resolved itself into the majesty of a Minotaur, "On Gay Wallpaper" locates an awesome transport in the whirlwind of some distinctly housebound weather:

> Three roses and three stems
> the basket floating
> standing in the horns of blue
>
> Repeated to the ceiling
> to the windows
> where the day
>
> Blows in
> the scalloped curtains to
> the sound of rain

The overall effect here is to raise the fantastic perception of "The Lily" to a more portentous level. There is incantation in the "threes, threes, threes" and supernatural imminence in the closing gust of wind and rain. We are, therefore, perfectly prepared for the apparitional landscape which opens the next poem, "The Source." Literally, the scene is simply a rural homestead on a mist-shrouded morning. But the context of the preceding poems places a heavy emphasis upon the scene's inherently phantasmic qualities. As "The slope of the heavy woods / pales and disappears / in the wall of mist," landmarks slowly and briefly define themselves: a barn, a pasture, balsam, then maple trees, and finally, a single powerfully animistic elm:

> A triple elm's inverted
> lichen mottled
> triple thighs from which
>
> wisps of twigs
> droop with sharp leaves
>
> Which shake in the crotch
> brushing the stained bark
> fitfully

The image recalls the sexual pose of the earlier "Young Sycamore," with its stag-like "eccentric knotted / twigs / bending forward / hornlike at the top." But clearly, the sequence has by this time penetrated much deeper into the animistic realm. Yet it is equally clear that the sequence has returned from the tropics of "The Jungle," a more usual setting for animism. Despite the appearance of the shaman-elm, the scene of "The Source" is very plainly a northern one, although not the spare, vaguely urban one of "Young Sycamore." This landscape exudes a primeval richness. No sooner has the elm-god appeared than the poem's second section presents

> soft underfoot
> the low ferns
>
> Mounting a rusty root
> the pungent mould
> globular fungi

And then with miraculous suddeness, a spring appears, touching off the refreshment that opens the poem's third section:

rock strewn a stone
half-green

A spring in whose depth
white sand bubbles
overflows

3.

clear under late
raspberries
and delicate stemmed
touch-me-nots

And finally, the stream, "The Source," surges forth with bodily force:

where alders follow it marking
the low ground
the water is cast upon

a stair of uneven stones
with a rustling sound

An edge of bubbles stirs
swiftness is moulded
speed grows

the profuse body advances
over the stones unchanged

There is a druidic wonder about this profoundly animate place that can be fully realized only in the context of the entire sequence, for "The Source" arrives with a phenomenological and lyrical authority that surpasses the separate beauties of the independent poem. From the very outset of the volume—with the first mention of the vaguely tropical paradise of her youth that the old woman, "with herself alone / and growing old up here," had so longed for— the sequence has demanded an adequate answer to her implicit complaint about the aesthetic inadequacy of "up here." In these terms, "The Source" is the most compelling vindication of the northern latitudes thus far, and the wondrous realm of rare and pure beauty is not only compelling in its own right; it is also powerfully and specifically superior to the almost invisible Puerto Rico of the old woman's nostalgic revery.

The next two poems more sharply confirm this confident sense of specifically northern beauty. With neatly parsed couplets, "Nantucket" draws an interior window scene that is brilliant in its uncluttered use of color and highly lucid in its state of awareness:

> Flowers through the window
> lavender and yellow
>
> changed by white curtains
> Smell of cleanliness—

It also reintroduces the glass pitcher image of "Brilliant Sad Sun," only now without rhetorical complication of any sort. No longer simply the occasion for the speaker's reproach of the old woman's depressive indifference to the beauties of her present world, the pitcher stands now as part of an irreducible visual, aesthetic, and emotional purity:

> Sunshine of late afternoon—
> On the glass tray
>
> a glass pitcher, the tumbler
> turned down, by which
>
> a key is lying—And the
> immaculate white bed

The cleansing effect of the visual clarity quickly translates into the cleaving "winds of this northern March" in the next poem, "The Winds." The couplets of "Nantucket" give way to a single continuous stanza full of enjambed lines which literally rend the covers off of things as they separate syntactic partners of all sorts—all in a grand, forceful act of physical, perceptual, and sexual renewal:

> flowing edge to edge
> their clear edges meeting—
> the winds of this northern March—
> blow the bark from the trees
> the soil from the field
> the hair from the heads of
> girls, the shirts from the backs
> of the men, roofs from the
> houses, the cross from the
> church, the clouds from the sky

the fur from the faces of
wild animals, crusts
from scabby eyes, scales from
the mind and husbands from wives

At this point, the sequence has achieved a broad sense of power—natural, aesthetic, and emotional power. And it is entitled to the certain amount of self-delight that in the next poem attends the sudden reemergence of the dramatic speaking voice from the earlier poems. "Lines on Receiving the Dial's Award" is in fact comical, especially in its sarcastic opening remark:

In the common mind, a corked bottle,
that Senate's egg, to-day the prohibition
we all feel has been a little lifted

The reference is, we later discover, to a "fat quartflask" which an ill tradesman (presumably for medical services rendered) has proffered the speaker. But for a moment, the lingering context of "The Winds" could easily refer the wisecrack about a "corked bottle" to that poem's perhaps too self-serious poetic hurricane. In any case, the opening remark initiates a more relaxed mood as the speaker fully engages himself in the sensual examination of the bottle's physical lineaments:

What a beauty! a fat quartflask of
greenish glass, *The Father of His Country*
embossed upon one side of it
in glass letters capping the green profile
and on the other
A little more Grape Captain Bragg

There is no mistake about it: humble as it is, this flask is both an achievement in craft and a pleasure in perception. "Out of the sand, good to hold and to see— // It approaches poetry and my delight," says the speaker as he raises it in a mock toast to "*The Dial* and its courtesy." There are awards, and then there are *awards*.

It is all a very winningly unprententious and powerfully authentic sense of arrival. And it is from this happy disposition that the sequence can return its attention to the contemporary, local, and personal environs in which the sequence opened. Only now that locale ripples everywhere with unimpeachable contentment and delicious beauty. "The Red Lily," which like "The Young Syca-more" "between the wet / pavement and the gutter" resides near a common and heavily trafficked "crossroads," surpasses the tree's beauty in the clear impression of superior value that everywhere attends the poem:

> To the bob-white's call
> and drone of reaper
>
> tumbling daisies in the sun—
> one by one
>
> about the smutting panels of
> white doors
>
> grey shingles slip and fall—
> But you, a loveliness
>
> of even lines
> curving to the throat, the
>
> crossroads is your home.

And again,

> Sometimes a farmer's wife
> gathers an armful
>
> for her pitcher on the porch—
> Topping a stone wall
>
> against the shale-ledge
> a field full—

So that when the poem panegyrically concludes "everywhere/Red Lily // in your common cup / all beauty lies," there is an absolute authority in the claim.

So too, "The Attic Which Is Desire" surpasses the restaurant of "Brilliant Sad Sun" in the intensity of attention it manages to muster for its considerably more spartan and dreary interior setting. Instead of the merely appetizing signs of "LEE'S LUNCH," we encounter an awesome, enormous, "transfixed" marquee:

> the unused tent
> of

bare beams
beyond which

directly wait
the night

and day—
Here

from the street
by

```
        *  *  *
        *  S  *
        *  O  *
        *  D  *
        *  A  *
        *  *  *
```

The ascetic scene and the meditational ecstasy here make the
title of the poem no exaggeration; a powerfully alive "Desire" of
the imagination *has* been validated in the sequence. And it is exactly this sort of transfixed desire which accounts for the equanimi-
ous appreciation of both the dingy and the pretty in "Interests of
1926." A visiting doctor ascends "filthysweet" stairs to where he
sees "the miniature/ bright poplar leaves/ at a grimy window/ wad-
ing." And then, with his own obvious tenderness, the speaker can
quietly notice

in the clear smile of
the boyish husband
all compassion for
her injury . . . and
                    such is the
celebrated May

The smile recalls the young black girl's of "The Jungle," and so
does the equation of a large seasonal or earthly state with a muted
human expression. But now the exotica and the overstatement of
the earlier poem are entirely gone, and only the most common sort
of ease in the world's moment remains.

    With that perfect ease in turn comes a comical confession in
"This Is Just to Say." The speaker here creates a world in which
guilt itself is inseparable from an innocent pleasure in both some
stolen plums *and* in the admission to that transgression:

> I have eaten
> the plums
> that were in
> the icebox
>
> and which
> you were probably
> saving
> for breakfast
>
> Forgive me
> they were delicious
> so sweet
> and so cold

Obviously unrepentant, the speaker injects into the sequence the possibility of a pure *and enduring* delectation of even the most minor sensory episodes. This is a world truly and completely possessed—liberated from the debilitations of memory that had so divorced the old woman of "Brilliant Sad Sun" from the pleasures of her own present moment. Yet it remains for that world to be claimed by the old woman herself, to whose implicit presence the sequence finally returns in its three-part summative poem, "Birds and Flowers."

The first part of "Birds and Flowers" opens with a clear statement of the sequence's evolved position:

> It is summer, winter, any
> time—
> no time at all—but delight
>
> the springing up
> of those secret flowers
> the others imitate and so

Then it goes on with some robust floral description and even a retrospective nod to the "clusters on a wall" of "On Gay Wallpaper." Yet at the end, its excitement must give way to a very sad disappointment at a stubborn audience:

>   Come!
> And just now
>
> you will not come, your

ankles
carry you another way, as

thought grown old—or
older—in
your eyes fires them against

me—small flowers
birds flitting here and there
between twigs

Part II then develops the regret of this intractable estrangement while at the same time furthering the speaker's resolve to overcome it with the intensity of the subjective, joyful perceptual equipment which the sequence has so diligently acquired:

What have I done
to drive you away? It is
winter, true enough, but

this day I love you.
This day
there is no time at all

more than in under
my ribs where anatomists
say the heart is—

And just to-day you
will not have me. Well,
to-morrow it may be snowing—

For now, however, he can only resort to a more mild version of the reproach that he had originally expressed in "All the Fancy Things":

I'll keep after you, your
repulse of me is no more
than a rebuff to the weather—

If we make a desert of
ourselves—we make
a desert . . .

Of course, the woman's "clean air, high up" is now more accurately, and convincingly, defined for what it truly is—"a desert."

And with the assurance of his own personal outlook so thoroughly validated throughout the sequence, the speaker can boldly conclude the poem with a brilliant, positively brilliant, bursting acclamation of belief and color:

> Nothing is lost! the white
> shellwhite
> glassy, linenwhite, crystalwhite
> crocuses with orange centers
> the purple crocus with
> an orange center, the yellow
> crocus with a yellow center—
>
> That which was large but
> seemed spent of
> power to fill the world with
> its wave of splendor is
> overflowing again into every
> corner—
>
>   Though the eye
> turns inward, the mind
> has spread its embrace—in
> a wind that
> roughs the stiff petals—
>
> More! the particular flower is
> blossoming . . .

Finally, the entire sequence concludes in "Full Moon" with a hopeful if suspended appeal to the night's brightest source of illumination:

> Blessed moon
> noon
> of night
>
> that through the dark
> bids love
> stay—

The intended affect here is probably better measured by the additional ten lines that originally concluded the poem and that were in fact later restored. They are passionately hopeful:

curious shapes
awake
to plague me

Is day near
shining girl?
Yes, day!

the warm
the radiant
all fulfilling

day.

This is deliverance itself, full of expectation, intimacy, and affirmation of the all-sustaining day, even in the very absence of that day; it is abiding love.

So we emerge from the opening "collection" of poems in *Collected Poems 1921–1931* with a rather profound experience wrapped around us—we do, that is, if we have been attentive and continuous in our reading. If we have not, then we probably have noted a few choice poems—probably "Young Sycamore," "Poem," "This Is Just to Say"—as particularly charming and strangely effective for all their lack of gorgeous or profound language. But if we have been attentive, then we ourselves are now powerfully equipped readers, thoroughly versed in the book's design and aesthetic: the design is clearly sequential, and the aesthetic insists upon translating the drab and ephemeral world into the eternal immediacies of poetic beauty.

More important, though, we share the lyrical disposition of the book. Its affective imperative for a healing display of beauty for a profoundly disturbed loved one; its vigorous commitment to the genuine beauties of its own immediate northern world; its great pleasure in those beauties—all these qualities become the defining affective context which we bring to bear upon the rest of the book as it wends its way through the increasingly challenging and stressful episodes of the middle sequences.

3

Broadening the Scope, Entrenching the Feeling: "Primavera," "Spring and All," and "The Descent of Winter"

Buoyant as they are, the closing notes of "Poems" clearly represent something of a happy conclusion to that sequence. But they do not signal as well a complete lyrical closure. The sanguine aesthetic spirit comprising those happy notes·is inherently a forward-looking one, and it quite naturally turns itself in the volume's succeeding three sequences to the broader and more challenging context of a larger world—a world beyond the private aesthetic argument between mother and son.

Ironically, it is a shift in orientation that will ultimately lead to a defensive entrenchment of that aesthetic optimism. More immediately, however, it is a shift that the passage between "Poems" and "Primavera" makes certain to establish as the continuous fate of a single disposition. "The mind / has spread its embrace—in / a wind that / roughs the stiff petals" announce the penultimate lines of "Birds and Flowers," and then the last promise "More! the particular flower is / blossoming." And so spring emerges in "April," the first poem of "Primavera," in such vivid images as "The green shoot come between / the red flowrets/ curled back" and "the wind is howling / the river, shining mud."[1]

Certainly, the same delight in floral beauty and the same sense of hopeful expectation that conclude the former sequence lead quite naturally to the excited anticipation of a nascent spring in "April." But there are also clear differences here. There is far greater force in the beauty of the latter poem: color breaks and bends its way through, and the cleansing wind is a wild thing. And this is all very different from the gentler if more splendid profusion of crocus color in "Birds and Flowers." "Primavera" begins, in short, with the sense of a far more aggressive beauty, and the difference translates into a broad sense of ambition for the aesthetic impulse that emerged in "Poems."

At the same time there is also in the new sequence a slackening in the sense of personal intensity. The ecstatic look to the encouraging moon of the earlier "Full Moon" of "Poems," for instance, has composed itself into a casually amiable and thoughtful reconsideration of a new start for the world:

> April

> the beginning—or
> what you will:
> > the dress
> in which the veritable winter
> walks in Spring—

> Loose it!
> Let if fall (where it will)
> —again

And the festering polemical burden of "Poems" (the implicit refutation of the old woman's initial complaint in the opening poem) expresses itself now in a more overt and less contentious form. There are lines like "—the moral is love, bred of / the mind and eyes and hands—" and a full stanza of patient exposition near the opening poem's end:

> The forms
> of the emotions are crystalline,
> geometric-faceted. So we recognize
> only in the white heat of
> understanding, when a flame
> runs through the gap made
> by learning, the shapes of things—
> the ovoid sun, the pointed trees

Such explicitness also makes it clear that the fundamental lyrical and aesthetic issue of a sustaining joy in the immediate world remains unchanged from that of "Poems." The overall effect of this more deliberative frame of mind, however, is not to debilitate the poem with thematic abstraction, but to widen its focus and loosen its idiom enough to include even more of the public world in which the poem so clearly resides. Combined with a generally more assertive sense of beauty itself, the attention of the poem broadens the tokens of spring to include realty signs as well as emergent flowers;

a manifesto of modernist "Morals" as well as privately perceived landscape and weather; contemporary political oratory as well as intimate declarations of love—all of it an expression of a supremely generous spirit:

iris blades unsheathed—

BUY THIS PROPERTY

. . . .

—the wind is howling
the river, shining mud—

Moral
    it looses me

Moral
    it supports me

Moral
    it has never ceased
    to flow

Moral
    the faded evergreen

Moral
    I can laugh

Moral
    the redhead sat
    in bed with her legs
    crossed and talked
    rough stuff

Moral
    the door is open

Moral
    the tree moving diversely
    in all parts—

. . . .

I believe
    in equality for the negro—

THIS IS MY PLATFORM

I believe in your love

the first dandelion
flower at the edge of—

In short, the initial world of "Primavera" is perhaps less intimate and intense than that of "Poems," but it is also more publically alert and amiable, more genuinely at home in the world-at-large that it invokes.

Nowhere is this more clearly seen than in the reappearance of key motifs from "Poems." Take, for instance, the meek figure of the young Negress at the doorway in "The Jungle." In that poem, she materializes out of a tropical delirium; in "April," she assumes Amazonian proportions, her exoticism coupled with a comic voluptuousness, and she takes as her cue a set of traffic commands:

STOP : GO

—she
opened the door! nearly
six feet tall, and I . . .
wanted to found a new country—

For the rest, virgin negress
at the glass
in blue-glass Venetian beads—

a green truck
dragging a concrete mixer
passes
in the street—
the clatter and true sound
of verse—

And the menu of "Brilliant Sad Sun" becomes here less a privately perceived expression of apetite and more a comic recitation of public treats:

I believe

Spumoni	$1.00
French Vanilla	.70
Chocolate	.70
Strawberry	.70
Maple Walnut	.70
Coffee	.70
Tutti Frutti	.70
Pistachio	.70
Cherry Special	.70
Orange Ice	.70
Biscuit Tortoni	

25¢ per portion

Finally, and perhaps most important, the sexual trees of "The Source" lose their savage mystery in the face of a jocular lewdness:

Maple, I see you have
a squirrel in your crotch—

And you have a woodpecker
in your hole, Sycamore

—a fat blonde, in purple (no trucking
on this street)

There is all the casual pleasure in this poem of a happy walk (or drive) to work. And indeed, as the poem closes, all the general scenery and sounds of a commuter's jaunt narrow finally to a very specific arrival at the corridors of a hospital:

I believe

Woman's Ward

⟶

Private

⟵

The soul, my God, shall rise up
—a tree

Of course, all of these transformations signal more than just a simply amiable disposition. They also represent a larger vision of beauty in the casual world, and as such they are a direct expression of the greater aesthetic ambition established earlier in the poem. The association of traffic noise with extraordinary sexual appeal; the dwelling upon the variety of sensory flavors in a menu; the discovery of sexual vivacity in the wildlife of some trees; and the intuition of spiritual improvement (as well as sexual interest) in the directional signs to the lady's room and to private quarters—such things are bold efforts to enliven the most mundane details of the immediate and ordinary world through the power of the imagination.

It is as if after having discovered and passionately embraced the transfigured face of his beloved world, his "shining girl," the speaker steps back for perspective and an excited and rapid view of her overall form. And in fact, much of the opening "April" affects a summative character: the litanies of "Morals," the credo of "I believe's," and even the tabulation of the ice-cream menu are the most striking effects in this vein. But the roving attention of "April" must and does give way to a more careful examination of that world's individual parts, both banal and gorgeous, and in the succeeding three poems the sequence begins to complicate its happy disposition with the more problematic aesthetic conditions of the world at large. It is a shift that the transition between "April" and the succeeding "The Trees" makes seem almost inevitable as it moves a single motif to the fore and very exactly redirects it into a plainly angry moment.

After the lewd address to the maple and sycamore, for instance, "April" resumes its more serious strains and clarifies into a spiritual inquiry. First the transcendent soul is figuratively equated with a tree; then comes a challenge to an otherwise absentee deity; then all human experience defines itself literally as the bodies and motions of the trees themselves. But then directly on the heels of this arrives the distinctive rhyming personification that opens the poem "The Trees":

> The soul, my God, shall rise up
> —a tree
>
> But who are You?
> in this mortal wind
> that I at least can understand
> having sinned willingly

> The forms
> of the emotions are crystalline,
> geometric-faceted. So we recognize
> only in the white heat of
> understanding, when a flame
> runs through the gap made
> by learning, the shapes of things—
> the ovoid sun, the pointed trees
>
> lashing branches
>
> The wind is fierce, lashing
>
> the long-limbed trees whose
> branches
> wildly toss—
>
> THE TREES
>
> The trees—being trees
> thrash and scream
> guffaw and curse—
> wholly abandoned
> damning the race of men—

While the transitions of identical, exact, and near rhyme (trees/ trees; lash/thrash; toss/curse) as well as the title itself enforce a strong continuity between the poems, the shift in the succeeding poem's perspective nonetheless arrests the pseudotranscendental tendencies that close "April." Like earlier parts of "April" itself, "The Trees" returns the movement to a less pretentious vernacular but with a gruffer edge:

> Christ, the bastards
> haven't even sense enough
> to stay out in the rain—
>
> Wha ha ha ha
>
> Wheeeeee
> Clacka tacka tacka
> tacka tacka
> wha ha ha ha ha
> ha ha ha

There is also greater discontent here—not with the world itself, but with the modern race of men who have so outrageously devalued their erstwhile better halves. It is as though the aggrieved trees refuse to be so easily charmed by the teasing speaker of "April," refuse to forget that certain scores must be settled:

> haw haw haw haw
> —and memory broken
>
> wheeeeee
>
> There were never satyrs
> never maenads
> never eagle-headed gods—
> These were men
> from whose hands sprung
> love
> bursting the wood—

Finally, though, this lover's defensiveness nestles down into a more affectionate consideration of the trees themselves and, harkening back to the lyrical geography of "Poems," in decidedly winterish terms:

> Trees their companions
>
> —a cold wind winterlong
> in the hollows of our flesh
> icy with pleasure—
>
> no part of us untouched

And the affection then immediately gives rise to the delicate love talk of "The Bird's Companion," replete with a charming play upon the closing "companion" motif of the previous poem:

> As love
> that is
> each day upon the twig
> which may die
>
> So springs your love
> fresh up
> lusty for the sun
> the birds' companion—

Of course, in the mixed world that has been defined by the long, dominant opening poem of the sequence, it is probably inevitable that such delicate moments must jostle up against their more clownish neighbors. Just so, the dangling dash at the end of "The Bird's Companion" furnishes just enough suspension to create a real surprise when sun and bird surrender the stage to a carnival act in "The Sea-Elephant":

> Trundled from
> the strangeness of the sea—
> a kind of
> heaven—
>
> Ladies and Gentlemen!
> the greatest
> sea-monster ever exhibited
> alive
>
> .   .   .
>
> Sick
> of April's smallness
> the little
> leaves—
>
> Flesh has lief of you
> enormous sea—
> Speak!
> Blouaugh! (feed
>
> me) my
> flesh is riven—

For all its grossness, the sea-elephant is, like the trees, another instance of tenuously emerging life which suffers abuse from the world at large and which the single speaker relishes and celebrates throughout the sequence. Sadly, the only modern equivalent to the wonder of ancient sailors at their first encounter with the creature ("Gape. / Strange head— / told by old sailors— / rising // bearded / to the surface—and") is the speaker's own moral outrage at the displacement of the animal, a displacement that transforms his surfacings from an awesome marinal upheaval into a pathetic circus gambit for food from a trainer's hand:

> contort yourselves—
> But I
> am love. I am
> from the sea—

Blouaugh!
there is no crime save
the too heavy
body

the sea
held playfully—comes
to the surface
the water

boiling
about the head the cows
scattering
fish dripping from

the bounty
of . . . and Spring,
they say
Spring is icummen in—

The bitter sarcasm of the last lines gives way in "Rain" to a more interior brooding. The splash of the sea-elephant is replaced by sentimental rain drops; the public commotion of the circus ring is displaced by the quieter interior of a private home; and even the more solid quatrains of "The Sea-Elephant" become dispersed into an irregularly "dripping" pattern. Of course, however, there remains in the scene the traces of its predecessor, yet those traces are entirely transformed within the fabric of personal self-appraisal which has replaced the previous poem's public outrage: trees become sea-elephants by virtue of a guilty imagination:

There
          paintings
and fine
          metalware
woven stuffs—
all the whoreishness
of our
          delight
sees
from its window
the spring wash
of your love
          the falling
rain—

> The trees
> are become
> beasts fresh risen
> from
>   the sea—
> water
>
> trickles
> from the crevices of
> their hides—
>
> So my life is spent
>   to keep out love

The change here comes close to overturning the happy and extroverted aesthetic attention originally established for the sequence in "April." But ultimately, it is this same mildly despairing imagination that concocts the comforting figure of "a kind physician" venturing outside, "running in between / the drops // the rain." Unlike the irremediably boorish audience of "The Sea-Elephant," the sensibility here manages to redeem its own sense of emotional and aesthetic inadequacy by philosophically conceiving for itself a higher reality that exempts it from the otherwise humbling superiority of the rain's transformational potency:

> Unworldly love
> that has no hope
>   of the world
>
>   and that
> cannot change the world
> to its delight—
>
>   The rain
> falls upon the earth
> and grass and flowers
> come
>   perfectly
>
> into form from its
>   liquid
>
> clearness
>
>   But love is
> unworldly

      and nothing
comes of it but love

following

and falling endlessly
from
     her thoughts

The closing obeisance to "love" as though it were a graciously passing lady extracts a gallant dignity out of a fundamentally ignominious state, and it anticipates the terms of the broader recovery in the rest of the sequence as it seeks to overcome the defeat of casual beauty in the world by cultivating a more studied—and ultimately assertive—aesthetic refinement. Thus there follows the suddenly sweeping social graciousness of "The House:"

The house is yours
to wander in as you please—
Your breakfasts will be kept
ready for you until

you choose to arise!
.   .   .   .

This is the kitchen—
We have a new
hotwater heater and a new
gas-stove to please you

And the front stairs
have been freshly painted—
white risers
and the treads mahogany.

Come upstairs
to the bedroom—
Your bed awaits you—
the chiffonier waits—

This is hospitality of a fantastic sort—more an invitation to a newly refurbished life of color and pleasure than a wish for a merely comfortable stay. And though it seems an inexplicable exaggertion at first, the poem manages to define itself as a commensurately cheerful answer to the dismal house interior of "Rain." It

also reformulates in more genteel terms the comic vitality of the
portal "negress" in the opening "April," and it reorients the aesthetic ambition of the sequence away from the casual beauty of "a
green truck/ dragging a concrete mixer" and towards the special
beauty of more carefully prepared perceptions.

This reorientation receives its fullest expression in the sequence's final poem, "The Botticellian Trees." But more immediately there intervenes a poem that seems the very antithesis of
"The House." Instead of a gracious invitation to a new life, "Death"
begins with what has got to be one of the most confounding displays of discourtesy to the dearly departed ever written:

> He's dead
>
> the dog won't have to
> sleep on his potatoes
> any more to keep them
> from freezing—
>
> he's dead
> the old bastard—
> He's a bastard because
>
> there's nothing
> legitimate in him any
> more

Although superficially antithetical, the incredible rudeness here
really serves as a corollary to the special aesthetic manners of the
previous poem. Once empowered with a sense of special aesthetic
value, the sequence quite naturally defines all else in its terms.
Thus, death itself becomes shorn of every sentimental or religious
vestige. It is neither an occasion for routine sadness nor for mystical glorification; it is simply the worst sort of caricature of animated life:

> Put his head on
> one chair and his
> feet on another and
> he'll lie there
> like an acrobat—
>
> Love's beaten. He
> beat it. That's why
> he's insufferable—

because
he's here needing a
shave and making love
an inside howl
of anguish and defeat—

And burial is not a ceremonious disposal so much as the simply
necessary removal of a very rude fellow:

Dead
        his eyes
rolled up out of
the light—a mockery
                which
love cannot touch—

just bury it
and hide its face
for shame.

All this denunciation amounts to a restatement of the anger over
beauty's various defeats earlier in the sequence, only now the
anger is not complicated with any notes of personal guilt or self-
recrimination. We might well say, then, that despite the disturbingly darker notes that complicate the sequence, the implicit campaign of "Primavera" to apply the hopeful aesthetic outlook of
"Poems" to a broader and more public world has to some extent
succeeded. Life and death and the aesthetic possibilities they represent have been radically reconceived as, respectively, the most
gracious of hosts, the rudest of insults. And so "Primavera" closes
with a poem that is a conspicuous revision of the second in the
sequence. In place of the nondescript trees of "The Trees," we
have the more refined arbor of "The Botticellian Trees." And in
place of the former's angry resentment—the "thrash and scream/
guffaw and curse"—we have the exquisite delicacy of

The alphabet of
the trees

is fading in the
song of the leaves

the crossing
bars of the thin

letters that spelled
winter

and the cold
have been illumined

with
pointed green

by the rain and sun—
The strict simple

principles of
straight branches

are being modified
by pinched out

ifs of color, devout
conditions

the smiles of love—
.   .   .   .

And instead of a sulking winter tree trunk, we have the easy, unfet-
tered sensuality of

until the stript
sentences

move as a woman's
limbs under cloth

and praise from secrecy
with hot ardor

love's ascendancy
in summer—

In summer the song
sings itself

above the muffled words—

Clearly, there is some sense of positive accomplishment in "Primavera." At least in its formal surface, "The Botticellian Trees"—

with its well balanced couplets, its focused attention, and its mellifluous sounds—cannot but appear as a refinement of the comparatively sprawling, hectic, and sometimes even jarring "April." Yet
we should not mistake the structural articulation, no matter how
striking or balanced, with closure or with a permanent denial of
the sequence's darker strains—especially since the title of the succeeding sequence, "Spring and All," makes it equally plain that
"Primavera" was indeed only a beginning, a precursor to a more
encompassing and even more demanding spring.

   And indeed, "Spring and All" proves to be just about an overwhelming challenge to the book's spirit. The sequence's overall
development is an unrelenting passage from an idealized sense of
aesthetic ambition to an embittered social realism. "Flight to the
City," the opening poem of "Spring and All," immediately establishes both a lyrical continuity to and a further expansion of the
volume's poetic world. Recalling the courtly strains that closed
"Primavera," a troubadourian speaker is inspired by the aesthetic
call of an urban skyline at night, and he sets his mind on whisking
his beloved away to the larger world of the big city:

> The Easter stars are shining
> above lights that are flashing—
> coronal of the black—
>   Nobody
> to say it—
>   Nobody to say: pinholes
>
> Thither I would carry her
> among the lights—

The "her" is defined as the same feminine *principle* of beauty that
as an issue has preoccupied the entire volume thus far. But in
contrast to the arboreal "cloth" in "The Botticellian Trees," she is
now to be adorned with pronoucedly urban trinkets:

> a crown for her head with
> castles upon it, skyscrapers
> filled with nut-chocolates—

   The problem here, of course, is that such effects seem only hy-
perbolic and gaudy, perhaps even cynically so, after the quiet, refined sensuality of "The Botticellian Trees." Only the vaguely
anachronistic posture of the troubadour is at all convincing and
only *as* anachronism. The whole episode anticipates the more piti-

ful state recounted in "To Elsie," the final poem of the sequence, where "young slatterns" are "tricked out" with baubles conceived by impoverished imaginations. It also signals the disturbing aesthetic recalcitrance of a world that throughout the new sequence continuously challenges the optimistic spirit inherited from "Poems" and "Primavera." Nonetheless, the quixotic impulse to beauty has been expressed, and "Spring and All" sets about transforming the man-made world in beauty's image, starting "At the Faucet of June."

It is a good and a difficult place to start. As the title insinuates, nature and the aesthetic face of the seasons themselves seem everywhere regulated and spoiled by the manufactured. The very sunlight has become embedded and discolored "in a / yellow plaque upon the / varnished floor"; the breath of song is caricatured in a pneumatic measurement of "fifty pounds pressure"; and J. P. Morgan is a philistine Pluto who uses art like a wrench:

> pulling at the
> anemones in
> Persephone's cow-pasture
>
> When from among
> the steel rocks leaps
> J.P.M.
>
> who enjoyed
> extraordinary privileges
> among virginity
>
> to solve the core
> of whirling flywheels
> by cutting
>
> the Gordian knot
> with a Veronese or
> perhaps a Rubens—

The broad satire of the poem neatly magnifies the implicit foibles of contemporary civilization in "Flight to the City." But "Faucet" is not sheer lampoon. At the end, it discards cynicism for a carefully measured hope in the possibilities for genuine beauty that exist in even the preeminent motor vehicle:

> whose cars are about
> the finest on
> the market to-day—

And so it comes
to motor cars—
which is the son

leaving off the g
of sunlight and grass—
impossible

to say, impossible
to underestimate—
wind, earthquakes in

Manchuria, a
partridge
from dry leaves

Remote as it is, the possibility for the alignment of manufactured with natural expressions of excellence and power—the automobile with earthquakes, J. P. Morgan with a partridge—provokes in the next poem an invigorating glimpse of the new aesthetic order that the sequence seeks. It is, as the title makes clear, a study of a horticultured plant that, despite an unruly confusion at the top, manages to reveal as it descends brilliant clarities of color and form:

THE POT OF PRIMROSES

Pink confused with white
flowers and flowers reversed
take and spill the shaded flame
darting it back
into the lamp's horn

petals aslant darkened with mauve

red where in whorls
petal lays its glow upon petal
round flamegreen throats

petals radiant with transpiercing light
contending
                              above

the leaves
reaching up their modest green
from the pot's rim

> and there, wholly dark, the pot
> gay with rough moss

It is immensely significant that the oxymoron of the final stanza goes almost entirely unnoticed. In the way that the lyrical momentum of uplifting beauty simply engulfs even the objectively drab pot and makes it *convincingly* "gay," there is an implicit vindication of the previous poem's confidence in the possibility of transforming even the unsightly evidence of man's managing (or mismanaging) hand in the world.

In this regard, the deliberate visual trickery of the succeeding "The Eyeglasses" seems a more daring display of the same effect. Seamlessly merging the details of candy, flowers, field, and farmer, the opening stanzas make it impossible for us to discern whether the scene is an illustration from a candy box or an actually littered pasture. Then the speaker didactically breaks in to elucidate the confusion as simply the illustration of a perceptual necessity: "It is / this that engages the favorable // distortion of eyeglasses / that see everything and remain / related to mathematics." He follows his point with the surprising delight that precision in the examination of even the most routine things can engender:

> in the most practical frame of
> brown celluloid made to
> represent tortoiseshell—
>
> A letter from the man who
> wants to start a new magazine
> made of linen
>
> and he owns a typewriter—
> July 1, 1922
> All this is for eyeglasses

Against such precise and vivid features as "brown celluloid," "tortoiseshell," "linen," even "July 1, 1922," the opening blurs of the traditionally more rustic and poetic subjects pale; and the eyeglasses are one human contraption of genuine aesthetic worth. Yet, however persuasive his immediate argument, the speaker can only conclude with a sardonic comment upon their present disuse:

> to discover. But
> they lie there with the gold
> earpieces folded down
>
> tranquilly Titicaca—

"Composition" picks up the whimsical note of the last line and parlays it into a piece of fancy that is partially an adult analysis of design and partially a child's absurd fantasy—at once an artistic composition *and* a homework composition. We get both

> The red paper box
> hinged with cloth
>
> is lined
> inside and out
> with imitation
> leather

and

> Its two-inch trays
> have engineers
> that convey glue
> to airplanes

And again, we get both a serious aesthetic proposition—

> It is the sun
> the table
> with dinner
> on it for
> these are the same—

and a juvenile curiosity—

> What is the end
> to insects
> that suck gummed
> labels?

The overall effect is to create for the adult perspective a credible sense of fascination, even with the adornments of a cheap "red paper box":

> But the stars
> are round
> cardboard
> with a tin edge

> and a ring
> to fasten them
> to a trunk
> for the vacation—

No child ever treasured a cigar box more.

But the charm of that puerile enchantment quickly evaporates into the more absurd adult spectacle that "Light Becomes Darkness" lambasts. After the momentary reprieve of "Composition," the speaker resumes and intensifies the intellectual indictment he began in "The Eyeglasses." He sarcastically defines the proliferation of movie halls as the spring-like "efflorescent" expression of "The decay of cathedrals," and he disparagingly proposes a general equation between the decline of religion and the rise of cinema. Both are pathetic displays of an inadequate imagination:

> Nightly the crowds
> with the closeness and
> universality of sand
> witness the selfspittle
>
> which used to be drowned
> in incense and intoned
> over by the supple-jointed
> imagination of inoffensiveness

Then, in what has become a typical strategy, he secures his argument with an imagistic fillip: the entire grandiose agenda of the religious imagination—"to / attract the dynamic mob"—is suddenly and thoroughly reproved with the subtle, particular imagination of a Tolstoi:

> backed by biblical
> rigidity made into passion plays
> upon the altar to
> attract the dynamic mob
>
> whose female relative
> sweeping grass Tolstoi
> saw injected into
> the Russian nobility

And then, partially in delight with this counter-aesthetic (and perhaps partially to preclude any political significance to the invocation of the proletarian-minded Tolstoi), the sequence arrives at probably its most famous poem, "The Red Wheelbarrow":

> so much depends
> upon
>
> a red wheel
> barrow
>
> glazed with rain
> water
>
> beside the white
> chickens

There has probably never been such an irreducibly aesthetic farm implement. The precious imbalance of each couplet's line lengths, the emphatic separation of noun phrases in the enjambment, the vividness of the minimal detail—all highlight everything but the barrow's function. The dependency mentioned in the opening lines has nothing to attach itself to *except* the transfigured object that the wheelbarrow has become. If it does manage to successfully refer to anything else, it could only be the intellectual argument of the preceding poem. And that is really nothing more than a contemptuous expression of the same principle illustrated in delightful terms by "The Red Wheelbarrow."

If there were any doubt about art's fundamental capacity to enliven the manufactured as well as the natural world, "The Red Wheelbarrow" removes it. In the best human imagination even the most humble of man's handiwork can be rendered as a beautiful thing. Thus, after such perfection, the sudden subway-like jolt of the crass cynicism that opens "Rapid Transit" must seem nothing less than defilement itself:

> Somebody dies every four minutes
> in New York State—
>
> To hell with you and your poetry—
> You will rot and be blown
> through the next solar system
> with the rest of the gases—
>
> What the hell do you know about it?

The reduction of life to an idiot statistic contrasts sharply with the rich minimalism of "The Red Wheelbarrow." In this world, beauty survives only in the preposterous diction of street-smarts— "AXIOMS // Do not get killed"—or in the gratuitous alliteration of a civic slogan—"Careful Crossings Campaign / Cross Crossings Cautiously." Even the pleasures of the "open country" have been relegated to the promotional cliches of an advertisement authored by a corporation:

> Don't stay shut up in hot rooms
> Go to one of the Great Parks
>
> Pelham Bay for example
> It's on Long Island Sound
> with bathing, boating,
> tennis, baseball, golf, etc.
>
> Acres and acres of green grass
> wonderful shade-trees, rippling brooks
>
>> Take the Pelham Bay Park Branch
>> of the Lexington Ave. (East Side)
>> Line and you are there in a few
>> minutes
>
> Interborough Rapid Transit Co.

Prefaced by the city slicker cynicism of the opening lines, the penultimate stanza of train directions can only appear facile—modern transportation's empty promise of a suspiciously easy escape to an idyllic world. It is also an effect that disturbingly recalls and illumines the "troubadour's" invitation to elopement in "Flight to the City."

Against this glib offer of a day-trip spring stands the self-assured refusal of "The Avenue of Poplars." In couplets that recall "The Red Wheelbarrow" and a subject that echoes "The Botticellian Trees," the speaker appears to dismiss the purported marvels of the subway and the "Great Parks" in favor of his own more intimately known and friendly tree-lined street:

>> The leaves embrace
>> in the trees
>>
>> it is a wordless
>> world

without personality
I do not

seek a path
I am still with

Gypsy lips pressed
to my own—

It is the kiss
of leaves

without being
poison ivy

or nettle, the kiss
of oak leaves—

It is probably unavoidable that such an erotically charged communion with the world should begin to sooner or later sound like Whitman, and indeed, the remaining couplets could be *Leaves of Grass* without the sprawling lines:

He that has kissed
a leaf

need look no further—
I ascend

through
a canopy of leaves

and at the same time
I descend

for I do nothing
unusual—

I ride in my car
I think about

prehistoric caves
in the Pyrenees—

the cave of
Les Trois Frères

The beautiful relaxation of the idle daydreaming in the last few lines creates both lyrically and literally a greater sense of transport than the preceding IRT. Equipped only with a car, a roadway, and an intensely alive sensibility, we penetrate through to both the heights of the transcendental and, with quick wit, the innermost realms of primitive art.

The conceit of an "idle" imagination powerfully in love with its world and its own handiwork in that world is elaborately explored in "At the Ball Game." First the speaker leisurely elucidates yet another human totem of spring in the distinctive couplets that have become increasingly reserved for only the best expressions of the human imagination:

> The crowd at the ball game
> is moved uniformly
>
> by a spirit of uselessness
> which delights them—
>
> all the exciting detail
> of the chase
>
> and the escape, the error
> the flash of genius—
>
> to no end save beauty
> the eternal—[2]

Then, there is a sudden moment of tension as some vulgar usage emerges:

> So in detail they, the crowd,
> are beautiful
>
> for this
> to be warned against
>
> saluted and defied—
> It is alive, venomous
>
> It smiles grimly
> its words cut—
>
> The flashy female with her
> "mother" gets it—

> The Jew gets it straight—it
> is deadly, terrifying—

But like the quick punctuation of baseball plays themselves, the tension just as quickly dissipates as the relaxed intellectual tones resume, and the poem finally closes with a calm restatement of the scene and theme:

> It is the Inquisition, the
> Revolution
>
> It is beauty itself
> that lives
>
> day by day in them
> idly—
>
> This is
> the power of their faces
>
> It is summer, it is the solstice
> the crowd is
>
> cheering, the crowd is laughing
> in detail
>
> permanently, seriously
> without thought

This isometric relaxation prepares us perfectly for the supremely peaceful "Rigamarole." It is night, and all the suburban earth has settled down into a slow orchestration of visual, aural, and tactile details, each perfectly at rest:

> The veritable night
> of wires and stars
>
> the moon is in
> the oak tree's crotch
>
> and sleepers in
> the windows cough
>
> athwart the round
> and pointed leaves

> and insects sting
> while on the grass
>
> the whitish moonlight
> tearfully
>
> assumes the attitudes
> of afternoon—

Then, out of this luminous transformation of the night, there arises the nocturne of an enchanted peach tree that precisely and sensually embodies the principle of an imaginative renewal, a renewal that is identical with the physical renewal of nature and that is what the entire sequence has been seeking for the man-made world as well:

> But it is real
> where peaches hang
>
> recalling death's
> long promised symphony
>
> whose tuneful wood
> and stringish undergrowth
>
> are ghosts existing
> without being
>
> save to come with juice
> and pulp to assuage
>
> the hunger which
> the night reveals

Finally, the speaker himself takes comfort in the fortitude that this highly imaginative vision provides against a hideously abrasive daylight:

> so that now at last
> the truth's aglow
>
> with devilish peace
> forestalling day
>
> which dawns tomorrow
> with dreadful reds

>the heart to predicate
>with mists that loved
>
>the ocean and the fields—
>Thus moonlight
>
>is the perfect
>human touch.

The "rigamarole" of the title, of course, refers ironically to the metaphysical figure of the peach tree—that and the concluding conceit of the last three lines. There is also perhaps a milder ironic reference to the conspicuous lyricism of the piece. The phrasing is exquisitely mellifluous: the rhymes are delicately subtle; the rhythmic rise and fall of each couplet is so perfectly measured that it could be the breath of sleep itself. The effects are in fact *so* fine that they may approach an untenable preciousness—a state of poetic rigamarole.

And indeed "Rigamarole" *is* something of a false conclusion to the sequence. For all its quietude, the peace in this poem reveals itself as a bit gratuitous and illusory. The special tokens of the modern man-made world that have governed the imagery and motifs of the poems until now are peculiarly absent from "Rigamarole." Except for the inconspicuous utility wires in the opening image of the night sky, there is little to suggest that the transforming "human touch" of the last line has reached much beyond a private if timeless meditation. Instead, as the echo of "oak tree's crotch" implies, we remain very much in the vegetative world. Of course, the speaker himself has not pretended much more; the poem's ending does include a distinct, although controlled, note of anxiety at the prospect of "day // which dawns to-morrow / with dreadful reds." The night imagination offers only respite from, not transformation of, the hard realities of the public world.

It is this anxious discomfort which emerges as the real concluding affect of "Spring and All." Stripping away the fey luster of "Rigamarole," "To Elsie" returns to the disturbing facts of the human world with a vengeance. The slightly glib proposal for elopement in "Flight to the City" now reappears a part of a positively devastating social dilemma. "The pure products of America" are painfully called forth as a hideous roster of the indigent, the diseased, the demeaned—"deaf-mutes, thieves / old names"—all bereft of any sustaining "rigamarole":

>and young slatterns, bathed
>in filth

> from Monday to Saturday
>
> to be tricked out that night
> with gauds
> from imaginations which have no
>
> peasant traditions to give them
> character
> but flutter and flaunt
>
> sheer rags—succumbing without
> emotion
> save numbed terror
>
> under some hedge of choke-cherry
> or viburnum—
> which they cannot express—

The broad cultural defects spawned by the country's very youth (spring and all indeed) then slowly resolve themselves into failings of a more personal sort. "Rescued by an / agent," the Indian-blooded Elsie is

> sent out at fifteen to work in
> some hard-pressed
> house in the suburbs—
>
> some doctor's family, some Elsie—
> voluptuous water
> expressing with broken
>
> brain the truth about us—
> her great
> ungainly hips and flopping breasts
>
> addressed to cheap
> jewelry
> and rich young men with fine eyes

The angry personal sarcasm of "some hard-pressed / house in the suburbs" finally cools, but only into an even more profoundly disturbing state—a frustrated and helpless complaint about the dereliction of those who presumably hold the responsibility for the country's imagination:

as if the earth under our feet
were
an excrement of some sky

and we degraded prisoners
destined
to hunger until we eat filth

while the imagination strains
after deer
going by fields of goldenrod in

the stifling heat of September
Somehow
it seems to destroy us

It is only in isolate flecks that
something
is given off

No one
to witness
and adjust, no one to drive the car

So the final note of "Spring and All" is quite different from those of the two sequences that precede it. The intimate tension between personal temperaments that had served as the imaginative impetus in "Poems" ultimately leads to the resolution and tenderness of "Full Moon" with its happy and gentle question, "Is day near / shining girl?" Similarly, the personal aesthetic ambition that had inspired the exertions of "Primavera" lead to the graceful pleasure of "The Botticellian Trees." But the larger cultural agenda that challenges the imagination in "Spring and All" leads only to the public disgrace and personal demoralization of "To Elsie."

It is, therefore, entirely natural that the disappointing spring of "Spring and All" gives way in the succeeding sequence to the dormancy's more proper expression—"The Descent of Winter." A sulky mood emerges to retrench the volume's aesthetic ambition, and although ultimately, this mood manages to muster a far more realistic, more mature faith in the possibility of a new aesthetic world order, it more immediately signals retreat rather than advance. It is as if imagination itself were hunkering down in preparation for the season's distress. The poems of the sequence shed even the inherent flamboyance of genuine titles, and they are left instead with the mere dates of composition; imagination has abdicated to the calendar.

"9/29" opens the section with a claustrophobic description of a ship's state room:

> My bed is narrow
> in a small room
> at sea
>
> The numbers are on
> the wall
> Arabic 1
>
> Berth No. 2
> was empty above me
> the steward
>
> took it apart
> and removed
> it
>
> only the number
> remains
> • 2 •

The numbers on the wall, grown magnified under a completely involved attention, especially shrink the sense of space, as does the contracting three-line stanza itself. Together, they confirm the equivalently heightened sense of time that the date/title suggests. But even out of this neurotic state, the concrete beauty of the number plaque manages to assert itself:

> on an oval disc
> of celluloid
> tacked
>
> to the white enameled
> woodwork
> with
>
> two bright nails
> like stars
> beside
>
> the moon

Thus, the sequence begins with an intensely alive sensibility under siege, in retreat. "10/10" and "10/21 (the orange flames)" continue this remarkable complex of beauty and stress while shifting the emphasis a bit. Rather than the fugitive beauty of the number plaque at the end of "9/29," we encounter as foremost in "10/ 10" the beauty of a vividly colored flower:

> Monday
> the canna flaunts
> its crimson head

But as the overly time-conscious notation of the day perhaps suggests, this flower, especially its thrice repeated color, is languishing:

> Crimson lying folded
> crisply down upon
>
> the invisible
>
> darkly crimson heart
> of the poor yard—
>
> the grass is long
> October tenth
>
> 1927

The entire affective state here might best be termed neurasthenic, and indeed the paradoxical coupling of a heightened sense of the immediate moment with the near amnesia of longer periods (such as those insinuated by the unmentioned intervals between poems/entries) *is* a classical symptom of clinical neurasthenia. So is the depressive fascination with a fire in "10/21 (the orange flames)" (explicitly identified in other printings of the poem as a rubbish fire). An entire nine-line, blockish stanza pensively mulls over the color and motion of the blaze:

> the orange flames
> stream horizontal, windblown
> they parallel the ground
> waving up and down
> the flamepoints alternating

> the body streaked with loops
> and purple stains while
> the pale smoke, above,
> continues steadily eastward—

Then in the second stanza it turns into an equally obsessive and now explicit grouse about the infirmities of old age:

> What chance have the old?
> There are no duties for them
> no places where they may sit.
> Their knowledge is laughed at
> they cannot see, they cannot hear.

And on for eight more lines—"Their feet hurt, they are weak / they should not have to suffer"—until the speaker pathetically insists, "there should be a truce for them."

But the only "truce" in sight is the embarrassing one between hunter and prey that prompts the entry for "10/22 (and hungers still return)." The picture here is of literal failure—hunters returning empty-handed—yet underneath it all is that same vigorously alive sensibility that has been hunkering further and further down throughout the sequence. Note, for instance, how the single fine detail of the hunters' swagger through the municipal precincts creates a convincing basis for the mythic transfiguration that is hinted at in the final lines of the poem:

> and hunters still return
> even through the city
> with their guns slung
> openly from the shoulder—
> emptyhanded howbeit
> for the most part
>   but aloof
> as if from another world[3]

This same imaginative vitality then takes the theme of cultural ineffectuality and translates it into the paradoxically vivid Gerontion-like doldrums of "10/28 (On hot days)":

> On hot days
> the sewing machine
>   whirling
>
> in the next room
> in the kitchen

and men at the bar
    talking of the strike
and cash

The relationship here between the elements of beauty and those of enervation is almost the exact inverse of the earlier "10/10." There, the literally beautiful canna seemed overwhelmed by a languorous affect; here the denoted lethargy seems buoyed by the beauty of the vivid physical impression, especially of the "whirling" sewing machine. We sense, then, that a certain equilibrium has been attained in this season of "descent"—exactly at its middle poem/date. Sustaining beauty is no longer the fugitive presence at the end of a poem, as it was in "9/29"; it is now the very substance of the entries.

And so, when "10/29" picks up the motif of class conflict from "10/28 (On hot days)" ("talking of the strike"), it parlays it into a forthright manifesto of the ascendant sensibility's own redemptive aesthetic:

The justice of poverty
    its shame its dirt
are one with the meanness
    of love

Its organ in a tarpaulin
    the green birds
the fat, sleepy horse
    the old men

The precise details and vivid language of the second stanza are now aligned with the affirmation of the literal statement in the first, and the sense of confident consolidation is further reinforced by the first appearance since the opening poem of a visually regular stanza. This time, however, the more balanced quatrains stand in exact contrast to the shrinking triplets of "9/29." Everything serves to save from idiocy the detailed spectacle of a genuine human effort at enacted beauty:

The grinder sourfaced
    hat over eyes
the beggar smiling all open
    the lantern out

And the popular tunes—
    sold to the least bidder
for a nickel
    two cents or ·

> nothing at all
> or even
> against the desire
> forced on us

The final stanza, especially its last line, neatly suggests the incipient boldness of which even the hurdy-gurdy's necessarily minimal aestheticism proves capable. In "11/1," that boldness grows more plainly robust. There is a literally comic expansion of scene that sharply contrasts with the claustrophobic interior of the opening "9/29," and the grotesque gigantism of the decor in that poem also contrasts with the naturally large embroidery which some meadow reeds create on the night's horizon:

> The moon, the dried weeds
> and the Pleiades—
>
> Seven feet tall
> the dark, dried weedstalks
> make a part of the night—
> a red lace
> on the blue milky sky

Within this idyllic enlargement of view and feeling, there is the sudden ejaculation of a creative imperative—"Write"—followed immediately by an abrupt contraction of the visual field:

> Write—
> by a small lamp

Then, the sudden sense of getting down to business expands into a deliberation upon the relative effects to be had with different measures of illumination; and the "small lamp" of the previous stanza retroactively acquires an ironic inadequacy as it pales in the presence of two immensely healthy boys revealed by the greater illumination of a billboard:

> the Pleiades are almost
> nameless
> and the moon is tilted
> and halfgone
>
> And in runningpants and
> with ecstatic aesthetic faces
> on the illumined

> signboard are leaping
> over printed hurdles and
> "1/4 of their energy comes
> from bread"
>
> two gigantic highschool boys
> ten feet tall

These two bounding youths with their "aesthetic faces" appear as something like the champions of both their own printed legend ("1/4 of their energy. . .") and the imaginative initiative which that very script and their own image represent. However commercial the billboard's origin, its reality is an exuberantly, gigantically aesthetic one.

Indeed, the boys are rather effective champions, for they and their slogan prepare us exactly for the appearance of an equally expansive title at the head of the next day's entry:

11/2

A MORNING IMAGINATION OF RUSSIA

One can almost see the unending Asiatic steppes at sunrise! The entry itself is just as expansive. In full proselike lines and at relatively huge length (the poem is over three full pages), a speaker opens the "IMAGINATION" by first translating the exterior immensity of the boys into a more subjective awakening and amplification of spirit:

> The earth and the sky were very close
> When the sun rose it rose in his heart
> It bathed the red cold world of
> the dawn so that the chill was his own

This sense of inner expansion immediately defines itself as part of the sequence's established lyrical emergence out of the fact of seasonal distress and into the mitigating beauty of its very wreckage:

> The mists were sleep and sleep began
> to fade from his eyes. Below him in the
> garden a few flowers were lying forward
> on the intense green grass where
> in the opalescent shadows oak leaves
> were pressed hard down upon it in patches
> by the night rain. There were no cities

The brilliant colors especially recall and confirm the sensory boldness that had persisted in the crimson canna and whirling sewing
machine of "10/10" and "10/28 (On hot days)." Then with hardly a
pause, the speaker deploys the vaguely proletarian suggestions of
the title, and constructs a broad cultural perspective that will incorporate the opening sense of personal liberation and govern the rest
of the poem:

> . . . There were no cities
> between him and his desires
> His hatreds and his loves were without walls
> without rooms, without elevators
> without files, delays of veiled murderers
> muffled thieves, the tailings of
> tedious, dead pavements, the walls
> against desire save only for him who can pay
> high. There were no cities—he was
> without money—

Thus, the first stanza. Out of the opening claustrophobic, ship-
board passage of "9/29," we have finally arrived in a newly liberated, revolutionary country. Here the decadent titillation of urban
wealth is swept away by the restored delights of a peasant pleasure
in the natural world:

> Cities are full of light, fine clothes
> delicacies for the table, variety,
> novelty—fashion: all spent for this.
> Never to be like that again—
> the frame that was. It tickled his
> imagination. But it passed in a rising calm
>
> Tan dar a dei! Tan dar a dei!
>
> He was singing. Two miserable peasants
> very lazy and foolish
> seemed to have walked out from his own
> feet and were walking away
> with wooden rakes
> under the six nearly bare poplars, up the hill

The objective credibility of this proletarian utopia may, of
course, be unconvincing. But the envisioning of it is a powerful
projection of the imaginative strength that has literally been awak-
ened in the sequence. In place, for instance, of the morose brooding

over the fire in "10/21 (the orange flames)," we now have a whimsical moment of distraction that attaches the central sensibility to a
whole new world order:

> There go my feet.
>
> He stood still in the window forgetting
> to shave—
>
> The very old past was refound
> redirected. It had wandered into himself

And there is an equally refreshing moment a few lines later as the
speaker nobly resolves to himself

>   . . . He would go
> out to pick herbs, he graduate of
> the old university. He would go out
> and ask that old woman, in the little
> village by the lake, to show him wild
> ginger. He himself would not know the plant.

It is with this lyrical, not political authority that our hero can
convincingly conceive of himself with even a literally astronomical
exaggeration:

> Nothing between now.
>
> He would go to the soviet unshaven. This
> was the day—and listen. Listen. That
> was all he did, listen to them, weigh
> for them. He was turning into
> a pair of scales, the scales in the
> zodiac.

This is not megalomania; it is simply the commensurate response
to the claustrophobia and cosmic shrinkage with which the entire
sequence had begun—to the "two bright nails / like stars / beside."
    Given the extreme nature of the antithetical states involved here,
it is probably equally inevitable that a certain siege mentality per-
sist even beyond what appears to be something of a successful
resolution for the sequence, as is in fact the case. Even amidst the
revolutionary pride at discharging his own menial duties, the hero
of this daydream cannot help but worry with paranoia:

He took a small pair of scissors
from the shelf and clipped his nails
carefully. He himself served the fire.
We have cut out the cancer but
who knows? perhaps the patient will die.
The patient is anybody, anything
worthless that I desire—my hands
to have it—instead of the feeling
that there is a piece of glazed paper
between me and the paper—invisible
but tough running through the legal
processes of possession—a city, that
we could possess—

                    It's in art, it's in
the French school.

"It's in art, it's in / the French school"—at once the alarm is the very height of a psychological hysteria and an aesthetic certitude; it is art in profound resistance to the forces of life which ennervate and denude the imagination. It is finally in these terms that the sprawling "A MORNING IMAGINATION OF RUSSIA" concludes.

Intensely aware of the precariously minimal nature of his revolutionary aesthetic advances, the speaker manages nonetheless to muster a heartening comaraderie with which to affirm the sustaining value of those efforts:

                    We have little now but
we have that. We are convalescents. Very
feeble. Our hands shake. We need a
transfusion. No one will give it to us,
they are afraid of infection. I do not
blame them. We have paid heavily. But we
have got—touch. The eyes and the ears
down on it. Close.

With encouragement like this ringing in our ears, it seems easy to close the entire sequence with the blithe defiance of "11/28":

I make very little money.
What of it?
I prefer the grass with the rain on it
the short grass before my headlights
when I am turning the car—

> a degenerate trait, no doubt.
> It would ruin England.

This is no mere impudence. After the slow profound trial of the entire preceding sequence, the primacy of grass over money is unimpeachable, and the smugness of the speaker is entirely earned. So too is his driver's seat, which is presumably the one left worrisomely vacant at the end of "To Elsie."

Of course, this closing sense of superiority depends for its full success largely upon the predefined motivation we are able to bring to bear upon the single entry of "11/28." In this regard, the narrative trappings of "A MORNING IMAGINATION OF RUSSIA" are especially useful; they introduce an explicitly narrative dimension into the poetic, lyrical body of the sequence. In doing so, they further confirm the continuous nature of experience that the very chronology of all the entries has been implying all along, and the poetic, lyrical experience of the sequence even more clearly *accumulates* throughout the text.

In ways such as these, "Descent of Winter" is the most articulated of the four sequences thus far in the book. "Poems," for instance, acquires whatever lyrical and thematic unity it finally has by virtue of the sheer contiguity of poems in an otherwise unformatted section. "Primavera" and "Spring and All," while deploying the very effective thematic cues of their titles, still require from the reader a studied attention to the lyrical and thematic pressures that each of the separately titled poems exert upon one another. By contrast, the chronological diary of "Descent of Winter" provides a diachronic memory that is almost as subliminally compelling as it would be in prose fiction.

That sense of a consolidated memory also creates for "Descent of Winter" a psychological immediacy and personal intensity that is, in retrospect, noticeably lacking in the preceding sections. The personal intimacy between mother and son that circumscribed "Poems" was, for all its moments of tenderness, an ultimately accidental feature to the aesthetic issue raised by the old woman's discontent with an alien northern world. And the passionate attachment to natural beauty in "Primavera" had been nearly entirely outward in its attention; we infer the attachment from the rendered quality of the external world.

In "Spring and All" as well, the thwarted personal desire to transform the man-made world into beautiful terms expressed itself primarily in the way that the intellectual proposals and beautiful exempla for that program clash with the intractable real world. But in "Descent," we have all of these elements more internalized. "9/29" is a profoundly neurotic moment—not the family difficulty of "All the Fancy Things"; the natural beauty of "10/10" is fraught with a neurasthenic struggle—not the animistic reproach of "The Trees"; and the world order of "A MORNING IMAGINATION OF RUSSIA" is a profound wish-fulfillment— not the disappointing reality of "To Elsie."

4

Retrenching Ambitions, Pacifying Feeling: "The Flower" and "(Prior to 1921)"

In many ways, "Descent of Winter" is really the climax of *Collected Poems 1921–1931*. Even its relative brevity makes for a sense of concentration that marks the maturity and consolidation of the volume's larger context. Similarly, "The Flower," the single poem that constitutes the penultimate section of the book, is much more than a single poem; it is more of a coda to the entire volume. The motifs of the poem resonate with all the lyrical and thematic significance they have acquired in the earlier sequences. Take for instance the single governing figure of "The Flower" with which the speaker attempts to circumscribe his entire life. Its first petal encompasses the same city horizon that seductively beckoned in the opening "Flight to the City" of "Spring and All," only now its glimpse is literally blanched with the more modest sense of appraisal developed by "Descent of Winter":

> A petal, colorless and without form
> the oblong towers lie
>
> beyond the low hill and northward the great
> bridge stanchions,
>
> small in the distance, have appeared,
> pinkish and incomplete—
>
> It is the city,
> approaching over the river. Nothing
>
> of it is mine, but visibly
> for all that it is petal of a flower—my own.

Another petal is an equally affected version of the jaunt through a burgeoning neighborhood in the "April" of "Primavera":

> garbage barrel. One petal goes eight blocks
>
> past two churches and a brick school beyond
> the edge of the park where under trees
>
> leafless now, women having nothing else to do
> sit in summer—to the small house
>
> in which I happen to have been born. Or
> a heap of dirt, if you care
>
> to say it, frozen and sunstreaked in
> the January sun, returning.

Yet in the center of these two less than cheery petals obstinately remains the flower itself—that same individual imagination that has tenaciously sought beauty in every corner of its world and even now affirms it in a dump with a vivid chromatic image of a scavenging dog:

> It is a flower through which the wind
> combs the whitened grass and a black dog
>
> with yellow legs stands eating from a
> garbage barrel. One petal goes eight blocks.

Other petals appear: the visionary Russian motif from "Descent of Winter" abruptly jostles its way into the poem as a famous revolutionary's renunciation of the various social "opiates":

> to say it, frozen and sunstreaked in
> the January sun, returning.
>
> Then they hand you—they who wish to God
> you'd keep your fingers out of
>
> their business—science or philosophy or
> anything else they can find to throw off
>
> to distract you. But Madame Lenine
> is a benefactress when under her picture
>
> in the papers she is quoted as saying:
> Children should be especially protected
>
> from religion. Another petal

And the revolutionary fervor flies off into the transcendental petal of a promising new start in California:

> from religion. Another petal
> reaches to San Diego, California where
>
> a number of young men, New Yorkers most
> of them, are kicking up the dust.

But finally, in the center of the poem and directly upon the heels of the reasserted revolutionary aspirations, there is the "heart" of the flower. It is a clear reconception of the refreshingly sexual female figure from one of the "Morals" of "April"—"the redhead" who talked "rough stuff":

> A flower, at its heart (the stamens, pistil,
> etc.) is a naked woman, about 38, just
>
> out of bed, worth looking at both for
> her body and her mind and what she has seen
>
> and done. She it was put me straight
> about the city when I said, It
>
> makes me ill to see them run up
> a new bridge like that in a few months
>
> and I can't find time even to get
> a book written. They have the power,
>
> that's all, she replied. That's what you all
> want. If you can't get it, acknowledge
>
> at least what it is. And they're not
> going to give it to you. Quite right.

The refreshing directness of the woman's sexual situation and the forthrightness of her opinions create an intensely arresting moment of honesty in the poem. It is a state that the succeeding lines immediately seize and fuse into a complex of revelation, full of rapid reappraisal and self-reproach:

> For years I've been tormented by
> that miracle, the buildings all lit up—

> unable to say much to the point
> though it is the major sight
>
> of this region. But foolish to rhapsodize over
> strings of lights, the blaze of power
>
> in which I have not the least part.
> Another petal reaches

Out of this telescoped moment of truth, there surfaces yet a single last configuration to the flower of the speaker's imaginative life. And it is nothing less than the pristine beauty that was the implicit object of the old woman's longings in "All the Fancy Things." Only now that beauty is neither discredited as part of an unhealthy nostalgia nor cancelled by a stronger vision of northern beauty. It is instead respectfully and lovingly restored, finally, as the unimpeachable legacy of genuine if tropical beauty that it has probably always been:

> into the past, to Porto Rico
> when my mother was a child bathing in a small
>
> river and splashing water up on
> the yucca leaves to see them roll back pearls.
>
> The snow is hard on the pavements. This
> is no more a romance than an allegory.

The last note here of concession to the old woman's distaste for northern hardships is very close to an outright apology, and it declares the broader and really thorough tolerance and generosity into which the volume as a whole has grown after its humbling episodes of truth-telling and reappraisal. And in the same way, the final lines of "The Flower" restate the personal artistic modesty that has come to replace the varieties of aesthetic optimism in the earlier sequences. The aesthetic ambition to transform the world is reduced to the self-directed lampoon of a preposterous interpolation in a otherwise humble and honest program, i.e., "I plan one thing—. . .—to write":

> I plan one thing—that I could press
> buttons to do the curing of or caring for
>
> the sick that I do laboriously now by hand
> for cash, to have the time

> when I am fresh, in the morning, when
> my mind is clear and burning—to write.

As summative as it is in the way that it speaks to the book's preceding themes and affects, "The Flower" creates a considerable sense of closure. But closure of any kind is physically precluded by the inclusion of the volume's truly final sequence: "(Prior to 1921)," a group of eight previously uncollected poems from the ten-year period 1913–23.[1]

The title, like those of the preceding sequences, is functional. It at once broadens the frame of the book back out to the spacious overview originally suggested by the title *Collected Poems 1921–1931*. And at the same time, the parentheses of the heading serves nicely to establish its own nature as an afterbeat, a reverberation. Yet that reverberation proliferates into the *past—prior* to 1921— rather than in the future. The perspective is especially confounded in light of the future-oriented "plan—. . .—to write" announced at the end of "The Flower."

So the book returns to something like the situation established with the "Poems" sequence at the opening of the book. Confused a bit by chronological cues and deprived of any thematic ones, we have little choice but to proceed one poem at a time, making sense as we can. Only now there is a substantial context which can and indeed must be brought to bear upon those poems. And this established context exercises a profoundly revisionary influence as the older work of the final sequence is redefined along the lines of the more recent work that has preceded it in the volume.

The first poem of "(Prior To 1921)," for instance, speaks splendidly to its precedents in the volume:

AT NIGHT

> The stars, that are small lights—
> now that I know them foreign,
> uninterfering, like nothing
> in my life—I walk by their sparkle
> relieved and comforted. Or when
> the moon moves slowly up among them
> with a flat shine then the night
> has a novel light in it—curved
> curiously in a thin half-circle

The paradoxical sense of relief at a diminished sense of the self corresponds precisely with the healthy reappraisal established at the end of "The Flower." And the equally diminished half-moon quite accurately recasts the lunar deity of "Full Moon" in the terms of the sobering realism that has evolved between that poem and the current one. Thus, this first poem quite quickly clarifies any initial confusion about literary perspective. It restates the concluding lyrical moment of "The Flower," and places it in a more relaxed and broadly retrospective key.

The next poem, "To Mark Anthony in Heaven," sustains the continuity with a strong transitional trick in its first lines. The peaceful night passes on to an even more contented day:

> This quiet morning light
> reflected, how many times
> from grass and trees and clouds
> enters my north room
> touching the walls with
> grass and clouds and trees.

Again, particularly noticeable are the stray motifs from earlier poems—the floral interior of "On Gay Wallpaper"; the summer freshness of the hotel room in "Nantucket"; and the general pleasure in the natural world that permeates the entire book. And then the poem's idle reverie mixes these established elements with the explicitly sexual theme that emerged as the "heart" of the immediately preceding "The Flower":

> Anthony,
> trees and grass and clouds.
> Why did you follow
> that beloved body
> with your ships at Actium?
> I hope it was because
> you knew her inch by inch
> from slanting feet upward
> to the roots of her hair
> and down again and that
> you saw her
> above the battle's fury—
> clouds and trees and grass—

Despite the classical reference, this is the same candid sensuousness that depicted the "naked woman, about 38, just / out of bed, worth looking at both for / her body and her mind." Yet that sensuousness now seems almost empty-headed rather than refreshing. The attraction of the forthright "naked woman" in "The Flower" had been inseparable from the concomitantly unindulgent side of her nature; ultimately, her candor lead to an equally bold indictment of the speaker's aesthetic motivation. But the imagined enjoyment of Cleopatra too easily overshadows the complications of her presence; the dishonor of Anthony's flight from battle is literally glossed over. And there is something literally juvenile in the sexual simplicity that leads to the poem's final stanza:

> For then you are
> listening in heaven.

"At least he died with a smile on his face" might say as much.

Certainly, the sensibility of "To Mark Anthony in Heaven" seems quite removed from the morally and aesthetically complicated one of "The Flower." In fact, the former seems an almost impossible sequel to the latter. It is perhaps just at this point, when that impossible relationship becomes clear, that the retrospective cue of the sequence's title becomes truly functional: the poems of "(Prior to 1921)" are precisely what their group title suggests-- parenthetical, retrospective afterbeats. These poems are the aesthetic salad days of the book's central sensibility, brought into line with the broad moment of aesthetic and biographical reappraisal that culminates in "The Flower."

That is, the entire scheme profoundly revises the poems as it recovers them. They assume the definitions of their present context, a context far more mature and substantial than any that existed originally for them. And in the process, the poems gain lyrical weight. The adolescent fantasy of "To Mark Anthony in Heaven" is redeemed from simple silliness and achieves an engaging naiveté as the imagination behind it assumes as well all the lyrical and aesthetic complications that its adult life will endure after 1921 and already has endured earlier in the present book. And so too does the sophomoric dialogue of "Transitional" seem a retrospective foreshadowing of the contentious exchange between the speaker and the old woman that in "All the Fancy Things" impels the difficult and costly search for a valid beauty throughout the book:

> First he said:
> It is the woman in us
> That makes us write—
> Let us acknowledge it—
> Men would be silent.
> We are not men

Therefore we can speak
And be conscious
(of the two sides)
Unbent by the sensual
As befits accuracy.

I then said:
Dare you make this
Your propaganda?

And he answered:
Am I not I—here?

Not even the comic profundity of the closing double-talk can completely dispel the larger seriousness that attends this poem. The entire affect belongs to the richest sort of recall, tolerant of youthful foibles and enamored of the innocence that breeds them.

Of course, "Transitional" is also, as all the poems always are, responsive to the local pressures of its most immediate context. And while the title does suggest the fleeting preciousness of the juvenile quest for truth, it also points to the conspicuous bridge that the poem attempts to build between its neighboring poems. Look, for instance, at the passage from "To Mark Anthony . . ." and "Transitional":

For then you are
listening in heaven.
                    (from "To Mark Anthony . . .")

First he said:
It is the woman in us
                    (from "Transitional")

And then note the transition between "Transitional" and the succeeding "Man in a Room."

And he answered:
Am I not I—here?
                    (from "Transitional")

Here, no woman, no man besides,
Nor child, nor dog, nor bird, nor wasp,
                    (from "Man in a Room")

The devices are not especially subtle—the play on "listening" and "said"; the immediate repetition of "here"—but they are effective

at both directing our attention again to the sequential continuity of
the sequence *and* at reminding us, again, of the prototypical nature
of these transitions in the broader context of the more subtle lyrical
sequences written after 1921 and published here in front of "(Prior
to 1921)."

In any event, the most immediate lyrical effect of "Transitional"
is to take the silly sexuality of "To Mark Anthony in Heaven" and
place it into equally silly philosophical terms and then to pass it
on to the histrionic foresakeness of "Man in a Room":

> Here, no woman, nor man besides,
> Nor child, nor dog, nor bird, nor wasp,
> Nor ditch-pool, nor green thing. Color of flower,
> Blood-bright berry none, nor flame-rust
> On leaf, nor pink gall-sting on stem, nor
> Staring stone. *Ay de mi!*
> No hawthorn's white thorn-tree here, nor lawn
> Of buttercups, nor any counterpart:

Again, despite the almost ludicrously excessive catalog of deprivation, we cannot help but discern something stunning and precise
in some of the phrasing and images. "Ditch-pool," "flame-rust,"
"pink gall-sting on stem"—all are evidence of the more durable
and disciplined renditions of natural beauty that inhabit and miti-
gate the more credible difficulties of the post-1921 sequences earlier in the book. But here and now, the imaginative capacity of
"Man in a Room" seems just able to muster a clear, all too "poetic"
dichotomy between the real and the beautiful, the inside and the
out:

> Bed, book-backs, walls, floor,
> Flat pictures, desk, clothes-box, litter
> Of paper scrawls. So sit I here,
> So stand, so walk about. Beside
> The flower-white tree not so lonely I:
> Torn petals, dew-wet, yellowed my bare ankles.

Nonetheless, the central sensibility here apparently succeeds in
transporting himself out his person-room, for in the next poem,
"A Coronal," he is traipsing off with Lady Beauty herself. There
is again a certain pomposity in the basic conceit of the poem and
in some of its hyperbole:

> Anemones sprang where she pressed
> and cresses
> stood green in the slender source—

But there is also within all that an undeniable beauty of sound, image, and rhythm that validates the blithe romantic escapism. There is a delightful variety of "s" rhymes, for instance, and real freshness of phrasing in "cress / stood green in the slender source." And the opening stanza is the first really effective deployment of the sort of modern motif that figured so importantly in the middle sequences of the book:

> New books of poetry will be written
> New books and unheard of manuscripts
> will come wrapped in brown paper
> and many and many a time
> the postman will blow
> and sidle down the leafplastered steps
> thumbing over other men's business.

The elements of tired indifference in these lines—the absence of all urgency in "and many and many a time"; the careless equation of "books" and "manuscripts" with routine business correspondence; the postman's uninspired professional tread in the fallen foliage—such things effectively motivate and prepare for the fantastic frolic that follows:

> But we ran ahead of it all.
> One coming after
> could have seen her footprints
> in the wet and followed us
> among the stark chestnuts.

Even the element of youthful folly expressed in the preceding poems of the section appears to be more masterfully controlled here. The *carpe diem* logic of the first two stanzas, for instance, is admittedly handled in relatively amateurish fashion. With an almost fatuous schematism, there is a simple segregation into the first stanza of the drab pedestrian testimonies to a life of art; into the second go the more fanciful notions of that life. But in the last stanza, the two realms do finally fuse into an intoxicated dedication to the life—and labor—of poesy:

> Anemones sprang where she pressed
> and cresses
> stood green in the slender source—
> And new books of poetry
> will be written, leather colored oakleaves
> many and many a time.

This is all still much more naive than the sober and very adult "I plan— . . . —to write" which concludes "The Flower." But the poem's transformation of "manuscripts / . . . wrapped in brown paper" into "leather colored oakleaves" is clever enough to warrant at least some of the youthful optimism in the final lines. And that optimism is in turn enough of a basis against which the following "Sicilian Emigrant's Song" can define itself as something more than a clownish display of rustic buoyancy:

<blockquote>

O—eh—lee! La—la!
   Donna! Donna!
Blue is the sky of Palermo;
Blue is the little bay;
And dost thou remember the orange and fig,
The lively sun and the sea-breeze at evening?
   Hey—la!
Donna! Donna! Maria!

O—eh—li! La—la!
   Donna! Donna!
Gray is the sky of this land.
Gray and green is the water.
I see no trees, dost thou? The wind
Is cold for the big woman there with the candle.
   Hey—La!
Donna! Donna! Maria!

O—eh—li! O—la!
   Donna! Donna!
I sang thee by the blue waters;
I sing thee here in the gray dawning.
Kiss, for I put down my guitar;
I'll sing thee more songs after the landing.
   O Jesu, I love thee!
Donna! Donna! Maria!

</blockquote>

In the context of the more natural idiom deployed in the other sequences, the archaic "dost thou's" represent an amateurish attempt at idyllic conventions; the quintuply stoppered refrains ("O—eh—lee! La—la!") are nearly unsingable; and "The lively sun and the sea-breeze at evening" must have been tired phrasing even in 1900. But the poem does at least attempt to carry forward from "A Coronal" both a pastoral motif and a note of sexual and aesthetic optimism. Yet its bittersweet memory of a Mediterranean paradise in the face of a drearier new land recalls as well the more painfully nostalgic tropical paradise of the old woman in "All the Fancy Things." So the hints of a harsh reality awaiting the emigrant's excited anticipation are exaggerated, and the entire episode really forebodes the difficult and distressing search for a northern beauty in the new American land that has driven the entire book.

Increasingly, then, the sequence has managed to grow happier and happier more and more unconvincingly. The governing affect might almost be called *fatuous*. But it is also not to be entirely denied, this intensely adolescent contentment. Indeed, the penultimate poem to the sequence (and to the entire book) confirms just that element. The opening of "The Revelation" repeats something like the awakening moment of "To Mark Anthony in Heaven" along with the relaxed anticlimax of "At Night," but it is all more thoroughly imbued with the youthful ingenuousness that has surfaced in "Transitional," "Man in a Room," "A Coronal," and "Sicilian Emigrant's Song":

> I awoke happy, the house
> Was strange, voices
> Were across a gap
> Through which a girl
> Came and paused,
> Reaching out to me—

This retrospective revelation is quite different from the one at the "heart" of "The Flower." Instead of "a naked woman, almost 38" with her caustic truth, there is only the most caressing of young girls; and rather than the agonizing moment of self-appraisal, she initiates only the secret, bashful communion of puppy love:

> Then I remembered
> What I had dreamed—
> A girl
> One whom I knew well
> Leaned on the door of my car
> And stroked my hand—

> I shall pass her on the street
> We shall say trivial things
> To each other
> But I shall never cease
> To search her eyes
> For that quiet look—

Somewhere in the lyrical and thematic memory of the book rests the certain knowledge that this moment cannot last—and that knowledge (of all that in the book has preceded this moment and in the historical future will succeed it) makes it even more precious. Thus, there cannot be but a certain happiness when the sequence and the book finally conclude with just the mildest of deflations to this youthful bliss that will surely, as the book has already testified, give way to higher moments in the years to come.

In fact, the closing poem, "Portrait of a Lady," is downright humorous. As a young gallant grows more and more fanciful and sensual in praise of his lady's beauty, something thwarts him and prods him instead to an increasingly frustrated search for the artistic sources of his figures. Perhaps it is the speaker's impatience with the romantic hyperbole of his own serenade; perhaps it is the lady's coy deflections of his amorous meaning. But whatever its source, the frustration grows and overcomes the poem:

> Your thighs are appletrees
> whose blossoms touch the sky.
> Which sky? The sky
> where Watteau hung a lady's
> slipper. Your knees
> are a southern breeze—or
> a gust or snow. Agh! what
> sort of man was Fragonard?
> —as if that answered
> anything. Ah, yes—below
> the knees, since the tune
> drops that way, it is
> one of those white summer days,
> the tall grass of your ankles
> flickers upon the shore—
> Which shore?—
> the sand clings to my lips—
> Which shore?
> Agh, petals maybe. How
> should I know?
> Which shore? Which shore?
> I said petals from an appletree.

It is a richly old-fashioned country episode. The fine talk of some boy, making impossible equations of "a southern breeze" with "a gust of snow" and constantly verging on the sexual in its connotation, finally collapses into a comical exasperation with itself. If he had a hat in hand, the fellow must surely have thrown it down at the last line. Certainly, though, the mounting frustration here deserves no more violent punctuation. For, as we already know, it will only be this speaker's very first difficulty with a female figure whose presence manages to challenge his automatic notions of art and beauty—his first difficulty with the "Lady" who must inevitably replace the dreamt-of "girl"; with the old woman of "All the Fancy Things" who opens the book itself.

5

An Accomplished Book

Williams really had much reason to be pleased with *Collected Poems 1921–31*. The book really did "come up to the attention as a whole." Just as important, it recovered much of his poetic record and placed it within an entirely new and lyrically coherent context. Unfortunately, however, almost no one else seemed to appreciate that fact. Most reviewers dwelt merely on Williams's imagistic technique and his social or aesthetic values.

But two other poets—Marianne Moore and Basil Bunting—came closer to recognizing something beyond the fragmented "singling out of the brief moment" by which Babette Deutsch had characterized the book. Seizing upon the "struggle" which she believed was a "main force in William Carlos Williams," Moore saw as one of its chief effects the "breathless budding of thought from thought . . . With an abandon born of inner security, Dr Williams somewhere nicknames the chain of incontrovertibly logical [yet] apparent non-sequiturs, rigmarole" (103). It was an observation that Williams himself particularly appreciated. He wrote immediately to her, "the thing that I like best about your review of my book is that you have looked at what I have done through my own eyes. I assure you that this is so. Had it not been so you would not have noticed the 'inner security' nor the significance of some of the detail—which nobody seems to value as I have valued it" (*Selected Letters* 147).

While Moore, and even Williams himself, *seemed* to be confirming as notable the structural achievement of the book, Bunting was more direct about the matter. After praising Williams's skills at "mosaic" and quoting the "isolate flecks" passage from "To Elsie," Bunting noted "the technique that makes such flecks cohere into a To Elsie [sic] is a master's: the collection and arrangement of flecks." But at the same time, Bunting was happy to see that

Williams however does not provoke the clash between the poet and the indulger in literary tidbits to such an extent as some of his contemporaries. None of his poems is long enough to get bewildering. It is when mosaic is practiced on the scale of Pound's "Cantos" or Zukofsky's "A" . . . that the academic reader begins to grumble, not finding the point of focus for himself and consequently unable to look steadily at any large portion of the poet's subject. . . . Williams is readily visible: if not at the first glance, at the second or third for sure.

This attractive transparency [arises] partly from limitations recognized and acquiesced in. The poems are all short, the subjects all circumscribed, self-complete, so that no loose ends need be left. This implies no lack of scope, seeing that all the poems are American and just as the separate chunks of fact in each poem project a foreseen design, the separate poems, or nearly all of them, are ready to unite at the right focus into the unfinished and finishable design of their common theme, America. (153)

Bunting's identification of "America" as the unifying principle for *Collected Poems 1921–1931* was too broad to be really correct, but his comparison of the book's structural intent with those of Pound's *Cantos* and Zukofsky's *A* was about as accurate a piece of poetic taxonomy as was to be had at the time. All three of the works *were* unified, lyrically based attempts at extended poetic sequences. The real difference between Williams's work and the others' was not one of scale, as Bunting claimed, but of structural orientation. The *Cantos* and *A* were decidedly open in structure, eschewing the traditional devices of closure and instead preparing for ever more books at the close of each finished one. *Collected Poems 1921–1931,* on the other hand, ends with the clearly retrospective pressure of "(Prior to 1921)." There is really little to add to this rather complete book—at least not in the way of further lyrical or thematic development.

Nonetheless, in 1938—just four years after the appearance of *Collected Poems 1921–1931*—Williams published *The Complete Collected Poems of William Carlos Williams 1906–1938,* and in doing so, he once again redefined his poetic record, this time along considerably different lyrical lines.

Part II
The Complete Collected Poems
1906–1938

6

"Completing" the Collected Poems

Of course Williams's first volume of "collected" poetry was not at all complete. It ignored entirely his first three volumes—*The Tempers, Al Que Quiere!,* and *Sour Grapes*—even though the last of these was in fact published in 1921, the first of the eleven years surveyed by the book's title. And obviously, Williams did go on to publish other individual volumes. Within two years of the 1934 publication of *Collected Poems 1921–1931,* for instance, Williams had already produced *An Early Martyr* (1935) and *Adam & Eve & The City* (1936). So within just a few years of his first collection, there were still good practical reasons to publish the much more comprehensive *Complete Collected Poems of William Carlos Williams 1906–1938.*

Certainly, practical considerations must have been foremost for James Laughlin, who at Pound's charge was set upon becoming the official publisher for the modernist masters and thus was probably eager to acquire and reissue under his own imprint the entirety of Williams's work. In any event, it is certain that Williams himself initially viewed the volume with only a minimal regard. "The poems won't be hard to get together," he wrote Laughlin early in 1938.

> I want them to come out in subdivisions of the original books as they appeared, chronologically. A very few alterations will have to be made and a few of the poems will need to be omitted for lack of value but the rest had better just follow along as they first appeared. You fix the date of their appearance to suit yourself. I don't give one whoop in hell—so long as you are interested (Williams and Laughlin 31).

But in the nine months between this note and the actual appearance of *The Complete Collected,* Williams apparently became more interested and changed his mind about how the book ought to be arranged. While in general he observed the actual chronology of the original volumes as he arranged them into the "subsections" of *The Complete Collected,* he rearranged radically the poems of

137

"Al Que Quiere," shuffled the poems of "Sour Grapes" around a bit, reassigned many of the poems from "Adam & Eve and The City" to a new section entitled "Recent Verse," and—most curiously—assembled as the final section of the book another new gathering entitled "Longer Poems," made up of seven poems from earlier volumes along with three newer uncollected ones. Once again, Williams seemed to be attempting to compile something more than a simple archival reprint.

Exactly what Williams sought is not immediately apparent. Significantly larger than its predecessor, *The Complete Collected Poems* faces a significant problem in focus. There is such a large expanse and variety of literal and lyrical material that it all becomes difficult to hold in the mind at the same time without the aid of some dominant subject or motif such as the city/hero Paterson. *Collected Poems 1921–1931* had been after all a comparatively brief work; even its middle sections, ostensibly reprints of earlier works, were radically condensed and tailored to a single curve of feeling and theme that quickly established its dominance in the book. But the 1938 volume deliberately diffuses the focus. For instance, it restores to their original lengths "The Descent of Winter," "Della Primavera Transportata al Morale," and "Spring and All," and it even enlarges by a few poems the latter two.

Of even greater effect is the roughly chronological ordering of the volume. *Collected Poems 1921–1931* had begun with Williams's most recent and mature work, and by position and sheer bulk it dominated and brought into its own lyrical and thematic orbit the more abbreviated works (themselves at most only ten years distant) which followed. But *The Complete Collected Poems* begins with the beginning, with the earliest, least stable period of Williams's work.

In terms of sheer surface style, for instance, there is a much greater difference between the affected classical archaism of the 1913 *The Tempers* and the slightly vulgar familiarity of the 1917 *Al Que Quiere!* than between the equally contemporary and American idioms of the 1931 "Poems" and the 1935 *An Early Martyr and Other Poems.* Thus, there is initially more disjunction than continuum apparent in *The Complete Collected Poems,* and the individual "subdivisions" tend to define themselves as autonomous chapters in a canon that is unified in only the broadest, biographical sense—until, that is, we encounter the anomalous "Longer Poems" sequence that serves as the volume's eleventh and final section.

With a relatively evident and concise lyrical and thematic structure of its own, this unique arrangement of ten poems defines the sequential dynamics of the preceding ten sections as well. Each of the ten longer poems reaches back not only to clarify the lyrical character of its corresponding section in the preceding series of ten sections but also to provide a reference against which can be measured the relative achievement of each section within the over-all development of Williams's poetic record. Thus, it will be useful if we frame the very broad development of *The Complete Collected Poems 1906–1938* with the more narrow and immediately compre-hensible one of "Longer Poems."

7

The Closing Sequence of "Longer Poems": Fixing the World's Modernity—and the Volume's Lyrical Dynamics

Quite appropriately, "Morning" opens the ten poem section of "Longer Poems" with an extended moment of awakening and epiphany. The details of early morning in a hilltop shantytown are slowly revealed—first the horizon and the neighborhood itself, then its emerging inhabitants: two old immigrant Italians descending the hill, a young shopkeeper peering from his shop window, a forager in a rubbish lot, and finally a perennially "mourning" widow at a church altar.

But the poem is more than a simple tableau. There builds throughout it a general sense of transfiguration that finally culminates in a sacred regard for the widow's dirty tears:

> alone on the cold
> floor beside the candled altar, stifled
> weeping—and moans for his lost
> departed soul the tears falling
> and wiped away, turbid with her grime.
>
> Covered, swaddled, pinched and saved
> shrivelled, broken—to be rewetted and
> used again.

The off rhyme of "stifled" and "grime" calls attention to the fundamental place of deprivation in this sacramental transformation. And the final series of participles consecrates into a chant the notion of recovering some cherished resource bred from human loss.

It is really what the poem has been about from its opening expression of wonder at the transformational power of the incipient shantytown day:

MORNING

> on the hill is cool! Even the dead
> grass stems that start with the wind along
> the crude board fence are less than harsh.

This is, of course, an axiomatic conversion of dormancy into a state of refreshment, and as such it is rather tendentious, but it nonetheless directs our attention to the transfigured qualities of the more concretely realized images that follow. The winter illumination of houses, for instance, intensified by the surrounding leafless trees and grapevines, suggests something of supernal immanence. The colors of some flapping laundry, the stuffing of a mattress, and the clothlike winter dressing of a garden—they all assume a sky-like softness, an almost heavenly serenity:

> Pully lines
> to poles, on one a blue
> and white tablecloth bellying easily.
> Feather beds from windows and swathed in
> old linoleum and burlap, fig trees. Barrels
> over shrubs.

It is particularly interesting to note how the "b" alliteration works in this stanza. The key "soft" words of "blue," "bellying," and "beds" in the second through fourth lines help extend the plainly ethereal affect of those lines into the somewhat coarser images of the fifth line by networking with "burlap" and "Barrels." The overall effect of merging the sublime with the squalid is a less obvious instance of the same lyrical logic that sanctifies the widow's dirty tears at the end of the poem.

Earlier in the poem it associates "houses badly numbered" with an "immensely wide" sky and later, outhouses with a church tower. There is in fact a progression throughout the poem in the intensity and the audacity of these associations, and that progression becomes in turn identified with the increasing signs of stirring life in the literal street scene, so that finally, the act of awakening itself becomes identical to the recognition of what Wallace Stevens would have called the poem's "anti-poetic" values.

This is most clearly seen in the passage of the several "characters" throughout the poem. The first are two old Italians engrossed in discourse as they stroll among some distinctly non-academic groves:

These Wops are wise

　　　　　　—and walk about
absorbed among stray dogs and sparrows,
pigeons wheeling overheard, their
feces falling—

Certainly, there is some sarcasm here, especially in the possibly disparaging "Wops" of the first line. But the succeeding stanza immediately dissipates that note with a roster of rather ignoble creatures that is too long to be much of a wisecrack. Instead its length appears to evidence a serious attention to the animals, and the "wise" absorption of the men's discussion is vaguely equated with a genuine pleasure in the unsanitary urban wildlife.

Within a few lines, the seriousness of attention is made even clearer by the concluding moment to the immigrants' episode. From the dirty highway pavement at the foot of the hill, they look back to a nearly spectral sight, almost as a part of their "absorbed" discussion itself:

Whence, turn and look where,
at the crest, the shoulders of a man
are disappearing gradually below the worn
fox-fur of tattered grasses—

　　　　　　　　　And round again, the
two old men in caps crossing at
a gutter now, *Pago, Pago!* still absorbed.

The very next moment introduces "a young man's face staring / from a dirty window—Womens Hats." The simple gaze of this just risen fellow corresponds precisely to the dawning sense of *awareness* that the poem is developing, and it leads directly into an even more forthright statement of the poem's ethos. As a determined scavenger pokes about in the rubbish, his fervid examinations give rise to a prayer, an invocation to just that immanence that seems only illusively present earlier in the poem:

scratching within the littered field—
old plaster, bits of brick—to find what
coming? In God's name! Washed out, worn
out, scavengered and rescavengered—

Spirit of place rise from these ashes
repeating secretly an obscure refrain:

> This is my house and here I live,
> Here I was born and this is my office—
>
> —passionately leans examining, stirring
> with the stick, a child following.
> Roots, salads? Medicinal, stomachic?

The obscure figure is almost miraculously transformed into a medicine man, and the rubbish into herbs. It is only a step from this sudden religiosity to the final sanctity of the widow's episode. Even more tellingly, the invocational prayer anticipates exactly the clear sense of injunction that ends the entire poem: "to be rewetted and / used again." So the broad annunciation that opens the poem, with its suggestions of some sort of renewal for "Even the dead / grass stems that start with the wind," has finally translated itself into an agenda.

Ultimately, that agenda is an aesthetic and cultural one. It arises out of an imaginative perspective increasingly attuned to the incipient life force in its environment, regardless (indeed by virtue) of the social shabbiness in that environment. And it commits itself to the further aesthetic cultivation of that environment. Of course, this is all an odd sort of "mourning." But odd or not, it defines a signal motif that helps the entire section to cohere as a sequence. Indeed, the very final moment of the final poem seems a direct development of the motif.

Addressing "the filthy Passaic," the "old queen" of "The Wanderer" concludes her elaborate dedication of the young poet to the river with a "mourning" that mixes similar elements of filth and water, sorrow and hope:

> Tallest oaks and yellow birches
> that dip their leaves in you, mourning,
> As now I dip my hair, immemorial
> Of me, immemorial of him
> Immemorial of these our promises!

The primitive mimesis of the dousing; the special prominence given to it as a form of "mourning" by the resurgence of the trochaic in that word at the end of an otherwise iambic line; the murmurous repetition of "immemorial"; the incremental metrical advance of the anapest in *that* word through the iambs of the last three lines—such things advance to a studied ritualism the spontaneous and tentative sanctity over the widow's tears at the end of "Morning" the poem.

Of course it is the intervening eight poems in the section that actually accomplish the passage between these two poles. "An Elegy to D. H. Lawrence" first confirms a generally continuous phenomenology to the sequence by playing its own variation upon the "mourning" complex. Commemorating the death of a cultural figure like Lawrence, the elegy both enlarges the scope of the sequence and complicates it with some troubling elements of cultural controversy and public denunciation. "Paterson: Episode 17" intensifies the distress with its more immediate and compelling (and profoundly confused) story of the ravished Beautiful Thing. Then "The Crimson Cyclamen" recovers some equanimity with a careful meditation upon the transporting natural beauties of the title's flower. "The Waitress" attempts to extend this uplifting attention to the more harrowed figure of its title, but the poem is finally overcome by its own sense of impossibility, and the sequence falls back to the sobering retrenchment of "The Flower."

From this point of relative calm, the next three poems launch a final and successful siege upon the untransfigured world. "Romance Modern" begins with an exuberant, adolescent fantasy of the forest, and then "Paterson" leavens the movement with and adult seriousness about the "facts" of urban life. "March" marshals both elements into a fierce elemental assault upon the dormant world of early spring. Finally, "The Wanderer" raises this elemental labor of renewal and transfiguration to epic proportions, and with an elaborate, magical rite of initiation, settles it all upon a single hero, a predestined youth who swaps souls with the Passaic itself.

Noteworthy enough as it is in its own right, the sequential articulation here is especially significant for the fact that it recapitulates and thus clarifies (or "fixes") the dynamics of the ten sequences that precede "Longer Poems." Each of the ten longer poems repeats, or more precisely, reconceives the essential affects and themes of its serially respective sequence in the ten that constitute the real body of the volume and of Williams's poetic record. Thus, for instance, the wondrous epiphany of contemporary aesthetic need in "Morning," the first longer poem, parallels in "The Tempers," the first sequence, an equally spontaneous and astonished awareness of the modern world's lack of anything like the aesthetic vitality associated with the classical world's mythically animated reality.

There is a similar correspondence between the other sections and longer poems: the troublesome fate of the famous artist commemorated in "An Elegy to D. H. Lawrence" reconceives the frustration of personal artistic ambitions of "Transitional"; the disturbing account of the world's perverted response to beauty in "Paterson: Episode 17" reconceives a local community's similarly discouraging response to the aesthetic overtures of its resident artist in "Al Que Quiere"; the ethereal meditation of "The Crimson Cyclamen" reconceives a fortifying retreat to private beauty in "Sour Grapes"; the sulking overture to the oppressed beauty of "The Waitress" reconceives a distressing assessment of abused beauty in the contemporary world of "Spring and All"; the personal artistic retrenchment of "The Flower" reconceives the besiegement of an aesthetic sensibility in "The Descent of Winter"; the exuberant recovery of "Romance Modern" reconceives the cheerful aesthetic optimism that drives "Collected Poems 1934"; the cooly efficient repossession of beauty from the contemporary, urban world in "Paterson" reconceives the rigorous, unsentimental extraction of beauty from a socially defective life in "An Early Martyr"; the arousing mobilization of elemental forces and aesthetic tradition in "March" reconceives a similar mobilization of power in the parental legacies and contemporary physics of "Adam & Eve and the City"; and finally, the glorious consecration of a poetic hero for modernity and for Paterson in "The Wanderer" reconceives the profound attachment to those same things in "Recent Verse."

As this abbreviated overview only vaguely suggests, the reciprocities here are not simply a matter of repetition. There is in the lyrical and thematic caliber and even in the rough chronology of the respective poems and sections a certain balance that works throughout the volume to validate every poetic episode with the *full* expression of Williams's overall development—with both the raw yet unaccomplished ambition of his earliest efforts *and* the more restrained but greater artistic intelligence of his maturity. So, for example, it is the very recent (in fact, premiering) "Morning" that serves as the counterpart to the very early, 1912 "The Tempers." And the extended moment of awakening in the longer poem involves a far more subtle, direct, and modern intuition of aesthetic immanence than does the classical posturing of "The Tempers."

Conversely, the very last of the ten sequences, "Recent Verse," involves a far quieter, more realistic, and more authentic commitment to the modern reality of Paterson than does the Romantic (or "Rococo") fantasy of initiation in the 1914 "The Wanderer." And in the very middle of the sequences and longer poems, there is a rough equivalence of caliber between the very modern, compelling, and protoconfessional honesty of the 1930 "The Flower" (the sixth longer poem) and the equally self-conscious journal entries of a modern sensibility under siege in the roughly concurrent sixth sequence, "The Descent of Winter."

The net effect of this entire arrangement is to suggest a single and constant baseline of superior accomplishment—whether in section or longer poem—against which every lyric and poetic impulse may be measured both for their immediate worth—that is, for the part each poetic moment plays in the dynamics of its immediate location within the volume—and for their overall worth—for the relationship each moment bears to the poetic growth of Williams's work through 1938.

With all these considerations in mind, then, we shall approach a comprehensive examination of the lyrical dynamics in *The Complete Collected Poems 1906–1938* by first giving detailed and serial attention to the whole of the summative "Longer Poems." This fuller exegesis will then provide the reference against which we may evaluate on a more selective basis the other ten sequences of the volume.

And so we note that after the opening poem's odd sort of "mourning" comes an equally odd sort of elegy. While full of the conventional details of seasonal nature, "An Elegy for D. H. Lawrence" has as its main burden a sense of cultural outrage rather than personal grief. It is "Sorrow to the *young* / that Lawrence has passed / unwanted from England" (emphasis added). And the prominent and distinctly unpanegyric notation of Lawrence's caddish failure to answer a piece of fan mail (presumably Williams's) precludes pathos in general. Instead, everything in the poem joins in a sustained reproach for England's rejection of Lawrence's aesthetic powers of regeneration. Testimony becomes phillipic; Lawrence's insignial snake becomes an inquisitor; flowers become shameful witnesses; and the season becomes a judgment:

> Poor Lawrence
> worn with a fury of sad labor
> to create summer from
> spring's decay. English
> women. Men driven not to love
> but to the ends of the earth.
> The serpent turning his
> stone-like head,
> the fixed agate eyes turn also.

> And unopened joquils
> hang their folded heads. No
> summer. . .

What the indignation of the entire poem does do is advance into a preliminary adversity the almost religious fervor over the widow's dirty tears that closed the previous poem. For more than sorrow at Lawrence's passing, this elegy introduces a broad sense of the real difficulty that faces the newly invoked and perhaps quixotic task of renewal. It also translates the terms of that renewal into the broader generative terms of Lawrence's famous sexual life force. The common denizens of the shantytowns in "Morning," for instance, are replaced by the more exotic and erotic virgin and gypsy from Lawrence's story of that name. And the first poem's details of place become those of Lawrence's zoetic expatriate geography:

> Remember, now, Lawrence dead.
> Blue squills in bloom—to
> the scorched aridity of
> the Mexican plateau. Or baked
> public squares in the cities of
> Mediterranean islands
> where one waits for busses and
> boats come slowly along the water
> arriving.
>
> But the sweep of spring over
> temperate lands, meadows and woods
> where the young walk and talk
> incompletely,
> straining to no summer,
> hearing the frogs, speaking of
> birds and insects—
>
> Febrile spring moves not to heat

The squills are assigned as generous bequests to the sultry southern lands, while nothing but a suspended disappointment settles upon the northern world. The merit here, of course, is the capacity to take full pleasure in life. The implied Mediterranean delight in the deliberately prolonged motions of coming and going—the relish behind the separated word "arriving"—stands in sharp contrast to the insensibility of the northern youths to even the blatant excitement of rutting frogs. They prefer instead the cool chatter of naturalists. It is, in short, an unaroused world that answers the sequence's initial perception of a vague redemption available in the very filth of that world; thus rather than the usual solace, this elegy can ultimately work its way only toward some cynical overstatement:

> Violently the satiric sun
> that leads April not to
> the panting dance but to stillness
> in, into the brain, dips
> and is gone also,
> And sisters return
> through the dusk
> to the measured rancor
> of their unbending elders.

The deep psychic assault upon and stern censure of beauty's sexual expression that are anticipated here are actually enacted in the more literal, and disturbing, account of "Paterson: Episode 17." At the center of this poem is the story of "Beautiful Thing," a young woman first beat up and then molested in the course of a three-day drunken debauch. The basic story itself does much to capture the crudeness and perversity in the modern world's response to beauty. After "the guys from Paterson / beat up / the guys from Newark," they quite needlessly add a nose-breaking punch to the Newark gang's moll "for good luck and emphasis." That, of course, leaves little for the fellows from Newark to do but besot the lady and ravish her for "Three days in the same dress / up and down."

In summary, the entire affair, like its participants, is simply vulgar. But within the basic empathy of the actual poem, the vulgarity in the episode assumes a transfiguration greater than that glimpsed in "Morning": the woman is nearly canonized as the "Beautiful Thing" that serves as the poem's enraptured refrain. Even more important, however, is the odd ambivalence that adulterates that empathy. With something like the uncontrollable stupidity of the Newark gang that only knows how to rape its damaged goods, the voice of the poem seems to twitch with abusive gestures throughout its expressions of endearment. Note for instance how the mixture of phrases in the imperative voice mix in the first stanza with those of the purely indicative to create an utter precariousness for Beautiful Thing. We might almost imagine her flinching.

> Beat hell out of it
>   Beautiful Thing
>   spotless cap
> and crossed white straps
> over the dark rippled cloth—
>   Lift the stick
> above that easy head
> where you sit by the ivied
> church, one arm
>   buttressing you
> long fingers spread out
> among the clear grass prongs—
>   and drive it down
>   Beautiful Thing
> that your carressing body kiss
>   and kiss again
> that holy lawn—

"Beat hell out of it"; "Lift the stick"; "and drive it down"—murderous commands set off as the three starting points for the syntax of the stanza so that all the tender regard for the lady's person in the rest seems a perverse sort of delicacy.

This is a profoundly confused, and modern, response to beauty, and it more than justifies in retrospect the apprehension of the Lawrence elegy. It also marks a tremendous contrast to the hardy transcendental disposition in "Morning" that could trace the figure of a church spire in the construction refuse around an outhouse. Now there is instead a religiosity that first makes a violent sacrificial altar of a peaceful churchyard grove and then goes on to celebrate the "sacrament" of victimization itself:

> And again! obliquely—
> legs curled under you as a
>   deer's leaping—
> pose of supreme indifference
>   sacrament
> to a summer's day
>   Beautiful Thing

The rather perverse flippancy of the alliteration in the penultimate and antepenultimate lines especially emphasizes the absence of any redeeming veneration to this act. Nor is there even the possibility of any common compassion. As is usual in rape, there is only a vague blame available to this priest's victim: "It would take / a

Dominie to be patient / Beautiful Thing / with you." It all remains a simply inexplicable brutality, at least in its fact.

In its awareness, the brutality is guiltily cognizant of itself. Around its constant attention to the sublime features of Beautiful Thing, the speaking sensibility alternates between the vicarious violence noted above and an intellectual analysis of her predicament:

> The incredible
> nose straight from the brow
> the empurpled lips
> and dazzled half sleepy eyes
> Beautiful Thing
> of some trusting animal
> makes a temple
> of its place of savage slaughter
> revealing
> the damaged will incites still
> to violence
> consumately beautiful Thing
> and falls about your resting
> shoulders—
>
> Gently! Gently!
> as in all things an opposite
> that awakes
> the fury, conceiving
> knowledge
> by way of despair that has
> no place
> to lay its glossy head—

Despite its clearly intellectual character, the mood here is as ecstatic as the preceding sacrificial passages. The same indented alternation of short lines with longer ones that created the responsorial effect of the earlier stanzas continues on through these that follow. And at the heart of them all there is the same beatific recitation of the "Beautiful Thing" refrain itself. At the same time, the recurrent "l" rhymes in "incredible," "animal," and "temple" culminate in the internal rhyme of "will" and "still" and make a poetic climax out of a line of abstract insight. Finally, however, this sort of clarity is useless, bound up as it is with the orgasmic urge of a perverted sexuality. And at the end of the poem, after the full account has been given of the woman's defilement, the speaker can only confess to human frailty and yet begin again the complex and pathologic possession of Beautiful Thing:

> It would take
> a Dominie to be patient
> Beautiful Thing
> with you—
>
> The stroke begins again—
> regularly
> automatic
> contrapuntal to
> the flogging
> like the beat of famous lines
> in the few excellent poems
> woven to make you
> gracious
> and on frequent occasions
> foul drunk
> Beautiful Thing
> pulse of release
> to the attentive
> and obedient mind.

It is hard not to note the sudden introduction in these closing lines of poetry as a subject. Poetry in fact quite clearly becomes identified with the aroused attention to beauty that alternates with the "flogging" that is "for the damaged will" the inevitable achievement of that arousal. This equation does two important things. First, it develops further the increasingly specific nature of the central endeavor in the sequence: from the general aesthetic imperative for transfiguration and renewal in "Morning", to the explicitly literary testament to that imperative commemorated in the Lawrence elegy, to the specifically poetic struggle with that imperative enacted in "Paterson: Episode 17." Second, it injects a small note of hope for that endeavor by virtue of its precedents, the "few excellent poems" that are somehow associated with the discipline of "the attentive / *and obedient* mind." Thus, the closing lines here prepare perfectly for the prolonged and highly disciplined examination of beauty in "The Crimson Cyclamen" that follows.

"The Crimson Cyclamen" is in fact very much a meditation. Beginning with both precise botanical observation and the abstract language of intellectual analysis, it traces the growth of the flower in large verse paragraphs until about two-thirds of the way through the poem, when along with the flower's bloom, the form breaks out into exclamation-filled quatrains of "ecstasy" [*sic*]. Then the poem falls back into somewhat briefer verse paragraphs to note in more subdued tones the flower's final wilting. The obvious counterpoint that this controlled, cerebral pulse provides to the orgasmic spasms of "Paterson: Episode 17" underscores and corrects the essential pathology of the preceding poem. There is no violent complication to the incipient transfiguration with which the poem opens—only a scientific accuracy:

White suffused with red
more rose than crimson
—all a color
the petals flare back
from the stooping craters
of those flowers
as from a wind rising—
And though the light
that enfolds and pierces
them discovers blues
and yellows there also—
and crimson's a dull word
beside such play—
yet the effect against
this winter where
they stand—is crimson—

It is miraculous . . .

This sort of observational precision is enhanced in the poem by a strain of Platonism that also elevates the more gusty appetites for beauty established earlier in the sequence. Embedded throughout the clear sensuousness are phrases and ideas that both establish metaphysical principles and resonate with physical tangibility. Note for instance how teleology blends with the visual luminosity of the image "thought mirrors" in the passage that follows the one cited above:

It is miraculous
that flower should rise
by flower
alike in loveliness—
as thought mirrors
of some perfection

Even at the height of excitement with the blooming of the cyclamen's flowers, there remains the same philosophical basis to the very tactile pistil and stamens, and full transfiguration occurs as a function of deliberate study as much as of accidental beauty:

> Fast within a ring
> where the compact agencies
> of conception
>
> lie mathematically
> ranged
> round the
> hair-like sting—
>
> From such a pit
> the color flows
> over
> a purple rim
>
> upward to
> the light! the light!
> all around—
> Five petals

There is in fact a very explicit equation with thought itself developed throughout the examination of the cyclamen. "The leaves / freakish, of the air / as thought is," are placed within a very definite scheme of cogitation: the variegation of the leaves is equated with "an abstraction / playfully following / centripital / devices, as of pure thought"; the furcation of veins on the underside of the leaves is "to link together / the unnicked argument / to the last crinkled edge"; and the actual edge of the leaf, "where the under and the over / meet and disappear / and the air alone begins / to go from them" is a "conclusion left still / blunt, floating." Blossoming "must / put thought to rest," and the unfolded flower itself is "passion / earlier and later than thought / that rises above thought."

Regardless of its ultimate diminishment of thought as an idea, this extended systemization—combined with the precise observation and the general philosophic perspective—creates a pervasive impression of mental discipline that transforms the eventual excitement over the cyclamen's flowers from mere sensuous arousal to genuine spiritual rapture. Thus, it is no exaggeration when the "empurpled lips" of Beautiful Thing reappear in "an ecstacy / from the empurpled ring" of the cyclamen. Neither is it simply crepuscular when in the closing relaxation of the poem, the etiolated flower becomes bathed in a twilight purple that redeems everything with beauty and a truly contemplative serenity. For both those states are everywhere validated by the "attentive / and obedient mind" that was heralded at the end of "Paterson: Episode 17":

> The day rises and swifter
> briefer
> more frailly relaxed
> than thought that still
> holds good—the color
> draws back while still
> the flower grows
> the rose of it nearly all lost
> a darkness of dawning purple
> paints a deeper afternoon—
>
> The day passes
> in a horizon of colors
> all meeting
> less severe in loveliness
> the petals fallen now well back

The last few lines that follow quite clearly rephrase (with the sublimer dusk replacing invigorating dawn) the opening axiom of aesthetic refreshment from "Morning," and they thus emphasize the thematic continuity and the lyrical progress in the sequence. The issue at hand is still very much the aesthetic renewal of a shabby world, and the general sense of inchoate transfiguration evoked in "Morning" has advanced to the fully manifest beauty of the cyclamen and to the unabashed proclamation of aesthetic supremacy as a principle:

> the frail fruit
> by its frailty supreme
> opening in the tense moment
> to no bean
> no completion
> no root
> no leaf and no stem
> but color only and a form—

Thus, it is no real surprise when the next poem, "The Waitress," returns in a wholly rehabilitated way to the female figure of beauty that was so brutalized in "Paterson: Episode 17." The confused sacrifice of Beautiful Thing has been replaced by the pure adoration of a servingwoman. And the major physical trauma suffered by Beautiful Thing gives way to what in comparison seems merely a bad case of dishpan hands. Even the loud and obsessive outrage of the Lawrence elegy has been restrained to just a quick satiric insinuation of society's disregard for this unassuming idol of beauty:

> The benefits of poverty are a roughened skin
> of the hands, the broken
> knuckles, the stained wrists.

Things are, in short, better all the way around. They are also enlarged in a very fundamental way. More than simply marking progress, "The Waitress" conveys the essential euphoria of "The Crimson Cyclamen" out of the realm of rarefied meditation and into that of an ordinary and spontaneous attention. The previous concentration upon precise physical details and to their incipient transfiguration now attaches itself to the most fleeting and usually invisible of presences—the waitress of the title:

> Serious. Not as the others.
> All the rest are liars, all but you.
>   Wait on us.
> Wait on us, the hair held back practically
> by a net, close behind the ears, at the sides of
> the head. But the eyes
>   but the mouth, lightly (quickly)
> touched with rouge.
>
> The black dress makes the hair dark, strangely
> enough, and the white dress makes it light.

The expression of a fortunate discovery from among an unpromising pack; the eagerly repeated plea for the favors of the woman's service; the redundant flutter of meaning and suffix in "lightly (quickly)—all add a deep thrill to the medallion-like profile drawn by the outline of a restaurant hairnet and to the apparitional effect created by the chiaroscuro of her uniform.

There is the same sort of excited perception extended to the incidentals of the actual dinner—to the fragments of a social club's parliamentary motions, to the bustle of the hotel bellhop, and to the sea-view at the window. They all carry an exhilaration that culminates in the religious ecstasy of oracle:

O unlit candle with the soft white
plume, Sunbeam Finest Safety Matches all together in
a little box—

And the reflections of both in
the mirror and the reflection of the hand, writing
writing—
Speak to me of her!

This transfiguration of the truly mundane is more properly the sort of achievement only vaguely intuited in "Morning." Yet it is nothing like a fully accomplished vision; it is finally and fundamentally only a glimpse, defined at beginning and end by a grammatical litany of negatives. Those negatives—"No wit," "none needed," "no way," "nobody else and nothing else," "none of us," "Neither by you," "nor by me"—recall the similarly negative roster of the aesthetic proclamation in "The Crimson Cyclamen," and they do share some of the especial intent of that proclamation. But while in both poems most of the negatives ostensibly serve to single out their respective replicas of transfigured beauty, those in "The Waitress" appear to collapse finally under the weight of their own sheer denial. The transporting presence of the waitress yields de facto to the garish titillation of neon signs, and the poem concludes with a bittersweet relinquishment of transfigured beauty to the realm of the elusive:

THE WAITRESS

No wit (and none needed) but
the silence of her ways, gray eyes in
a depth of black lashes—
The eyes look and the look falls.

There is no way, no way. So close
one may feel the warmth of the cheek and yet there is
no way. . .
.   .   .   .

—and nobody else and nothing else
in the whole city, not an electric sign of shifting
colors, fourfoot daisies and acanthus fronds going from
red to orange, green to blue—forty feet across—

Wait on us, wait
on us with your momentary beauty to be enjoyed by
none of us. Neither by you, certainly,
nor by me.

By comparison, then, the rapture of "The Crimson Cyclamen" proves perhaps too precious and untenable a medium for the exaltation of the common moment. It is one thing to exalt a flower, and quite another a waitress, despite the equation to the contrary which the last line of "The Crimson Cyclamen" ("merging into one flower—") makes with the immediately succeeding title of "The Waitress." And so there is an element of disappointment at the end of "The Waitress," and it is to this note of failure that the succeeding "The Flower" most strongly addresses itself.

Just as "The Waitress" reached back to "Paterson: Episode 17" to redraw the female figure of Beautiful Thing in light of the intervening ecstasy of "The Crimson Cyclamen," so too does "The Flower" reach back to "The Crimson Cyclamen," reconceiving the flower motif in the somewhat more disenchanted light of "The Waitress." "The Flower" in fact more literally fulfills in its title the promise of the last line in "The Crimson Cyclamen" than does the intervening "The Waitress." And the echo of that line's last word ("flower") recalls in particular the structural principle of centripetal contiguity in the bouquet image of the earlier poem's closing lines: "the petals fallen now well back / till flower touches flower / all round / at the petal tips / merging into one flower—."

With such retrospective cues, the opening line for "The Flower"—"A petal, colorless and without form"—seems an especially dramatic contrast to the "color only and a form" of the aesthetically transfigured cyclamen. Thus, but for somewhat different contextual reasons, the sober reassessment in "The Flower" retains much of the special impact it had in its original setting of *Collected Poems 1921–1931*. The purely figurative use itself of the motif adds in its new context an even more pervasive sense of failure to the basic affect of the poem. Similarly, the various details of the individual petals manage to locate new lyrical and literal precedents from among the other new poems that precede them. For example, the central recognition in "The Flower" of a very personal and specifically literary defeat at the hands of a city-building civilization repeats in more immediate and compelling terms the defeat of Lawrence by imperial Britain that was the occasion for a rather facile indignation in the earlier elegy.

The greater sense of defeat extends as well to the defoliated winter trees and public benches in "The Flower" as they restate in less numinous terms the memory of summertime idleness in "Morning." Where "Sun benches at the curb bespeak / another season, truncated poplars, / that having served for shade / served also later for the fire," there is now a perjorative cast to "the edge of the park where under trees / leafless now, women having nothing else to do / sit in summer." In the way the initial placement of "leafless now" in the middle line tends to make it read as a figurative introductory modifier to "women," the "leafless" might as well read "useless," and the women are no doubt old and idle.

This is a rather drastic reconception of woman for the sequence. The other women in the poem revise even more clearly the figures of earlier poems. Madame Lenine's deliberately provocative Bolshevik sentiments about religion contrast with the appealing "silence of her ways" and with the quite muted irony about the "benefits of poverty" in "The Waitress." And the disabusing "naked woman, about 38, just / out of bed, worth looking at" recalls both the ravished Beautiful Thing and the ultimately disillusioning waitress. The female figure of beauty has, in short, become entirely more complicated than it has ever been. The women of "The Flower" are together at once old and young, idle and revolutionary, retiring and forthright.

It is, of course, the "naked woman, about 38" who individually embodies all these things at once, who in the flower is "at its heart (the stamens, pistil, / etc.)." And she is as well the greatest source of the discomfiture that governs the poem. Her blunt indictment of the speaker's dishonorable motives (not for art but for pure "power") goads him into the guilty self-ridicule that closes the poem. The original aesthetic imperative in "Morning" for the widow's tears "to be rewetted and / used again" becomes the considerably more modest "I plan one thing— . . . —to write"; and in the middle of that less grandiose imperative, there lies the lampoon of a preposterously ambitious scheme to earn a physician's livelihood by pushing buttons.

"Romance Modern" seizes the spirit of that embedded lampoon, and raises it to a positive vandalism as it bristles under a vague but strong sense of stricture and confinement, very much equivalent to the sense of retrenchment in "The Flower." The poem opens with some fey effects of light and rain upon a mountainous landscape, glimpsed from the rear-seat windows of a touring car. At first addressing the landscape ("the other world") in the secrecy of back-seat adolescent passion ("Talk to me. Sh! they would hear us"), the speaker puerilely fantasizes leaping from the car to join the "detached dance of gnomes" he sees. But he quickly grows more impulsive and begins to sound more like a juvenile delinquent:

> Lean forward. Punch the steersman
> behind the ear. Twirl the wheel!

> Over the edge! Screams! Crash!
> The end. I sit above my head—

The mock sound effects and the comical disincarnation make
this a hyperactive episode, and they introduce the mania that dominates the rest of the poem. Equating the car crash with a bold break
through to "the other world," the speaker blurts out declarations of
arousal and love in a revelry of liberation:

> . . . All stuff of the blind emotions.
> But—stirred, the eye seizes
> for the first time—The eye awake!—
> anything, a dirt bank with green stars
> of scrawny weed flattened upon it under
> a weight of air—for the first time!—
> or a yawning depth: Big!
> Swim around in it, through it—
> all directions and find
> vitreous seawater stuff—
> God how I love you! . . .

This exciting sense of aesthetic renewal is something like what
the sequence has been seeking since "Morning," and that identity
is asserted with the reappearance of the earlier poem's most basic
motif, placed now within the newly defining ardor of the present
poem's moment:

> Love you? It's
> a fire in the blood, willy-nilly!
> It's the sun coming up in the morning.

In the same way, the sexual treatment of the actual body of the
renewed world—the landscape—makes of that body a clear repetition of Beautiful Thing from "Paterson: Episode 17." Directly on
the heels of some manic chatter about some new sportswear, there
comes what appears to be a rededication to Beautiful Thing's broken nose:

> Oh get a flannel shirt, white flannel
> or pongee. You'd look so well!
> I married you because I liked your nose.
> I wanted you! I wanted you
> in spite of all they'd say—

Of course, the sudden remark about the beloved's nose has,
like the preoccupation with the sportswear, a distinct measure of

thorough triviality to it—"the fillip of novelty. It's a fire in the blood," as the speaker puts it. And that element is ultimately the governing flaw in the poem. Like all teenage passions, this one is overdone, and all too predictably, the transcendental moment becomes a silly suicide pact:

> Rain and light, mountain and rain,
> rain and river. Will you love me always?
> —A car overturned and two crushed bodies
> under it.—Always! Always!

The poem simply has nowhere to go from the sheer indulgence of its fantasy, and so it can only fall off into a sheer dizziness with visual effects and an adolescent sense of jealous betrayal by them. "You are sold cheap everywhere in town!" exclaims the speaker before finally exhaling a futile wish that it all were truly transcendental and not just the optical illusions of the hour and place.

"Romance Modern" is essentially what the archaic syntax of its title suggests—a piece of melodrama, an overreaction to the sense of failure and inadequacy in "The Flower." And as such, it in turn calls for some sort of correction. The debunking poem that follows does just that. "Paterson" retains something of the vigor from "Romance Modern" but returns it to the steadier honesty that dominates the end of "The Flower." The very first line seems a reproof to the landscape antics of the previous poem: "Before the grass is out the people are out." And the emphatic refrain of "Paterson" is really a more businesslike restatement of the same principle of renewal that informs the preceding histrionic poem:

> A good head, backed by the eye—awake!
> backed by the emotions—blind—
>
> > (from "Romance Modern")
>
> Say it! No ideas but in things.
>
> > (from "Paterson")

Thus, the "things" so promoted by "Paterson" are not the romantically shimmering landscape of "Romance Modern" but a late winter neighborhood that strongly recalls the hilltop shantytown of "Morning," only made particular now, as particular as a specific town. Key motifs—nondescript houses, leafless trees, transfiguring light—reappear, only now with greater emphasis upon their physical bodies. Indeed, the truncated tree of the earlier poem has not only been restored but glorified in its very branches and bark, and light itself is asserted substance:

> —Say it, no ideas but in things—
> nothing but the blank faces of the houses
> and cyclindrical trees
> bent, forked by preconception and accident
> split, furrowed, creased, mottled, stained
> secret—into the body of the light—

This corporealness is developed into the central trope of the poem. Town and inhabitants become both the flesh and thought of a city animated to the dimensions of a living man. "These are the ideas, savage and tender," the lines above continue, "somewhat of the music, et cetera / of Paterson, that great philosopher." And later in the poem, "It is / his flesh making the traffic, cranking the car / buying the meat."

The transubstantiation here is distinctly not of the rarefied or sacred kind; the realm is of the same shabby sort as in "Morning." But the details are distinctly compelling in their precise articulation. Where the landscape of "Romance Modern" was persistently blurred with both literally visual distortions ("sliding mists sheeting the alders") and an emotional hyperbole, that of "Paterson" is boldly particular:

> abandoned to grey beds of dead grass
> black sumac, withered weed stalks
> mud and thickets cluttered with dead leaves—

The heavy alliteration and consonance of stop sounds in these lines—b's, d's, g's, k's—and the frequency of spondees confirm in clipped sounds the exceptional factual precision of the description here. The lusterless fields are forcefully and completely realized; there is nothing gushy or sentimental.

Neither is there in the portrait of Paterson's best thought, a luckless casualty by the name of Jacob:

> Divine thought! Jacob fell backwards off the press
> and broke his spine. What pathos, what mercy
> of nurses (who keep birthday books)
> and doctors who can't speak proper english—
> is here correctly on a spotless bed
> painless to the Nth power—the two legs
> perfect without movement or sensation

"Correctly"—more than any thing else, this world jolts the sentiment out of this anecdote. It asserts factual accuracy where we expect unstinting pity, and it transforms the blitheness of the nurses' diversions and the doctors' careless language into components of a larger and happier aesthetic respect for the victim, one in which his useless limbs can be newly calibrated to an aesthetic supremacy and with a mathematical accuracy (to the "Nth power").

This is the sort of truly clearer-sighted "wit" that the poem implicitly promotes against the impetuousness of "Romance Modern." It embraces the very evidence of aesthetic defeat among its subjects—the "cheap pictures, furniture / filled silk, cardboard shoes, bad dentistry"—and meets it all with a very deliberate resolve to redeem it:

> But never, in despair and anxiety
> forget to drive wit in, in till it
> discover that his thoughts are decorous and simple
> and never forget that though his thoughts are decorous
> and simple, the despair and anxiety

And when the poem settles down to some very cheerful images—gleeful children playing in the snow, a singing canary, some robust potted geraniums—there is through it all an expression not only of sheer beauty but also of vindication and explanation for a viewpoint. The first image is "The *actual,* florid detail of cheap carpet" (emphasis added); the flowers are noticeably canned rather than potted; and, in the final lines of the poem, all the images are proclaimed to be "the divisions and imbalances / of his whole concept, made small by pity / and desire, they are—no ideas beside the facts—."

This fundamental polemic that runs throughout "Paterson" permits an element of subdued anger to complement the uplifting perceptions of beauty. Take the imperative cited above, for example. Although the sheer length and symmetry of the imperative (along with its literal concern with "thought" as a subject) make clear its essentially rational and deliberate character, there is also something emotionally aggressive. The festering repetition of injuries suffered in the identical rhymes of the first and last lines; the special emphasis in the at first suspended and then repeated phrase "never forget"; and the insistent short "i" and "t" sounds in the aggressive infinitive phrase of the second line—this could all be the phraseology of vengeance, even war. And it is out of this latent note that the penultimate poem of the sequence grows.

Divided into five numbered parts, "March" both opens and closes on some rather ferocious notes. The first is a brief eight-line chronicle of seasonal austerity that restates the late winter/ early spring motif that has run throughout the sequence:

> Winter is long in this climate
> and spring—a matter of a few days
> only,—a flower or two picked
> from mud or from among wet leaves
> or at best against treacherous
> bitterness of wind, and sky shining
> teasingly, then closing in black
> and sudden, with fierce jaws.

At this point, the sense of menace is restricted to some clearly aesthetic effects of the elements. But by the final section of the poem, the imminent threat has been translated into a blatant war cry. "But! now for the battle! / Now for murder," cries the speaker as he addresses the winds and instructs them to "Fling yourselves upon / their empty roses— / cut savagely!" "March" seems as much a military command as the name of a month.

The double meaning is not gratuitous, for in a very fundamental sense, the entire poem is a poetic mobilization. The impending force in the images of the opening section is not immediately discharged but is instead deferred by a chummy second section that calls up three associations from the past of a broad cultural tradition and from some present personal experience. "March, / you remind me of / the pyramids, our pyramids / stript of the polished stone," fondly remarks the speaker, who then goes on to further associate his pal with Fra Angelico at work upon a fresco and with some rowdy younger poets. The collective invocation makes the theme of the poem the most explicitly aesthetic one in the entire sequence, and it inspires in the section itself a friendly and explicitly aesthetic declaration "to write poetry . . . a poem that shall have you / in it March."

That declaration leads directly to the celebrations of the three separate associations in the final three sections of the poem. The "pyramids" are unearthed in the proud excavations of III, and we witness the aesthetic testimony to ancient glories—a basrelief of the Assyrian king Ashurbanipal in a victorious hunt, and then a majestic procession of sacred animals to Nebuchadnezzar's Babylonian throne. Then the speaker assumes for himself an equal grandeur. Unleashing some of the pent-up force from the opening section, he boasts Faustian powers over nature, men, and time itself:

> Now—
> they are coming into bloom again!
> See them!
> marching still, bared by
> the storms from my calendar
> —winds that blow back the sand!
> winds that enfilade dirt!
> winds that by strange craft
> have whipt up a black army
> that by pick and shovel
> bare a procession to
> > the god, Marduk!

The fourth section answers this masculine bravado with the feminine delicacy of Fra Angelico's Virgin Mother. Opening in the reposeful tones of recollection ("My second spring— / passed in a monastery / with plaster walls—in Fiesole"), the heart of IV is the image of a Mary whose "intently serious" demeanor recalls in beatific terms the earthier "serious" waitress of the fifth poem as well as the titular "Beautiful Thing" of "Paterson: Episode 17." Yet though the essential temper of it has changed, there is in IV the same aggressive element as is in the other sections of the poem. The splendid visitation includes a small but very clear element of Lawrentian sexuality as the visual communion of angel and virgin are likened to that between rapacious snake and mesmerized bird.

Thus, the fifth section and its "third springtime" of marauding winds—"Winds! / lean, serious as a virgin" that "whirl up the snow / seeking under it" the first flowers of spring—constitutes a very deliberate culmination of the fundamental aesthetic expressions of power that have preoccupied the poem: male, female, and now elemental, all in a broad and nearly crazed search for the first evidence of renewed beauty, for "one flower / in which to warm myself!" At the same time, the final moment of the poem mixes in as cautionary notes the less tempestuous, accomplished *facts* (or aesthetic artifacts) of those other springs, those other awakenings:

> But though you are lean and frozen—
> think of the blue bulls of Babylon.
>
> Fling yourselves upon
> > their empty roses—
> > > cut savagely!

> But—
> think of the painted monastery
>   at Fiesole.

This combination of a diligent regard for tradition and a literally physical exuberance might best be described as zeal. And it is not all that different from that first tentative note of sacred mission that concluded "Morning." Nor are the cautionary notes here that much different from the broad moment of personal reappraisal in "The Flower." The mission has simply been paganized, its terms changed to purely aesthetic ones and its spirit made fearlessly heroic. Similarly, the reappraisal has been generalized and its discouragement turned into insight. "March" is, in other words, a recommencement, in more seasoned and bolder terms, to the same cultural and aesthetic imperative evolved out of the first poem in the sequence.

"The Wanderer: A Rococo Study" completes this recommencement with a grand eight-part suite of pagan, almost druidic initiation. The inchoate imperative of "Morning" becomes replaced by an explicit mission, as "all the persons of godhead" beckon to a predestined speaker. The Holy Spirit here, of course, appears as no Christian dove but as two common scavenger birds. The first is a crow that captivates the speaker's attention with the sheer physical exhilaration of its flushing and soaring. The arousal is enough to make the sensibility here articulate, and as the ferry-riding speaker stands at the prow gazing toward Manhattan, he poses to himself a very explicit question: "How shall I be a mirror to this modernity?" The question immediately prompts the metamorphosis of the bird figure into, appropriately, a talking seagull, who hails the speaker with boasts of strength and skill:

> How shall I be a mirror to this modernity?
> When lo! in a rush, dragging
> A blunt boat on the yielding river—
> Suddenly I saw her! And she waved me
> From the white wet in midst of her playing!
> She cried me, "Haia! Here I am, son!
> See how strong my little finger is!
> Can I not swim well?
> I can fly too!" And with that a great sea-gull

The heroic bravado in this pentecost seems a clear extension of "March," and it retrieves from its previous futility the feminine principle of defeated beauty that has run throughout the sequence.

The maternal element here, for instance—the address to "son," and the attention that the "m" alliteration gives to the punning "modernity"—evokes and adds genuine intimacy to an earlier association in "The Waitress" between the entrancing working woman and some screaming gulls at a nearby window. Yet the fundamental labor in the equation has been entirely preserved: this new goddess comes "dragging / A blunt boat."

In any terms, however, the apparition of the gull in this episode quite accurately anticipates the outright epiphany of the next movement, "Clarity." Literally enraptured into the sky as a metamorphisized gull himself, the speaker begins to prophesy a messianic salvation for the aesthetic body of the world:

> And as gulls we flew and with soft cries
> We seemed to speak, flying, "It is she
> The mighty, recreating the whole world,
> This is the first day of wonders!
>
> She is attiring herself before me—
> Taking shape before me for worship,
> A red leaf that falls upon a stone!

Like the pentecost, this prophesying literally redeems with sustaining purpose earlier lyrical moments in the sequence. The haiku-like delicacy of the falling red leaf, for instance, repeats within a broad revelational excitement the ultimately pensive red leaf motif of "The Crimson Cyclamen." And the suggestion of an altar in the end-line association of "worship" and "stone" highlights in a purely exalting context the disturbing victimology of "Paterson: Episode 17." Similarly, the further incarnation of the goddess as a beggar reconceives the scavenger figure of "Morning" with a now unequivocally divine if shabby demeanor:

> That high wanderer of by-ways
> Walking imperious in beggary!
> At her throat is loose gold, a single chain
> From among many, on her bent fingers
> Are rings from which the stones are fallen,
> Her wrists are a diminished state, her ankles

"Clarity" asserts the basic lyrical disposition for a sublime vision of the shabby, but it is the following two sections, "Broadway" and "Paterson—The Strike," that project the first authentic evidence of the shabby itself. The shift is literally shocking, as the first two lines of "Broadway" record a slap to the back of the head that recalls the rambunctious "Punch [to] the steersman / behind the ear" in "Romance Modern": "It was then she struck—from behind, / In mid air, as with the edge of a great wing!" The smack is, of course, now delivered with the more complete motivation of the preceding section, and lyrically it more resembles the disabusing realism of "The Flower" than the adolescent volitility of "Romance Modern." The goddess is stripping away a bit of the naiveté the pervades both "Advent" and "Clarity," and replacing it with the true features of the "modernity" the speaker has embraced in principle. Amidst a promenade of wasteland characters ("Empty men with shell-thin bodies"), the heretofore submissive "Beautiful Thing" becomes galvanized into a pugnacious Ugly Thing as the goddess assumes for herself the smell and face of a repulsively salacious old hag who shouts a challenge to the speaker's own Eliot-like aloofness from the scene:

> "Well, do their eyes shine, do their clothes fit?
> These *live* I tell you! Old men with red cheeks,
> Young men in gay suits! See them!
> Dogged, quivering, impassive—

The reproof brings the first real sense of personal distress to the poem, and the episode closes with the chastised speaker in a frantically extended bid for credibility with the muse. Flattering her with successive honorifics, he resubmits his plea for the "power to catch something of this day's / Air and sun into your service! / That these toilers after peace and after pleasure / May turn to you, worshippers at all hours!"

That note of personal desperation prepares exactly for the even more shocking display of public misery in "Paterson—The Strike." Assuming a now "wretchedly brooding" aspect, the muse dispatches the speaker into the slums of Paterson for some purging realism:

> "Faces all knotted up like burls on oaks,
> Grasping, fox-snouted, thick-lipped,
> Sagging breasts and protruding stomachs,
> rasping voices, filthy habits with the hands.
> Nowhere you! Everywhere the electric!

These are the same "facts" that were documented in the earlier poem "Paterson," only here they are distinctly horrific rather than "correct." Detached from the mitigation of the earlier poem's intellectual conviction, they are now perceived strictly in terms of desperation, and they are thus revealed in the real fullness of their brutality. Even the self-perception of the speaker grows monstrous:

> "Ugly, venomous, gigantic!
> Tossing me as a great father his helpless
> Infant till it shriek with ecstasy
> And its eyes roll and its tongue hangs out!—

The last image is more Bosch than baby, and like the unsettling anecdote of Jacob in "Paterson," it dispels all possibility of sentiment and stiffens the visual attention. Thus there is no facetiousness in the speaker's concluding statement to "Paterson—The Strike": "'I am at peace again, old queen, I listen clearer now.'" There *is* a greater clarity present now, a greater *aesthetic* clarity and one which in degree equals that extreme sense of explicit *understanding* in "Clarity" itself. On this thoroughly aroused basis, the last three movements of "The Wanderer" can convincingly emerge into the realm of the transcendental.

"Abroad" begins the process by removing the literal scene to a more idyllic setting. The streets of Paterson are replaced by a landscape strongly reminiscent of the mountainous terrain in "Romance Modern." But virtually all of the adolescent fantasy of that poem has been eliminated, and the woods have become the referent for the muse's most serious intention. In some impassioned, oratorical parallelism that repeats with greater animation the merely simmering "never forget" clauses in "Paterson," the old woman makes an impassioned social crusade out of an aesthetic agenda:

> Speak to men of these, concerning me!
> For never while you permit them to ignore me
> In these shall the full of my freed voice
> Come grappling the ear with intent!
> Never while the air's clear coolness
> Is seized to be a coat for pettiness;
> Never while the richness of greenery
> Stands a shield for prurient minds;
> Never, permitting these things unchallenged
> Shall my voice of leaves and varicolored back come free through!"

Similarly, the muse momentarily replaces the dirty denizens of Paterson with a shouted projection of some peasants suffering under a rustic oppression. The changes do not signal a return to pastoral values as much as they facilitate the general sense of dedication that "Abroad" develops. It is simply easier to sympathize with laboring farmers than with unemployed "fox-snouted" riffraff. The segment finally, and inevitably, returns to the urban landscape enriched with a leavening eye for natural beauty and with a note of fond personal nostalgia that would have been impossible or unconvincing for the brutal streets of "Paterson—The Strike":

> To the city, upward, still laughing
> Until the great towers stood above the marshland
> Wheeling beneath: the little creeks, the mallows
> That I picked as a boy, the Hackensack
> So quiet that seemed so broad formerly:
> the crawling trains, the cedar swamp on the one side—
> All so old, so familiar—so new now

The happy retrospective contrasts sharply with the brooding futility of the one in "The Flower," and instead of leading to retrenchment and future modesty as in the earlier poem, the slightly heightened sense of time that informs this moment prompts in the following segment, "Soothsay," some audaciously grandiose expectations. Repeating the wizardly command "Behold yourself old!" the muse envisages the speaker in broadly heroic terms:

> Sustained in strength, wielding might in gript surges!
> Not bodying the sun in weak leaps
> But holding way over rockish men
> With fern free fingers on their little crags,
> Their hollows, the new Atlas, to bear them
> For pride and mockery! Behold

These alliterative lines, with their emphasis upon physical mightiness, could be right out of *The Seafarer* were it not for the God's Titan name. And the honorifics grows even grander. The speaker becomes the prevailing forces of nature itself, replete with the purple and fanfare of royalty:

>   . . . Behold
> Yourself old! winding with slow might—
> A vine among oaks—to the thin tops:
> Leaving the leafless leaved,
> Bearing purple clusters! Behold
> Yourself old! birds are behind you.
> You are the wind coming that stills birds,
> Shakes the leaves in booming polyphony—
> Slow winning high way amid the knocking

Throughout all of this prophetic pomp, however, is a clear thread of treachery. The very opening lines of the segment record in forsaken tones the muse's desertion of the speaker, as "Eight days went by, eight days." And when the muse returns there is something insidious as well as exalting in her incantations. "Behold yourself old!" begins not as conjuration but as something of a cruel comeuppance to the slightly glib maturity the nostalgic speaker displays at the end of "Abroad." "Would you behold yourself old, beloved?'" teases the crone, and the speaker can overcome his hurt only with some deliberate Stoicism: "I was pierced, yet I consented gladly / For I knew it could not be otherwise." And certainly, the prophecy of victory only in old age (so accurate to Williams himself), of a dubious victory like that of a defeated Titan or as "slow" as that of a vine or wind— certainly such prophecy is foreboding as well as auspicious. There is ruin as well as renewal in this fate, and the muse is not merely glib herself when she concludes the segment by declaring an essential ambivalence at the heart of her possession of the speaker:

> "Good is my over lip and evil
> My underlip to you henceforth:
> For I have taken your soul between my two hands
> And this shall be as it is spoken."

The declaration extends to the moral agencies of muse and speaker the same principle of ambivalence that has governed the sequence since "Morning," where it appeared as the only vaguely felt aesthetic merging of the squalid with the sublime. And the same consecration that completed that aesthetic impulse in the opening poem completes it here in the last. Much as the widow's dirty tears were held as precious relics, so too is the speaker made over into something sacred by the agency of filth itself, by "The Passaic, that filthy river." In its waters, "St. James' Grove" performs the formal baptism for "The Wanderer."

It is a distinctly more elaborate ritual than the tentative gesture at the end of "Morning." The filth, for instance, is more deliberate and uncompromisingly horrible, and there is a satanic cast to the baptism over which the "old queen" presides. "Wailing and laughing," she defines intimacy as a common foulness, the boy as a propitiation, and possession as demonic:

> Lo, the filth in our hair, our bodies stink!
> Old friend, here I have brought you

> The young soul you long asked of me.
> Stand forth, river, and give me
> The old friend of my revels!
> Give me the well-worn spirit,
> For here I have made a room for it

There is even a suggestion of suicide as after the metempsychosis between river and speaker, he stands a compliant witness to his own body floating away under the river's current.

Yet, in keeping with the promise of "Soothsay," the vaguely evil and sacrificial elements are mixed with the more joyful initiatory ones. The episode nearly begins on a charming note of boyish preparation—"In my woolen shirt and the pale blue necktie / My grandmother gave me, there I went"—and there is a sort of tribal pride in the actual ordainment of the muse: "Then she, leaping up with a fierce cry: / 'Enter, youth, into this bulk! / Enter, river, into this young man!'" The river itself brings the "crystal beginning of its days" to the boy as well as "the utter depth of its rottenness." And there is genuine fortitude in the speaker's reaction to the specter of his departing body:

> I could have shouted out in my agony
> At the sight of myself departing
> Forever—but I bit back my despair

The last phrase recalls the balanced counsel of "Paterson": "never, in despair and anxiety / forget to drive wit in"—and it further signals the essential moral transfiguration that this entire rite constitutes in the simultaneity of its "good" and "evil" elements. The defilement here is everywhere ennobled with the utmost of human (and aesthetic) purpose. And in an enlarged and exalted way, "St. James' Grove" fulfills the initial movement of "Morning," where the mere glimpse of a transfigured world led to an impassioned but abbreviated *agenda* for renewal: "to be rewetted and/ used again." That is, the final emphasis of the sequence is not so much upon some accomplished fact of transfigured beauty, but upon the large possibility for it inherent in the deep dedication to it. Thus it seems not at all outlandish when "St. James' Grove" concludes with some literally fantastic promises of renewal by the muse to the river:

> Deep foilage, the thickest beeches—
> Though elsewhere they are all dying—
> Tallest oaks and yellow birches

That dip their leaves in you, mourning,
As now I dip my hair, immemorial
Of me, immemorial of him
Immemorial of these our promises!

The "mourning" of course repeats in newly positive terms—
"rewets," as it were—that of the perennially "mourning" widow
from "Morning," and the testament of specially preserved trees
restates on more abundant terms the relic of the widow's "pinched
and saved" tears. Other reciprocities of closure can be noted. The
church altar of widow's grief and the grime of her tears, for instance, are now respectively an arboreal temple and a sanctifying
stink: "Here shall be a bird's paradise ... hallowed by a stench /
To be our joint solitude and temple." But the final orientation of
"The Wanderer," like "Morning" itself (and very much unlike
Collected Poems 1921–1931), is not closure as much as it is com-
mencement. With the essential values and lyrical impulse of the
intervening poems throughout "Longer Poems," "The Wanderer"
seems to anticipate, even demand the great sequence of renewed
"facts" that would actually follow—*Paterson*. And "Longer
Poems" would be hardly better placed anywhere else than last in
The Complete Collected Poems 1906–1938.

8

The Cruder Counterparts to "Longer Poems": "The Tempers," "Transitional," and "Al Que Quiere"

On its own lyrical and phenomenological terms, "Longer Poems" is a remarkably coherent sequence. Yet within the context of the entire volume, this final section also serves as something like a reprise, bringing into sharper relief the lyrical and poetic movement throughout the other ten individual sections, each of which possesses an internal coherence of its own. Compare, for instance, how "The Tempers" anticipates, with a different but related subject matter, the lyrical character and curve of movement in "Morning."

Like the later poem, the opening section begins with a literal moment of awakening. Only instead of a slowly transcendental shantytown dawn, there is heralded in "Peace on Earth" an impetuous revival of the classical deities:

> The Archer is wake!
> The Swan is flying!
> Gold against blue
> An Arrow is lying.
> There is hunting in heaven—
> Sleep safe till to-morrow.
>
> The Bears are abroad!
> The Eagle is screaming!
> Gold against blue
> Their eyes are gleaming!
> Sleep!
> Sleep safe till to-morrow.
>
> The Sisters lie
> With their arms intertwining;
> Gold against blue
> Their hair is shining!

The Serpent writhes!
Orion is listening!
Gold against blue

His sword is glistening!
Sleep!
There is hunting in heaven—
Sleep safe till to-morrow.

Despite the call to a peaceful night's sleep, the ostensibly gladsome tidings of a mythically animated world—of the classical world, really—are loaded with uneasier notes. There is a ferocious predation in the hunting images, dangerous seduction in that of the serpentine sisters, and murderous intent in Orion's surveillance. Combined with the emphasis upon a very temporary personal safety in the refrain "Sleep safe till to-morrow," these touches make it unclear whether the human reassurance of the poem arises out of the deities' vigorous presence itself or out of their fortunate if only momentary preoccupation with more heavenly prey.

There are as well other elements in the poem's craft that make the superficial comfort it claims a questionable one. For one thing, the invocation of mythic figures here is a bit heavy-handed. While in the ancient world personifying the constellations into the supernatural actors of a poem may have readily allowed a convincing expression of genuine feeling, in a modern poem it smacks of archaic literary formula more than anything else. And other details of the poem create the same sort of impression. The first stanza, for instance, fetches "lying" as a rhyme for "flying," despite the fact that the word choice makes the "Arrow" of the heavenly hunter a curiously motionless missile; rhyme seems to have superseded poetic reason. Similarly, there is little imagistic sense in the refrain "Gold against blue." Perhaps the colors are intended to suggest something like the splendor of sun and sky on a clear day, but if so, the effect would seem pointlessly incongruous with the nighttime moment suggested for the poem by its other refrain, "Sleep safe till to-morrow," and by its implicit astronomical perspective. But there is no reason to believe that the colors refer to anything specific, and the refrain probably signals a vague pretension to an Attic color scheme more than it does any real affective state.

Overall, such faults suggest a rather uninspired, or at best, awkward quality to the poem, despite its clear aspirations to communion with a great classical tradition. And indeed, about the most generous thing one could say about the poem is what Pound (whose

analogous poem "The Return" so entirely surpasses Williams's)
said in his review of the original collection for *The Tempers*:

> [Williams] makes a bold effort to express himself directly and con-
> vinces one that the emotions are veritably his own, wherever he shows
> traces of reading, it would seem to be a snare against which he strug-
> gles, rather than a support to lean upon. It is this that gives one hopes
> for his future work.

Sincere but poetically naive seemed to be Pound's judgment.
And those characteristics are really very similar in kind if not
caliber to the innocent, wide-eyed wonder that pervades "Morning." The poems differ only in their formulations of a single lyrical
strain. "Morning" expresses its wonder as part of a compelling (if
inchoate) awareness of certain crucial aesthetic values present in
the immediate modern world; "Peace on Earth" places the wonder
at the center of a compelling *problem* in those values: their conspicuous absence. Both formulations, however, have the same
practical effect. Where the inspiration of "Morning" leads finally
to the aesthetic imperative that closes the poem, the problem of
"Peace on Earth" leads to the solution of an aesthetic enterprise
that closes "The Tempers" in "To Wish Myself Courage":

> On the day when youth is no more upon me
> I will write of the leaves and the moon in a tree top!
> I will sing then the song, long in the making—
> When the stress of youth is put away from me.

The effects here are noticeably better handled than those in
"Peace on Earth," more akin to those in "Morning." Classical affectations have been replaced by a more genuinely youthful directness and simplicity—the excitement, in other words, remains with
the moon and not Diana or some other handy personification. Similarly, the toying with epic invocation in the third line avoids pomposity by virtue of its parallelism with the unpretentious second
line. Such effects support rather than subvert the resolve at the
end of the stanza by placing it within a credible modesty. So it is
that in contrast to the untrustworthy refrains of assurance in
"Peace on Earth," these lines from "To Wish Myself Courage" ring
with more convincing commitment. Even the hint of procrastina-
tion in them suggests a precociously mature foresight and patience
more than anything else.

This is all not simply a matter of technical trickery. The basic
sensibilities differ here as well. The final stanza of "To Wish Myself

Courage" displays this difference perhaps most clearly. Note, for instance, the difference in idiom and rhyme between it and "Peace on Earth":

> But when the spring of it is worn like the old moon
> And the eaten leaves are lace upon the cold earth—
> Then I will rise up in my great desire—
> Long at the birth—and sing me the youth–song!

Instead of the grunting rhythm of the pseudoclassical ejaculations in "Peace on Earth," there is here one full and well-balanced sentence. And in contrast to the earlier poem's gratuitous "flying"/ "lying" rhyme, the "old"/"cold" rhyme here is natural and unobtrusive, embedded as it is within the parallel noun phrases that end the first and second lines. Rhythm, in other words, has taken its properly dominant place over rhyme.

So too has idiomatic phrasing prevailed against phony formalisms like "The Archer is wake." There is instead an effectively employed (because locally defined) phrase like "the old moon," which acquires in addition to its nominal calendar meaning a genuine sense of familiar reference by virtue of the moon's previous mention in the first stanza. Lastly, vague classical allusions like "The Archer" and "The Swan" have given way to more concretely meaningful figures like the lace metaphor, which vividly renders the *literal* sight of the perforate and also aforementioned leaves. In short, everything signals a sensibility more alert to the aesthetic possibilities of its own immediate world than to those of stale literary convention.

It is this same newly emergent sensibility that "Morning" later invokes and begins to apply to the various ignobilities of the immediate, modern world. And much as the tentative transfigurations of that later poem initiate and prepare for the overall aesthetic undertaking of "Longer Poems," "The Tempers" prepares as well for a further broad aesthetic effort throughout the volume at large by carefully developing the constituent elements of a *lyrically credible* transfiguring imagination. "Portent," for example, contributes to the final, superficial resolve of the section a deeper religious conviction, just as the scavenger's prayer does in "Morning." And so too "Hic Jacet" contributes to the seemingly easy optimism of the section a disciplined, unsentimental regard for mortality and loss, just as the widow episode does in "Morning." The section as a whole, in other words, makes the boyish initiative of "To Wish Myself Courage"—and of "The Tempers" as a whole—as serious and as compelling a thing as the nearly sacred imperative for renewal announced at the end of "Morning."

Actually, "The Tempers" is even more profoundly preparatory in its nature than is "Morning," for the essential issue around which the section lyrically develops is, in fact, a *methodological* one. There is throughout the poems a fundamental involvement with literary conventions and traditions as each group of poems advances from an awkward, unconvincing archaism to a more natural and confident involvement with the immediately present world. The three poems that follow "Peace on Earth," for instance— "Postlude," "First Praise," and "Homage"—express the opening poem's archaic orientation within troubadourian love poems that, while still clearly artificial, at least attach the classical posturings to some genuinely discernable human passion:

> Lady of dusk wood fastnesses,
>   Thou art my Lady.
> I have known the crisp, splintering leaf-tread
>   with thee on before,
> White, slender through green saplings;
> I have lain by thee on the grey forest floor
>   Beside thee, my Lady.
>
> (from "First Praise")

Despite the stylized "Thou" and "Lady," despite even the precious phrasing of "with thee on before," the floral details create a primary sensory excitement. There is in the longer lines a brightening contrast in colors, of white and green against grey, and an onomatopoetic play of plosive "sp" sounds. And networked by a single quiet rhyme ("before"/"floor") to the shorter lines, these touches make credibly passionate instead of purely formulaic the repeated asseverations of those shorter lines.

Obviously, such effects are not by definition distinctively modern, but in the local context of the section, they do distinguish themselves from the more vapid sort of archaism that was equated with classicism in "Peace on Earth." Indeed, many years later, Williams himself would annotate the poems of *The Tempers* for John Thirlwall in jus† such terms. While "Peace on Earth" would be chalked up simply to "just making a berceuse that would hold together, using material that I knew," "First Praise" was given a bit more credit for a serious if only partly successful attempt at an authentic lyrical expression:

> I was always building it up and conscious of this falseness. I should have written about things around me, but I didn't know how. I was

unhappy because I wasn't doing what I wanted. I was just on the verge of saying right, but I couldn't get it out. I knew nothing of language except what I'd heard in Keats or the Pre-Raphaelite Brotherhood. (quoted in Litz and MacGowan 473)

Despite the small improvement, however, it was only for a much later poem in the sequence—"Con Brio"—that Williams could express real personal satisfaction: "This I always liked because I was just beginning to find my way around, to say what I wanted—written without changing a word" (quoted in Litz and MacGowan 475). But earlier in the sequence the poems are still more full of conventional poses than not. More typical is the "O, prayers in the dark!/ O, incense to Poseidon! / Calm in Atlantis" that ends "Postlude" or the hackneyed troubadourian conceit that begins "Homage":

> Elivira, by love's grace
> There goeth before you
> A clear radiance
> Which maketh all vain souls
> Candles when noon is.

Such airs really do demand some sort of deflation, and that is exactly what the following two teasing poems provide. Affecting a Shakespearean manner itself, "The Fool's Song" mocks the attempt "to put / Truth in a cage!" With a bird standing in for the capitalized abstraction, the attempt of course results only in both an escaped bird *and* a broken cage, to the great delight and "heigh-ho!" of the singing jester.

As elusive "Truth" then gives way to an illusive sexuality that more directly addresses the preceding three fatuous love songs, "From 'The Birth of Venus', Song" furthers the taunt with some chimerical mermaids who beckon with sexual titillation at the erotic possibilities—and impossibility—of a taboo tryst:

> Come with us and play!
> See, we have breasts as women!
> From your tents by the sea
> Come play with us; it is forbidden!

The mermaids, of course, are clearly Homeric figures, but the very real sexual tension they introduce, especially in the blunt anatomical usage of "breasts," extends the unnerving effect of "The Fool's Song" and jolts the section out of the ersatz sexuality that has thus far characterized the archaic.

The next two poems advance even further in this regard. "Immortal" parodies troubadourian hyperbole with some ungallant cynicism: "Ignorance" becomes the "beloved," the "godly thing" that is "Richer than clear gems; wider than the sky." And then "Mezzo Forte," for the first time in the sequence, drops entirely the courtly charade and equates it with a much more blunt and distinctly modern rendition of fickle affections, circa early twentieth century:

> Take that, damn you; and that!
> And here's a rose
> To make it right again!
> God knows
> I'm sorry, Grace; but then,
> It's not my fault if you will be cat.

So "Truth" has descended to "Ignorance" and finally to a shrew named "Grace." The capitalized abstractions and the classical/courtly tradition they represent have clearly not fared so well. Having lost even the pretense of the transcendental, they are redefined in more modern, more vulgar, and more lyrically credible terms. So at this point in the section, there appears something basically analogous to the squalid contemporary world to which "Morning" more directly turns its attention. And the next group of poems in "The Tempers" furthers the correspondence by extending the play of a disappointing tradition and a disabusing modernity into some shamanistic terms that anticipate the numinous features of landscape in "Morning."

"Crude Lament" bemoans to the old "Mother of flames" who has "kept the fire burning" that the young hunters "that went ahunting" (perhaps those from "Peace on Earth") "are asleep in the snow drifts" while their young wives are left weeping. But more than sorrow, the speaker is left with a powerful sense of unworthy survival; "Would god they had taken me with them!" he concludes. "An After Song" then connects to this sense an explicit estrangement between genuine classical splendor and a disoriented modern sensibility:

> So art thou broken in upon me, Apollo,
> Through a splendour of purple garments—
> Held by the yellow-haired Clymene
> To clothe the white of thy shoulders—
> Bare from the day's leaping of horses.
> This is strange to me, here in the modern twilight.

The poem inverts the lyric and thematic predicament of the sequence. Where "Peace on Earth" affirmed in its statement a viable and reassuring involvement with the classical tradition, the poem's poetic character (and caliber) belied that involvement. "An After Song," on the other hand, claims only incomprehension of that tradition, yet the Pre-Raphaelite simplicity and brilliance of color in the poem's images prove it to be in fact very much in touch with the best of that tradition. And thus Apollo's commanding entrance is enough of a hopeful note to sustain the passage through the grotesque futility of the three poems that complete the fire motif begun in "Crude Lament."[1]

Beginning "O crimson salamander," "The Ordeal" petitions the creature in conjurational tones to retrieve from Hell some Orphic "fellow." "Appeal" seems then to speak magically as that fellow, transformed into a nearly extinguished faggot at the edge of the fire. With more desperation of the frightened living than with the ritual solemnity of the peacefully dead, he in turn requests of the salamander "one little flame" which he may give as a talismanic bracelet to "him that flung me here." Unfortunately, the "Fire Spirit" can only reply with a darkly comic disclaimer that sounds more like a Yiddish shtick than an otherworldly voice:

> I am old.
> You warm yourselves at these fires?
> In the center of these flames
> I sit, my teeth chatter!
> Where shall I turn for comfort?

With this blatant failure to rekindle the cultural spirit on a primal level, the sequence then resorts to a more effective idiom, one that more closely approximates the transfiguring capacity of that in "Morning." The typical intensity-seeking ode-like form of the earlier poems gives way to the longer colloquial lines of dramatic monologue in "The Death of Franco of Cologne: His Prophecy of Beethoven." And almost ironically that looser form seems to permit the most intense affect yet in the sequence. Although it opens on a note of surrender that echoes in its figurative usage of "spark" the literal futility of the fire poems, the monologue ultimately locates a literally transporting vision of artistic transmission. "It is useless, good woman, useless: the spark fails me," exclaims the composer (and inventor of musical notation) to his nurse before throwing her out in frustration. Then in private communion with the notes that he likens to "little children that go playing / Over the five-barred gate," he paternally chides them for their unruliness and then warns them:

> But, black eyes, some day you'll get a master
> For he will come! He shall, he must come!
> And when he finishes and the burning dust from
> His wheels settles—what shall men see then?
> You, you, you, my own lovely children!
> . . . .
> For I have seen it! I have seen it
> Written where the world-clouds screen it
> From other eyes
> Over the bronze gates of paradise!

Thus, facing extinction, the promise of a sustained and sustaining tradition rapturously asserts itself, and it does so as a function of a transfiguring imagination. More significantly, that promise is evolved out of a more natural, "modern" idiom and out of the more plausible lyrical pressures of a common but profound human fact—death—rather than from the precedent of some gratuitous and wornout literary conventions. This complex of a transfiguring imagination, a modern idiom, and a realistic world is in its essential constituents identical to the one that motivates the closing aesthetic imperative of "Morning" after the spectacle of the forever grieving widow. It is in fact only a short distance from this point in "The Tempers" to the unpretentious confidence and enterprise of "To Wish Myself Courage," and the next five poems secure that passage while at the same time redeeming the false expressions of the earlier poems.

"Portent" picks up both the messiah theme and the note of rapture that close "Franco of Cologne" and translates them back into the ode-like form of the earlier poems. This both enhances the closing affect of "Franco of Cologne" and rehabilitates (within the local context of the section) the ode form itself. It contains, for instance, the sort of primary, naturalistic detail that shall invigorate "To Wish Myself Courage," and there is even an exact anticipation of the tree motif in that poem. In a similar way, "Ad Infinitum" replays the sexual episodes of the earlier poems. Something like the ludicrous foibles of courtly devotion and the fickle emotions they involve now appear but within the governing context of a deliberately congenial sincerity:

> Still I bring flowers
> Although you fling them at my feet

> Until none stays
> That is not struck across with wounds:
> Flowers and flowers
> That you may break them utterly
> As you have always done.

"Contemporania" then reconceives the type of imaginatively animated world that "Peace on Earth" so self-seriously sought, and of course it is not filled with ominously threatening gods but with some pixy leaves, chattering away in the aftermath of a literal storm:

> I go back and forth now
> And the little leaves follow me
> Talking of the great rain,
> Of branches broken,
> And the farmer's curses!

The affect grows even more spritish as "Hic Jacet" restates in conscientiously mundane and entirely charming terms the fatally solemn, ritualistic preoccupation with mortality that had so driven the fire poems. Instead of death's more ominous traditional attendants, there appear the delightful antics of "The coroner's merry little children." Everywhere, in other words, the concerns of the sequence achieve a more common, genuine, and cheerfully invigorating expression.

Implicit in this development is the fundamentally modern character of that more common expression, and in the penultimate poem, that character is made fully explicit. Cast (as is "To Wish Myself Courage") in the long lines of "Franco of Cologne," "Con Brio" places an emphatically corrective and historical edge on the issue while further defining it very much as a matter of aesthetic temperaments, of "Tempers":

> Miserly, is the best description of that poor fool
> Who holds Lancelot to have been a morose fellow
> Dolefully brooding over the events which had naturally to follow
> The high time of his deed with Guinevere.
> He has a sick historical sight, if I judge rightly,
> . . . .
> Bah, this sort of slither is below contempt!
> In the same vein we should have apple trees exempt
> From bearing anything but pink blossoms all the year,
> Fixed permanent lest their bellies wax unseemly, and the dear
> Innocent days of them be wasted quite.

How can we have less! Have we not the deed?
Lancelot thought little, spent his gold and rode to fight
Mounted, if God was willing, on a good steed.

The equation is unequivocal; the too self-serious temperament of
courtly idealism makes for a distorted perception of literary tradition, "a sick historical sight." And by the same token, the robust
spirit that informs this highly colloquial repudiation of that distortion makes for an accurate one.

Whatever its logical merits, such a deduction is by this time
indisputable in the local lyrical terms of the sequence: the usual
expressions of classical and courtly tradition *are* discredited vehi-
cles of feeling; and, on the other hand, the boldness of simple
daily gusto is a credible and compelling foundation to the aesthetic
enterprise of "To Wish Myself Courage." And thus the entire volume is launched.

Ultimately, all the thematic and lyrical elements of preparation
in "The Tempers" focus upon the explicit aesthetic endeavor mentioned in the middle stanza of "To Wish Myself Courage":

How can I ever be written out as men say?
Surely it is merely an interference with the long song—
This that I am now doing.

"The long song"—the sole measure of definition has only to do
with length, with unusual continuity. In this regard, "The Tempers"
significantly differs from the equally prepatory "Morning," which
defines its closing agenda in the more substantive terms of aesthetic renewal: "to be rewetted and / used again." Of course, the
specific constituents of "the long song" *do* seek with their own
methodological emphasis the aesthetic renewal of the neglected
and disreputable. There is in "Con Brio," for instance, a revisionist
approach to the coarse and the bawdy as a proper foundation for
a sound literary tradition (no doubt a radical proposal to Williams's
contemporaries but old news to a predecessor like Chaucer). But
for the most part, the initiative of "Morning" is clearly more mature, more thematically defined and more lyrically cogent, than
that of "The Tempers."

This is only appropriate, for historically, the poem probably enjoys some twenty-five more years of Williams's poetic development, and that development is bound to be generally apparent in
a volume of collected poetry that observes in its primary organiza-

tion a roughly accurate historical chronology. But to the extent that "Morning" appears as a deliberate reprise rather than simple successor to "The Tempers," it also appears as a deliberate *product* of "the long poem" (in a very loose sense) that "The Tempers" only initiates and that the intervening sequences further assemble.

Although a similar sort of relationship exists between each succeeding section and its corresponding longer poem, its particular intent is early and most clearly seen in the change of titles for the second section in the volume. Primarily comprising the poems that had constituted "Prior to" in *Collected Poems 1921–1931*, the section seems to have been retitled—to "Transitional"—specifically to lose the retrospective emphasis it had in the earlier volume and to confirm instead the prepatory, methodological emphasis of "The Tempers" and the broader continuity of the newer volume as a whole.

Other changes in the contents of "Transitional" / "Prior to" suggest equal attention to inter-sectional continuity. "At Night," for instance—which in *Collected Poems 1921–1931* had served as lead poem in "Prior to" and spoke so neatly to the diminished sense of self that had immediately preceded it in "The Flower"—was removed and reassigned to another section entirely, leaving "To Mark Anthony in Heaven" to open the new "Transitional." Thus, the slightly high-strung eagerness that closes "The Tempers" in the 1938 collection is sustained and mellowed rather than foiled by the new opening note of mildly euphoric daydreaming. Similarly, the new lead poem's citation of Anthony and Cleopatra recalls more immediately the similar use of Lancelot and Guinevere in "Con Brio."

The prominent use of such transitional devices as these is very similar to the way the Lawrence elegy in the later "Longer Poems" conspicuously assumes the key "mourning" motif from "Morning"; in both cases, at least some sort of continuity is immediately and obviously suggested between the respective parts. But even more important, the transitional cues signal similar complications to the lyrical impulses that precede them.

Note for instance how the special convergence of aesthetic and sexual pleasure that was explored in "The Tempers" is developed in "Transitional." At first, the sensuous (if somewhat juvenile) musing upon Anthony and Cleopatra in "To Mark Anthony in Heaven" essentially repeats the same kind of confident aesthetic preoccupation with the sexual relationship of famous lovers that attended the study of Lancelot and Guinevere in "Con Brio." Only instead of a pugnacious challenge to some wrongheaded notion of literary tradition, there is now the leisurely relish with which the images of "grass and trees and clouds"—and by association the "inch by inch" examination of Cleopatra wishfully ascribed to Anthony— are slowly rotated in the poem's quasi-refrain.

By the conclusion of "Transitional," however, this special convergence of aesthetic sexual elements reappears in the more frustrated combination of "Portrait of a Lady." Despite his best efforts to flatter his lady's sexual beauty with aptly sensual metaphors, the speaker of that poem succeeds only in tripping himself up over the details of his choice and source of figures, and his initial arousal is finally superseded by a somewhat amusing irritation with his own poetic ineptitude. Fantasies about famous lovers seem to be one thing; courting a real live girl is quite another.

The entire episode is rather charming, yet there is nonetheless expressed in it a real sense of artistic difficulty that is quite different from the cheerful optimism with which "The Tempers" closes in "To Wish Myself Courage." And it is to this genuine difficulty and its attendant frustrations that the later public rage of "An Elegy to D. H. Lawrence" mostly corresponds. Rooted in the intractability of a national culture's insensibility to the aesthetic influence of Lawrence, the rage in the elegy is simply a more serious version of the speaker's exasperation with the intractable materials of his "Lady." The chief difference here is one of lyrical and thematic maturity, as it was between "Morning" and "The Tempers." In "Transitional," the frustration is typically adolescent, ultimately related to a thwarted personal concupiscence; by the time of the elegy, the impatience has come to be a more profound cultural one, and the sexual initiative commemorated is virtually mythic in its proportions.

A similar growth is evident throughout the rest of the section's poems as well. As, for instance, the sophomoric philosophic doubletalk of the second and title poem strains to create a serious sexual aesthetics after the pure sensuousness of the opening poem, it distinctly if ineptly anticipates a similar gesture in the later elegy.

> We are not men
> Therefore we can speak
> And be conscious
> (of the two sides)
> Unbent by the sensual
> As befits accuracy.
> . . . .

And he answered:
Am I not I—here?

(from "Transitional")

And sisters return
through the dusk
to the measured rancor
of their unbending elders.

Greep, greep, greep the cricket
chants where the snake
with agate eyes leaned to the water.

(from "An Elegy to D. H. Lawrence")

The early poem is all specious logic, ironically out of touch with the very "accuracy" of its own aesthetics. The subtler intelligence in the elegy, on the other hand, brings a really factual and sensuous accuracy fully to bear upon the aesthetic position it seeks to establish. The details of Lawrence's life and literature are powerfully animated as the estrangement of male and female principles becomes an episode of parental censure, its "measured rancor" expressed as the insistent rebuke of cricket calls and its necessary filial submission as the scornful stare of a snake.

So too does each of the remaining poems anticipate more mature expressions even as they move the lyrical current of the section closer to the difficulties of "Portrait of a Lady." The contrived Mediteranean sentiment of "Sicilian Emigrant's Song" that so pathetically affirms its buoyancy in the face of a depressingly "gray" land seems a precursor to the subtle and genuinely sustaining zoetic geography of Lawrence's exile; the sarcastic disregard for superficial conformity in "Le Médicin Malgré Lui" gives merely flip defiance to the same oppressive mentality that is later villified as a truly dangerous, disapproving cultural character; the self-regarding histrionics of forlornness in "Man in a Room" amounts to a rehearsal for the more devastating sense of Lawrence's aesthetic alienation; the straining aesthetic escapism from literary routine in "A Coronal" predicts the unflinching difficulty of Lawrence's truly original aesthetic achievement; and the hint of disenchantment in the post-dream moment of "The Revelation" gives way to the fully angry disappointment at "Lawrence no more in the world / to answer April's promise."

The corollary to this sort of lyrical equivalence between section and "longer" poem is that each succeeding (and therefore more "mature") section will more closely reflect not only the general affects of the corresponding "longer" poems but the particular caliber and character of their expression as well. Such is the case as the volume passes from the adolescent irritation of "Transitional" and on into "Al Que Quiere" with its more adult discontent over a positively devalued world in general. Compare, for instance, the poem "Dawn" with the "Beat hell out of it" passage from "Paterson: Episode 17."

DAWN

Ecstatic bird songs pound
the hollow vastness of the sky
with metallic clinkings—
beating color up into it
at a far edge,—beating it, beating it
with rising, triumphant ardor,—
stirring it into warmth,
quickening in it a spreading change,—
bursting wildly against it as
dividing the horizon, a heavy sun
lifts himself—is lifted—
bit by bit above the edge
of things,—runs free at last
out into the open—! lumbering
glorified in full release upward—
                      songs cease.

There is more resemblance between the straining ardor in this poem and the precariously violent excitement of "Paterson: Episode 17" than between anything in "Transitional" and the Lawrence elegy. Even the key repetitions of "beating" and "lifts . . . is lifted" predict the exact usage for the complicated mixture of tenderness and brutality that later forms the response to Beautiful Thing. And in the almost loutish sun that runs "lumbering / glorified" and in the *cessation* of bird song that is the final achievement of all this exertion, there is perhaps something just about as hobbled and subdued as Beautiful Thing herself.

Certainly, however, the approach to beauty here is nothing quite so brutally stupid as that of the Newark gang. Things have not gotten quite so serious yet, nor so complicated. Despite their generic similarity to those of "Paterson: Episode 17," the lyrical tensions in "Al Que Quiere" are more simplistically defined and separated. The driving force behind the entire section is in fact an implicit but very evident *opposition* (rather than confusion) of responses toward a nascently beautiful world. On the one hand is the self-righteous aesthetics of a superior speaker, and on the other are the recalcitrant devaluations of his "townspeople." The opening poem, "Sub Terra," poses it in terms of a greatly disappointed desire for aesthetic fellowship:

> Where shall I find you,
> you my grotesque fellows
> that I seek everywhere
> to make up my band?
> None, not one
> with the earthy tastes I require;
> the burrowing pride that rises
> subtly as on a bush in May.

The disappointment in turn prompts throughout the section a broadly based and essentially proselytizing appeal to the aesthetic intelligence of these "fellows," most explicitly in the famously homiletic poem "Tract." Finally, however, in the absence of a confirming response from them, the desire for aesthetic fellowship becomes more fully thwarted and falls back to the defensive, almost surly retirement of the antepenultimate "Dedication For a Plot of Ground":

> She grubbed this earth with her own hands,
> domineered over this grass plot,
> blackguarded her oldest son
> into buying it, lived here fifteen years,
> attained a final loneliness and—
>
> If you can bring nothing to this place
> but your carcass, keep out.

The simple pluck of the old woman commemorated in this poem is a commonplace version of the more sublime if passive resilience to adversity displayed by the later Beautiful Thing, whose regal stature ("till your head / through fruitful exaggeration / was reaching the sky") asserts itself almost in direct proportion to the stages of her defilement. The old woman is simply a much more down-to-earth figure, and her adversities (primarily shipwreck and bereavement) are a good deal less immediately intense than the gang rape of Beautiful Thing. Yet certainly in the local terms of the volume, "the living presence of / Emily Dickinson Wellcome" (Wil-

liams's English grandmother) marks a tremendous advance from
the poetically intractable female figure that had concluded "Transitional" in "Portrait of a Lady."

So too does the terrene motif that dominates "Al Que Quiere"
trace out an advance in seriousness for the volume. The speaker's
likening in "Sub Terra" of his "grotesque fellows" with the requisite
"earthy tastes" to locusts swarming up out of the ground; his speci-
fications in "Tract" for a properly unadorned and discomforting
burial; his cranky eulogy to the earth-mother figure in "Dedication
for a Plot of Ground"—like the soil and the momentous events of
death and resurrection to which they ultimately refer, these details
are intrinsically darker and more profound than the juvenile sexual
fantasies that run through "Transitional." There is, in other words,
a distinct sense of emotional growth from one section to the next.

This growth is something that Williams apparently sought to especially emphasize in the way he altered the original set of *Al Que
Quiere* the volume as he turned it into "Al Que Quiere" the section.
In the 1917 arrangement, "Sub Terra" was followed by "Pastoral
(When I was younger)," and the refractory pose in the latter poem's
preference for the beauty of slum backyards tended to sieze the
antic preferences in the closing lines of the opening poem.

> —God, if I could fathom
> the guts of shadows!
>
> You to come with me
> poking into negro houses
> with their gloom and smell!
> In among children
> leaping around a dead dog!
> Mimicking
> onto the lawns of the rich!
> You!
>
> > (from "Sub Terra")
>
> When I was younger
> it was plain to me
> I must make something of myself.
> Older now
> I walk back streets
> admiring the houses
> of the very poor:
> . . . . . .
> . . . all,
> if I am fortunate,

> smeared a bluish green
> that properly weathered
> pleases me best
> of all colors.
>
> (from "Pastoral")

Had this sequencing been preserved in *Complete Collected Poems 1906–1938*, it would have picked up the juvenile note of "Transitional" and turned it all into a childish sort of aesthetic impudence. But the actual 1938 arrangement introduces two new poems—"Spring Song" and "The Shadow"—in the second and third spots, and they accomplish something entirely different, something more adult.

First, "Spring Song" seizes the more serious elements in "Sub Terra"—the desire for an aesthetic fellowship and the terrene phenomenology of the ground-swarming locusts—and translates them into some sensuous love-talk of the grave. Appearing to directly address the same "fellows" of the opening poem, the speaker assumes a strange postmortem privilege of imagination. "Having died," he says, "one is at great advantage / over his fellows— / one can pretend." And so willy-nilly he detects "the smell of earth / being upon you too" and contemplates

> one last amour
>
> to be divided for
> our death-necklaces, when
> I would merely lie
> hand in hand in the dirt with you.

"The Shadow" then heightens this sense of sepulchral intimacy with an even more sexual cast. The earth becomes a bed, spring a woman's embrace, and her scent that of the damp soil:

> Rich as the smell
> of new earth on a stone
> that has lain breathing
> the damp through its pores—
> Spring closes me in
> with her blossomy hair
> brings dark to my eyes.

Of course, what makes this all more adult than "Transitional" is not the simple intimation of sex and death but the sustained evidence in the poems' sensory richness of a greater poetic intelligence, one that resembles the sensuously metaphysical one in Donne's "The Relic" more than the comically concupiscent one of "Portrait of a Lady." Thus, a clear measure of the volume's poetic growth is given. At the same time, however, the new opening set also consolidates the initial poem's desire for an aesthetically aroused fellowship of "earthy tastes" and transforms it into a compelling and defining force throughout the remainder of the section. When, for instance, "Pastoral (When I was younger)" comes along as the *fourth* poem of the section, its final notation of isolation in its nonconventional social and aesthetic evaluations ("No one / will believe this / of vast import to the nation") seems an expression of something more than a youthful sarcasm; it seems an expression of genuine and profound disappointment.

Taken together then, these first four poems probably form the section's most signal lyrical divergence from the corresponding earlier book. But they constitute by no means the only changes Williams made. He omitted three poems ("Woman Walking," "Foreign," and "History") entirely from the volume. He assigned one ("Appeal") to "The Tempers" and one ("The Wanderer") to "Longer Poems." He shuffled the rest around so thoroughly that only seven of some fifty or so remained in their originally contiguous positions. And in addition to "Spring Song" and "The Shadow," he added yet two other new poems ("The Young Housewife" and "Drink"). The lyrical effect of each of these changes, particularly with regard to how they address the highly consolidated affects of the opening three poems, would be confusing to describe individually. But the way in which the new arrangement as a whole tends to define itself in terms of the opening set is not.

The aforementioned "Pastoral," for instance, heads a group of four poems, ending with "Pastoral (The little sparrows)," that constitutes a spirited aesthetic program for the opening impulse towards aesthetic communion. In the first "Pastoral" there is a proud admission of the general disrepute in which the speaker's aesthetics is held; then two poems ("Chickory and Daisies" and "Metric Figure") promote as the aesthetic and lyrical touchstones for the sequence the vitality of some literally earth-shaking chickory, a child's ferocious treatment of some daisies, and a splendid sun among the trees; and lastly the second "Pastoral" returns to the somewhat explanatory mode of the first "Pastoral" by shaming the speaker's smug fellows, particularly a pompous Episcopal priest, with the exemplary figures of some chippering sparrows and an earnest old man collecting "dog-lime."

After this preliminary setting forth of a cheerful aesthetic position, the sequence restates in "Love Song" the intimate tones of the opening set, repeating as it does some of the key motifs (daisies, petals, stems, tree leaves) from the second group and reasserting the principle of a subterranean upheaval by concluding a lovers' stroll with the image of large uprooted oak trees. "Gulls" complements this intimacy with an earnest public appeal to the speaker's "townspeople" for their esteem or at least their tolerance of his patient devotion to them, and then a set of three poems plays out in somewhat schematic fashion the component affects of that appeal. There is a fearful skyscrape in "Winter Sunset" that suggests a certain oppression of the speaker's aesthetic perceptions; there is a soothing seascape in "In Harbor" that fortifies the speaker with some privileged news of the "high sea"; and then there is the vigorous "Tract" on burial practices ("the ground sense") that puts both these elements together along with the concerned public spirit of a homily.

The overall effect of this last movement is to transfer some of the intimacy and sincerity from the opening set to a more public orientation and to make that orientation something more than an abstract cause. Then, in a personal apologia to some "leading citizens" that exactly reflects these curiously personalized public terms, "Apology" earnestly restates the speaker's aesthetic position before the next two poems put forth in dualistically opposed versions of roadside travel the essential sensibilities at odds here.

"Promenade" is an extremely affectionate pre-dinner stroll of father and son, full of joyously aesthetic discoveries of the weather and flowers. The second—"Libertad! Igualidad! Fraternidad!"—is a rude encounter between a pedestrian and the driver of an "ash-cart," full of intractable social bitterness. The naturalism of the first of these two poems clearly extends the terrene motif begun in the opening poem (the "earthy tastes") and the aesthetic intimacy with which it is associated. The second poem clarifies the indifferent resistance to those elements as the same conventional social priorities that goaded the speaker of the first "Pastoral" to "make something" of himself and that necessitated his "Apology" to the "leading citizens." In sum, there appears to be a distinct contest between cheerful aesthetic enrichment and dour social convention for the hearts and minds of the "townspeople."

With this measure of definition, the remaining bulk of the section sets out to remake the world according to the former principle. There are four poems that together enact an erotic desire out of an aesthetically aroused attention to the world: "Summer Song" opens with a roguish nonchalance inspired by a dreamy moon;

"Young Housewife" adds a bit of lechery in the crushing of some leaves; another "Love Song (Sweep the house clean)" sings a carpe diem in a call to clean house; and the previously cited "Dawn" attains a positive ardor in the break of day. Then there are three macho poems that harden the desire in a schematic division of the world into three elemental realms: "Hero" hails some adventurous exploits at sea as fit preparation for sexual conquests; then "Drink" boasts of its favorite "whiskey" as "a tough way of life: // The wild cherry / continually pressing back / peach orchards"; finally, "El Hombre" testifies to a camaraderie with a single maverick star in the sunrise.

The two groups together prepare for the following group of three poems that, again according to a scheme of three earthly elements, fully impassion the world itself according to the most "earthy tastes": "Winter Quiet" projects a landscape as the writhing embrace of lovers; "A Prelude" creates a Sapphic communion with some tide pools; and "Trees" presents the horizon as a heaving, even groaning together of sky and tree-covered hillock. The passionate forces here are then translated in the next group into three portraits of the human imagination. "Canthara" exotically recalls the sexual initiation of an old black man by the dance of no less than six genital-exposing women. Against that full-bodied memory is the vain, world-weary, and agoraphobic pomposity portrayed in "M. B." Then "Good Night" reconciles the two dispositions by triggering a vivid fantasy of some enticing opera chorus girls with a very lazy drawing of a bedtime glass of water.

In the next four poems, this combination of sexual and imaginative vigor takes a bit of a darker turn before then developing into a highly robust state. "Keller Gegen Dom" resorts to a furtive sexual assignation for its more carnal details, including the smell of a vinegar douche. Then "Dance Russe" lightens the "dirtiness" a bit with the amusing if secretive antics of a closet nudist, and "Mujer" introduces a genuine charm about a cat's incorrigible pregnancies. "A Portrait of a Woman in Bed" makes the cat's apetites in turn seem squeamish as a lower-class lady named Robitza shamelessly displays her body and her scorn for all conventional notions of personal responsibility. Thus, she brings back to the fore after this long interlude since "Libertad! . . ." the basic "issue" of the volume.

Robitza (the woman portrayed in bed) has just about the most "earthy" tastes imaginable. And her appearance seems to prompt another explanatory poem of the sort that the two "Pastorals" and "Apology" constitute. Posing itself rhetorical questions and reciting a few key motifs from the previous dozen or so poems, "Virtue" lustily affirms the superior value of all beauty judged unprofitable by the world and then calls our attention to a menagerie of ragtag characters, all boys and men. The male focus seems to prepare for the distinctly male apetites that are posted in the next three poems.

Leading with a self-admonishing confession of some rather rank and lady-displeasing olefactory preferences, "Smell!" prepares for the two lecherous confessions of secret desire for some prepubescent girls in "The Ogre" and "Sympathetic Portrait of a Child." Of course, these highly excited musings upon the girls are not moments of simple lust; they are also testimonies to a powerful imagination, evidenced everywhere by a aesthetic delight in the precise sensory details of the girls. Then almost as though to clarify that distinction comes yet another of the section's explanations to the "townspeople" in "Riposte." Unabashedly proclaiming the free distribution of love to be as powerful a cleansing agent as poetry, the poem dispels any sense of guilt that may attend the candid admissions of pedophilic desire in the previous two poems.

This bold attempt to redefine the socially sordid in terms of some superior aesthetic evaluation is at the heart of the entire section, just as it is at the heart of the later "Paterson: Episode 17." And it advances even further in "K. McB." and "The Old Men," a pair of poems that promote the same effort as a public principle in, respectively, female and male terms. The first poem roots on an earthy girl named Kathleen, an "exquisite chunk of mud," to "teach them [presumably the townspeople] a dignity . . . of mud"; the second poem salutes the sexual and aesthetic vigor of some dirty old burlesque buffs. And in this same confident spirit, the following "Spring Strains" restates most of the previously established landscape motifs (especially the solar ones from "Metric Figure" and "Dawn" and the terrene ones from "Sub Terra" and the first "Love Song") in a tremendously energized scene of rising sun and tree branches that is unapologetically composed in purely geometric and chromatic—in aesthetic—terms:

> In a tissue-thin monotone of blue-grey buds
> crowded erect with desire against the sky—
>   tense blue-grey twigs
> slenderly anchoring them down, drawing
> them in—
>   two blue-grey birds chasing
> a third struggle in circles, angles,
> swift convergings to a point that bursts
> instantly!

                              Vibrant bowing limbs
        pull downward, sucking in the sky
        that bulges from behind, plastering itself
        against them in packed rifts, rock blue
        and dirty orange!
                              But—
        (Hold hard, rigid jointed trees!)
        the blinding and red-edged sun-blur—
        creeping energy, concentrated
        counterforce—welds sky, buds, trees,
        rivets them in one puckering hold!
        Sticks through! Pulls the whole
        counter-pulling mass upward, to the right,
        locks even the opaque, not yet defined
        ground in a terrific drag that is
        loosening the very tap-roots!

        On a tissue-thin monotone of blue-grey buds
        two blue-grey birds, chasing a third,
        at full cry! Now they are
        flung outward and up—disappearing suddenly!

In lyrical intensity and phenomenological placement, "Spring Strains" is the climax of the section's aesthetic enthusiasm, and thus the sustained note of discouragement in the immediately succeeding "A Portrait in Greys" is especially powerful as that enthusiasm's antithesis. A series of rhetorical questions that reproach a companion's drab preferences for what is "level and undisturbed by colors" directly thwarts the previous poem's excitement of "tissue-thin monotone of blue-grey buds / crowded erect with desire against the sky." The clash repeats with greater finality the section's initial disjunction between speaker and "townspeople," and, not surprisingly, seems to conjure another "Pastoral" (the third) to restate, as did the first two, the section's current thematic and lyrical positions:

                    If I say I have heard voices
                    who will believe me?

                        "None has dipped his hand
                        in the black waters of the sky
                        nor picked the yellow lilies
                        that sway on their clear stems
                        and no tree has waited
                        long enough nor still enough
                        to touch fingers with the moon."

I looked and there were little frogs
with puffed out throats,
singing in the slime.

Clearly, those positions are not harmonious. They involve a speaker's deep sense of public discredit for the "voices" that he hears and that speak of such emphatically aesthetic elements as "the black waters of the sky." He is finally left with only an audience of "little frogs / with puffed out throats, / singing in the slime."

The frogs and the slime are, of course, the finally meager evidence of the terrene arousal so sought in the sequence's opening set of three poems. Yet the section continues on for a half-dozen more poems. These six recapitulate the basic affects and tensions of the entire sequence and turn them towards a personal recovery of some sort. "January Morning" is a "Suite" of fifteen numbered moments that, despite the obvious public rebuff of the previous two poems, reasserts as essentially unshaken the speaker's joyously aesthetic evaluations of such common beauty as the scenery from an early morning's commute to Manhattan; and the fifteenth part, a direct address to some fondly regarded "old woman," assigns to the more appropriate circumstances of individuals the impulse to personal intimacy that the speaker of the opening set had directed toward his "townspeople."

"To A Solitary Disciple" continues this process by repeating in selenographic terms the same sort of preoccupation with geometry and color as informed "Spring Strains," only now it is all posed in the individually affectionate tones of a master's aesthetic directives to his novitiate. Then "Ballet" completes the section's withdrawal from the public arena in a lonely soliloquy that, echoing in more tired tones the strange intermental desire of "Spring Song" and "The Shadow," asks to be joined by a stark steeple cross and a solitary robin in being happily crushed into the earth of a roadway by the feet of passing horses.

The lyrical retrenchment of these last three poems prepares exactly for the final, cranky attachment in "Dedication For a Plot of Ground" to a somewhat reclusive, almost hermetic old woman. And that cumulative sense of reclusion predicates in a fundamental way the two expressions of contentment that actually conclude the section. "Conquest" restates the earlier image from "Metric Figure" of a sun rising amidst trees, only instead of unequivically resplendent, the beauty of that image is now involved with a territorial sense of exclusively private ownership, an ownership that in the light of the preceding poems can only seem the better half of an essential alienation. This emphasis upon aesthetic privacy continues in the second "Love Song" that is the last poem of the section, for there is something masturbatory in that poem's orgasmic smear of color ("Yellow, yellow, yellow") over the entire world at the thought of some distant "you far off there under / the wine-red selvage of the west!"

Thus, these last two moments of something like aesthetic bliss really conclude the section with a rather fugitive hope. They are both highly private resorts to beauty, and in this regard, they very much resemble the equally fugitive hope with which "Paterson: Episode 17" concludes, when "the stroke . . . like the beat of famous lines / in the few excellent poems / woven to make you / gracious" is discernable but really overwhelmed by the "flogging" that makes Beautiful Thing on more "frequent occasions / foul drunk." All these moments represent outposts of aesthetic intelligence in an aesthetically stupid world.

9

Toward a Greater Equivalence with "Longer Poems": "Sour Grapes," "Spring and All," and "The Descent of Winter"

As is eventually the case with "Longer Poems," the further expression of this notable exception to aesthetic stupidity is left to the immediately ensuing segment. At the heart of "Sour Grapes" is a group of four flower poems that constitutes the same sort of highly disciplined examination of beauty as "The Crimson Cyclamen." Note for instance these lines from the first poem of the group, "Daisy":

> round the yellow center,
> split and creviced and done into
> minute flowerheads, he sends out
> his twenty rays—a little
> and the wind is among them
> to grow cool there!
>
> One turns the thing over
> in his hand and looks
> at it from the rear: brownedged,
> green and pointed scales
> armor his yellow.
>
> But turn and turn,
> the crisp petals remain
> brief, translucent, greenfastened,
> barely touching at the edges:
> blades of limpid seashell.

Everywhere here botanical precision forms the basis for aesthetic exhilaration. The colors and shapes are exact; the focus is nearly microscopic, ratcheted up as it is by the synonyms of the third and fourth lines in something like discrete powers of magnification; the shifting perspective, the "turn and turn" examination from front, rear, and edge is as thorough as a scientific protocol. And the entire complex of careful observation literally triggers the arresting moment of refreshment in the fifth and sixth lines. Reaching back to rhyme with the "split" that begins the microscopic close-ups, the closing word of the fourth line, "a little," seems at first to continue the physical description of the flower and to enjamb the lines with an adjective in search of a following referent. But when the initial phrase of the succeeding line—"and the wind"— substitutes a new syntax of exclamation, it both creates an element of surprise at the refreshing wind and necessitates a reconstruction of the grammar for the preceding lines. "A little" thus becomes a tremendously conspicous adverbial phrase that emphasizes in both meaning and function the microscopic scrutiny of the preceding lines, and the equally conspicuous lyrical state of refreshment that the phrase helps create becomes intricately associated with the factual basis of that scrutiny. Indeed the association is so close that it ultimately makes the closing transfiguration of petals into "limpid seashell" a genuinely optical effect rather than a simply gratuitous metaphor.

Each of the poems displays this same sort of rigorously factual attention to the floral beauty of its subject and applies that beauty to the lyrical burdens the section inherits from or anticipates in the larger volume. The concluding transfiguration of "Daisy," for example, arrives out of an opening image of "The dayseye hugging the earth," its details of a "rainbeaten furrow. . .clotted with sorrel and crabgrass" strongly recalling the terrene motif that primarily (and unsuccessfully) carried the urge to aesthetic communion in "Al Que Quiere." Then opening with a cry of "Yellow, yellow, yellow, yellow!" that strongly recalls the orgasmic aesthetic smear of the "Love Song" that closed "Al Que Quiere," "Primrose" attaches the excitement of that refrain to the thorough and factual inventory of the color's expression in the natural world. Instead of the privately libidinal "stain of love" that "smears with saffron/ the horned branches that lean / heavily / against a smooth purple sky! . . . spoiling the colors / of the whole world," there is the accurate inventory of a season, replete with the imperious primrose itself, the most botanically exact of species, presiding:

> Yellow, yellow, yellow, yellow!
> It is not a color.
> It is summer!
> It is the wind on a willow,

the lap of waves, the shadow
under a bush, a bird, a bluebird,
three herons, a dead hawk
rotting on a pole—
Clear yellow!

.   .   .   .   .

It is disinclination to be
five red petals or a rose, it is
a cluster of birdsbreast flowers
on a red stem six feet high,
four open yellow petals
above sepals curled
backward into reverse spikes—

And in its fully sublime details of coloration, "Queen-Ann's-Lace" predicts the more problematically confused response to Beautiful Thing that in the later "Paterson: Episode 17" is the more intense counterpart to the preceding "Al Que Quiere." As precedent to the "spotless cap / and cross white straps," to even "the empurpled lips and dazzled half sleepy eyes" of the brutally ravished woman is the properly sublime bruising of the flower:

Here is no question of whiteness,
white as can be, with a purple mole
at the center of each flower.
Each flower is a hand's span
of her whiteness. Wherever
his hand has lain there is
a tiny purple blemish. . .

More referenced to their own counterparts among the "Longer Poems," however, are the precursory elements to "The Crimson Cyclamen" in "Sour Grapes." The broad philosophic concern with transience that laces the meditation in the later poem; the extended intellectual analogy it deploys; and the Platonic strain that informs some its figures—all these things make themselves felt early on in the section, specifically in the second poem, "A Celebration." The poem unfolds as an inspection of hothouse plants on the eve of an orchid competition. The scenario would seem to invite the same sort of rigorous botany that is displayed by the later flower poems, but it is instead everywhere involved with a spectral dimension that becomes identified with philosophical concerns like teleology and paradox. The opening two stanzas, for example, describe some brisk March weather that appears like an intelligent agency of Platonist reality:

> A middle-northern March, now as always—
> gusts from the south broken against cold winds—
> but from under, as if a slow hand lifted a tide,
> it moves—not into April—into a second March,
>
> the old skin of wind-clear scales dropping
> upon the mould: this is the shadow projects the tree
> upward causing the sun to shine in his sphere.

A little further on, some dormant oleanders provoke distinct tele-ology with a vaguely mystical cast, and some overly fragrant orange trees prompt a typically philosophic delight with figures of obscurity:

> It is clearer to me than if the pink
> were on the branch. It would be a searching in
> a coloured cloud to reveal that which now, huskless,
> shows the very reason for their being
>
> . . . .
>
>   It is that very perfume
> has drawn the darkness down among the leaves.
> Do I speak clearly enough?
> It is this darkness reveals that which darkness alone
> loosens and sets spinning on waxen wings—

All of this, however, proves to be an ironic preparation for the actual examination of the orchids, which themselves are swamped in a similar idiom. The earlier preoccupation with time and its flukes—with "March, now as always—. . . not into April—into a second March"; with extremes of botanical dormancy and bloom—asserts itself too strongly as an otherworldly calendar that defines the orchids more than do their colors. Despite fleeting mentions of the "full, fragile / head of veined lavender," there are more usually descriptions like these:

> This is an odd January, died—in Villon's time.
> Snow, this is and this the stain of a violet
> grew in that place the spring that foresaw its own doom
> . . . .
>
> This falling spray of snowflakes is
> a handful of dead Februarys
> prayed into flower by Rafael Arevalo Martinez
> of Guatamala.

The sad awareness of transience that in "The Crimson Cyclamen" is so in tune with the rigorous botanical beauty of that flower is here completely divorced from it, and almost inevitably, the lyrical spirit of "A Celebration" leads finally to an outrightly hostile impatience with the flowers themselves. Upon noticing the absence of an orchid for March, the speaker suddenly turns peevish at the foiling of his calendar: "Flowers are a tiresome pastime. / One has a wish to shake them from their pots / root and stem, for the sun to gnaw."

In this disjunction with "The Crimson Cyclamen," "Sour Grapes" very much resembles "Al Que Quiere" in its relationship with "Paterson: Episode 17." The lyrical dispositions toward beauty that the later poems concentrate and fuse are in the earlier sections kept distinctly separate, even opposed. Thus, the smooth blend of philosophy, pensiveness, and observational precision in "The Crimson Cyclamen" is distributed more according to its parts in "Sour Grapes" and more according to the stage of the entire volume's poetic development.

Nowhere is this more clearly seen than in the "terror" that substitutes in "Sour Grapes" for the ecstasy that attends the full bloom of "The Crimson Cyclamen." The section very nearly both begins and ends with intensely neurasthenic moments triggered by, of all things, a too intense springtime:

> If you had come away with me
> into another state
> we had been quiet together.
> But there the sun coming up
> out of the nothing beyond the lake was
> too low in the sky,
> there was too great a pushing
> against him,
> too much of sumac buds, pink
> in the head
> with the clear gum upon them,
> too many opening hearts of lilac leaves,
> too many, too many swollen
> limp poplar tassels on the
> bare branches!

The geometry of the sunrise in these lines from the section's third poem, "April (If you had come away with me)," has become an episode in paranoia, the phrase "against him" metrically isolated and underscored. Similarly, the botanical details of sumac, lilac, and poplar are translated into state of psychological agitation ("pink / in the head"), unbearable emotional exposure ("too many opening hearts"), and a generalized state of bodily discomfort ("too many swollen")—all measured against the repeated phrasing of insufferable excess: "too low. . .too great. . .too many. . .too much. . ." By the penultimate poem of the section, this sense of distress turns into an absolute hysteria. "Portrait of the Author" nearly flails about with anguish at the botanical evidence of spring:

> The birches are mad with green points
> the wood's edge is burning with their green,
> burning, seething—No, no, no.
> The birches are opening their leaves one
> by one. Their delicate leaves unfold cold
> and separate, one by one. Slender tassels
> hang swaying from the delicate branch tips—
>
> . . . .
>
> Save me! The shad bush is in the edge
> of the clearing. The yards in a fury
> of lilac blossoms are driving me mad with terror.

Clearly, "Sour Grapes" is not the perfectly controlled meditation upon natural beauty that "The Crimson Cyclamen" is, nor should it be. Like the poetic and lyrical intelligence of the preceding sequences, that of "Sour Grapes" is still an immature one, and the overall development of the sequence reveals it to be more of a struggle for than a tour de force of a disciplined examination of beauty.

In this regard, the opening poem, "The Late Singer," may in the statement and even the initials of its title allude back to the closing "Love Song" of "Al Que Quiere." It is perhaps a deliberate signal of involvement with the preceding sequence's closing sense of aesthetic defeat, a sense of defeat that the fuller lyrical character of "The Late Singer" more completely addresses. "What is it that is dragging at my heart?" the speaker asks as he reproaches himself for a tardy response to spring and to the same sort of aesthetically defined world that motivated the sensibility in "Al Que Quiere": "The sparrow with the black rain on his breast / has been at his cadenzas for two weeks past."

The lyrical effect of this brief note is to establish as a fundamental condition of the new sequence a personally difficult sense of aesthetic imperative. And it is to this sense of difficulty that the imperative gestures of "A Celebration" in turn address themselves.

The very deliberate injunction—"let us walk to the orchid-house"—and the equally deliberate adjournment to the poem—"Walk out again into the cold"—combine with the calendar scheme of the orchids to suggest a very deliberate initiative that will some-how order and encompass the beauty of the flowers. At the same time, that initiative seems constantly disabled by a pensive frame of mind that ignores their very beauty. Thus, the vague specters of the contestants begin to replace vivid descriptions of the plants themselves. In the end, "A Celebration" turns into an obligation as restlessness or perhaps even agitation truncates the inspection. "This day has blossomed long enough," impatiently announces the speaker, and there is something distinctly excessive about his "wish" to throttle the plants and expose them, "root and stem, for the sun to gnaw."

About the only sort of disturbance for which this extreme and spontaneous desire could serve as the objective correlative is the deep psychological pressure that immediately expresses itself in the third and succeeding poem, "April (If you had come away with me)." The determined examination of natural beauty begun in "A Celebration" appears here to recoil in a terror bred primarily of a personal incapacity. "If you had come away with me / into another state," bewails the speaker, "we had been quiet together." These first three lines emphasize the affect of the entire poem as a distinct episode of neurasthenia and not simply some aesthetic preference for a minimalist natural palette. And each of the next four poems extends this episode and develops even more the sense of struggle inherent in it and in the opening two poems. A brief and tenuous sense of reprieve from the objective beauty of "The stars, that are small lights" in "At Night" is immediately subverted in "Berket and The Stars" by a sarcastic regard for a collective family memory that preposterously seizes the impulsive theft of a single orange as a grand testament to some ancestor's joie de vivre in a youth more usually tedious and impoverished than carefree. And then the aes-thetically based, neurasthenic terror of "April (If you had come way with me)" returns in the nightmare insomnia of "A Goodnight" and the surreal dilations of time and space in "Overture to a Dance of Locomotives."

Just how essential this sense of struggle is to "Sour Grapes" the section is quite apparent in the changes from *Sour Grapes* the volume that the first six poems incorporate. The original arrange-ment, for instance, did not at all include "At Night" (which was the opening poem of "Prior to 1921" in *Collected Poems 1921–1931*). It did, however, include the imperial "March" (now the penultimate poem of "Longer Poems") as its second poem, right after "The Late Singer." And it placed "Berket and The Stars" as third, with "A Celebration," "April (If you had come away with me)," "A Goodnight," and "Overture to a Dance of Locomotives" following. The overall effect of this arrangement was to consolidate the section's original sense of initiative into the first four poems, with the very assertive "March" serving as a perhaps too enthusiastic response to the self-prodding of "The Late Singer" and "Berket and the Stars" tending as a result to seem more naively impressed with than skeptical of Berket's legendary act of mischief. The troublesome inventory of "A Celebration" then appeared as a transitional poem, leading to the full distress of the last three poems, and the overall opening movement enacted an overly confident aesthetic initiative quite thoroughly displaced by an aesthetic terror.

There is, in other words, far too much defeat in the original arrangement; the rekindled initiative of the opening is overwhelmed. The revised arrangement, however—with its elimination of the overstated "March" and its momentary recovery from the just discernable distress of "A Celebration" before falling into the abyss of the last two poems—establishes a stronger sense of an initiative that is from the start in difficult straits and balancing not between victory and defeat, but among varying degrees of an anxious approach to beauty.

Exactly the same sort of effect is emphasized in the way Williams rearranged a group of poems near the end of the gathering. Originally, two almost humorous poems—"The Nightingales," a fancy about the shadows of shoelace-tying fingers; and "Spouts," a mildly ribald admiration of a city fountain—preceded two rather serious poems—"Blueflags," a brooding sensory visit to some lush marshland; and "The Widow's Lament in Springtime," a pining desire for oblivion in a blooming meadow. This plainly overwhelming contrast from a feeble happiness to an overwhelming sadness was then repeated even more strongly by the last four poems in what looks lyrically like a stagger to emotional and mental defeat. The springtime spirits of "Light-Hearted William" returned briefly and unconvincingly to a buoyant mood before "Portrait of the Author" plummeted to its absolute terror. Then in the wake of this extreme state, the somewhat dumbfounded observation of passing schoolgirls on a stultifyingly hot day in "The Lonely Street" came like a case of shell-shock, and in the same way, the nearly hallucinogenic enlargement of "the figure 5" against the shrill urgency of a firetruck's passage in "The Great Figure" appeared to evoke the hyperawareness of anxiety itself.

In the revised arrangement for "Sour Grapes" the section, however, all of this is changed to create a greater sense of balance between the positive and negative lyrical states, a greater sense of standoff rather than defeat. The upbeat "Spouts" and "The Nightingales" were separated and intermixed with the heavier-hearted "The Widow's Lament" and "Blueflags" so as to highlight the *alternation* between states. Even more significantly, the saddest poem in the group, "The Widow's Lament," was moved from the fourth and final place in the group to the second, so that there is a genuine sense of *recovery* from the moment, even in the arrival of the only relatively less brooding "Blueflags."

The balanced pattern established by these poems extends as well into the new order for the final group of four poems. The mild stupor of "The Lonely Street" is moved from after the hysteria of "Portrait of the Author" and placed instead just before it and just after the whimsical "Light-Hearted William." Thus, counting the previous four poems, fully six poems in alternating lyrical states now precede the major terror of "Portrait of the Author," and the structural habit of their pattern helps in turn to redefine radically the nature of the hyperawareness in "The Great Figure" that follows that terror. We are, in other words, so attuned to an alternation of lyrical disposition by the time we arrive at the last two poems of the section that the final urgencies of colors, sounds, and shapes in "The Great Figure" appear more like extreme aesthetic countermeasures to aesthetic terror rather then simple symptoms of that terror. In short, the new structural context transforms the final note of the sequence into one of aesthetic survival.

The deliberate intent of this final impression can be best measured by the sort of changes that Williams made at other places in "Sour Grapes." Most tended to further consolidate poems into lyrically similar groups and to distinguish between one group and another as distinct stages in the forward development of the sequence. "Epitaph," for example, was moved from after "Memory of April," with which it shares a distinctly asseverating tone and love conceit, and placed some four poems later, so that the newly intervening poems appear to be bracketed by the close reciprocities of the previously contiguous ones. Those poems happen to be the four flower poems already mentioned, and their special accomplishment in the section is thereby focused even more as a distinct lyrical moment. And in something of a similar fashion, "The Disputants," a study of the confused yet "composed" colors and shapes in a vaseful of cut flowers, was extracted from the midst of a group of four poems of unequivocal domestic happiness and placed at their head to more clearly mark the nature of the passage from the guilty domestic and sexual disloyalties of the preceding four poems. There is established, in effect, a keener *equation* rather than opposition between the two states, and in this regard, the equipoised lyrical alternations that begin with the immediately succeeding "Spouts" and continue on into the end of the section is perfectly prepared for.

In total, then, "Sour Grapes" appears to have been tailored to fit the contours of its immediate context within *The Complete Collected Poems*. With all its difficulties, it represents a significant advance in the lyrical spirit of the volume, and the evidence of that advance can be perhaps best seen in a single summary of the section's development. "The Late Singer," for instance, with its opening echo of the reclusion and defeat that close "Al Que Quiere," declares the basic continuity of the volume. The psychologically pressured, intellectually deliberate examination of natural, especially floral beauty in "A Celebration" then establishes both the defining endeavor and the distinctive lyrical disposition for the section. From there on, the poems of the section gather themselves around these keynotes.

The first group is the prolonged neurasthenia that begins with "April (If you had come away with me)" and ends with "Overture to a Dance of Locomotives." The sharply perceived details of natural beauty and finally even space and time themselves are here entirely unleashed as almost incomprehensible yet painfully intense phenomena. Then, there is in the succeeding group a return to the sort of reclusion that typified the end of "Al Que Quiere." A series of very private, pensive, and undisturbed landscapes ("The Desolate Field," "Willow Poem," "Approach to Winter," "January," and "Blizzard") quiet the section's agitation before the next group, a series of seven poems, begins to challenge the hermetic inclination those landscapes reflect. "Complaint" grumbles at a physician's call to service on a cold midnight but then grows compassionate over the patient, a woman in her tenth childbirth. Then "To Waken an Old Lady" summons a presumably moribund and torporific woman to the cheerful, gregarious beauty of a flock of "small, / cheeping birds."

The brooding landscapes return in "Winter Trees," "Dark Day," "Spring Storm" and "Thursday," only this time with very clear elements of explicit self-justification. Finally, the explicit demands of medical practice that were noted in "Complaint" return in "The

Cold Night," but this time, there is signaled a momentary reconciliation of private aesthetic pleasures with the body of public need;
the two become identical:

> It is cold. The white moun
> is among her scattered stars—
> like the bare thighs of
> the Police Sergeant's wife—among
> her five children . . .
>
> . . . .
> In April I shall see again—In April!
> the round and perfect thighs

This last excitement shows just how much this section is an
extension of "Al Que Quiere" and its thwarted desire for an aesthetic fellowship. And it in turn prepares for the extended movement of pity for the defeated fellows of an aroused life that follows.
"Time the Hangman," "To a Friend," and "The Gentle Man" play
out an empathetic spirit in some generous compassion for a once
proud but now enfeebled old "nigger"; for a promiscuous and preg-
nant young girl seeking a paternity judgment; and finally in the
speaker's own moving identification with these two.

Out of this episode, the sequence moves into four epigrammatic
poems that leaven the pathos of the preceding three. "The Soughing Wind" appears to fashion a rather flip analogy for the unlucky
fates of the earlier figures, with early falling leaves substituting for
the defeated old man and young girl and late hanging ones standing
in for the still struggling speaker. Then adopting an attitude of
cavalier self-regard, "Spring" indulges in a frivolous bit of vanity
over the speaker's hair, and "Play" affects an ironic taste for mental
idleness. Finally, a more serious note returns as struggling with
the need to maintain distinctions, "Lines" fastidiously differenti-
ates the various green of leaves and broken grass.

With this last poem's return to the leaves motif of "The Soughing
Wind," the group effects some measure of closure and marks a
small improvement in its original corrective reaction. Instead of
the temperamental distance of personal indifference, there is in
"Lines" the disciplined distance of precise observation: "Leaves
are greygreen, / the glass broken, bright green." In turn, the conclusion introduces very nicely the following two odd poems, each of
which pivots upon an uncompromising insistence upon fact. "The
Poor (By constantly tormenting them)" proudly testifies to the
eventual affection engendered between a school physician and the
parents of lice-infested students by his relentless citation of the

bugs, regardless of any attendant social embarrassment. Then "Complete Destruction" brings even more rigor to the fore in the very exact and thorough cremation of a cat that permits not a single flea to escape.

In other words, a rigorous disposition has evolved in the sequence right here, and it is entirely appropriate that the next group of poems be the flower poems that so forecast the highly rigorous examination of beauty in "The Crimson Cyclamen." Preceded by "Memory of April," which in its title and content signals an explicit challenge to the terror-driven approach to beauty of the earlier "April (If you had come away with me)," the next four poems display their relatively disciplined and inspiring vision of beauty before concluding with the brief "Epitaph," which repeats in contented tones the same sort of approach to beauty as in "Memory of April." Not all in this central group is tranquil, however. The very last flower poem, "Great Mullen," introduces some troubling hints of sexual infidelity and bitter recriminations. Within the poem itself, those elements are entirely mastered and bent to the exquisite sense of growth and physical beauty in the mullen itself. But outside of the botanical discipline of the flower poems, those troubling elements immediately resurface in a full-blown way.

"Waiting," "The Hunter," "Arrival," and "To a Friend Concerning Several Ladies" create a positively oppressive sense of guilt at the speaker's disaffection from his family and his obdurate infidelities. A broad and very personal sense of failure, primarily moral, comes over the sequence and signals a even greater challenge to its aesthetic spirit. So against this challenge comes first the prototypical reconciliation of turmoil and harmony that is evident in the natural floral beauty of "The Disputants," and then the lyrical countermeasures to the guilt: the happy domestic tranquilities of "Youth and Beauty," "The Thinker," and "The Tulip Bed," all of which effectively rectify but do not eliminate the earlier sense of domestic estrangement. It is finally from this point of relative equipoise that the section launches the concluding alternations of lyric states that have already been described.

These alternations of lyric states, as we have already seen, establish as the final overall affect of "Sour Grapes" a sense of struggle, specifically a struggle with the demands of a profound aesthetic arousal. Equally evident from the final group, however, is the fundamentally personal nature of this struggle. There is an element of privacy that runs throughout the section and that especially informs the closing poems. The lighter poems in the final group, for example, extend the distinctly *domestic* happiness of the immediately preceding poems, and the hermetic desire for a private escape into natural beauty and then the darker horror that the last few poems place against that happiness is outrightly psychological in its character. Both instances, of course, anticipate the entirely more successful and even more private meditation of "The Crimson Cyclamen" later on in the volume, and as in that poem, the sense of a private aesthetic fortification in "Sour Grapes" leads directly to a more public involvement with beauty.

There is simply more of the world at large in the succeeding "Spring and All" section. The previous personal aesthetic burden changes, for instance, into the sense of a larger cultural issue that runs throughout the section. There is a discernable worry over the aesthetic dereliction from which the urban skyline suffers in "Flight to the City," and that worry eventually becomes in "To Elsie" a full outrage over the social devastation wrought upon "the pure products of America" by their aesthetic impoverishment. There is social satire as well in the figure of the industrialist "J. P. M." who uses art like a wrench in "At the Facet of June" and in the spectacle of pseudoreligion that constitutes the modern cinema in "Light Becomes Darkness." And there is a socially disturbing note of popular hostility to art, specifically poetry, in "Rapid Transit."[1]

All these elements parallel the boorishly indifferent public background in "The Waitress"—the parliamentary motions, the hotel traffic, the giant neon display—against which the fleeting glimpses of the servingwoman's transporting beauty are held. And likewise, the visions of female beauty throughout the earlier sequence in turn parallel that servingwoman's publically demeaned state. The housemaid in "To Elsie" is perhaps the most obvious instance of this parallel, her literal station, tawdry tastes, and common carriage forecasting the waitress's similar characteristics:

> some doctor's family, some Elsie—
> voluptuous water
> expressing with broken
>
> brain the truth about us—
> her great
> ungainly hips and flopping breasts
>
> addressed to cheap
> jewelry
> and rich young men with fine eyes
> (from "To Elsie")

There is a mole under the jaw, low under
the right ear—

And what arms!

                        The glassruby ring
on the fourth finger of the left hand.

                  —and the movements
under the scant dress as the weight of the tray
makes the hips shift forward slightly in lifting
and beginning to walk—
                (from "The Waitress")

There is, of course, very much of a lyric difference between the two passages here. The first is bound up in what amounts to a diatribe against the culture at large, and thus, although it asserts its delight in the woman, it overwhelms that delight by isolating its essential phrases—"voluptuous water," "her great," and "jewelry"—and bracketing them with the fuller expressions of the women's debasement—the ironically generic treatment of personal identity suggested in the "some" phrasing of the first line, for instance, or the alliterated mental defect of "broken // brain" emphasized in the enjambment between stanzas.

The latter passage reverses the proportions somewhat as it manages to subsume its annoyance with the social dilemma that necessitates the waitress's labor within an unencumbered excitement over her immediate beauty. Social sarcasm is set forth in a stanza about "the benefits of poverty" and then the exciting examination of the woman's features and even her jewelry is given greater amplitude and especially greater precision. Instead of a broad caricature of "ungainly hips and flopping breasts," there is the close mapping of a particular facial mole. Instead of a generically "cheap/ jewelry" there is a particularly colored and located ring. And instead of a general sense of lumbering movement there is a detailed physics of balance. And finally, instead of a line arrangement that obscures the delight with the woman, there are spontaneous line breaks that follow rather than constrain the emotional excitement and that place as a centerpiece an exclamation over the waitress's arms. In other words, all in the later poem underscores the pleasure, not the distress, at the woman's presence.

There is a similar instance in the way "To an Old Jaundiced Woman" anticipates the odic notes of "The Waitress." In the later poem, those notes constitute an unadulterated expression of desire and adoration, but in the earlier poem, they are involved with such a pathetic display of womanhood that they suggest more of a bitter realism about the woman's impossible situation:

> O unlit candle with the soft white
> plume, Sunbeam Finest Safety Matches all together in
> a little box—
>
> And the reflections of both in
> the mirror and the reflection of the hand, writing
> writing—
> > Speak to me of her!
> > (from "The Waitress"

TO AN OLD JAUNDICED WOMAN

O tongue
licking
the sore on
her netherlip

O toppled belly

O passionate cotton
stuck with
matted hair

elysian slobber
from her mouth
upon
the folded handkerchief

I can't die

—moaned the old
jaundiced woman
rolling her
saffron eyeballs

I can't die
I can't die

Even the ultimate impossibility of ever possessing the glimpsed female beauty that fundamentally restricts the excitement of "The Waitress" appears more worrisome, more problematical in the precursory expression of "Spring and All." Instead of the fully clear and unequivocal litany of negatives ("Never. . .No way. . .")

against which the positive joy in the poem can at least define itself, there is a confused and delusional fantasy about deflowering an old hospital coworker in "Young Love" that ultimately leads only to a deep regret over failing to take possession of the lady's all too fully available virginity.

All of these differences are signal conditions of the *volume's* lyrical state at this point. With only the determined but precarious command of beauty established by "Sour Grapes," there is little foundation as yet for the sort of clear sighted and unshakeable grasp of beauty that persists at the center of the fatalism in "The Waitress." Lyrically more plausible is the more thoroughly troubled awareness of beauty that pervades "Spring and All," and this is a linkage that the section's opening poems quite noticeably promote.

The opening, title poem, for instance, with its landscape of stunned awakening life, seems to translate the personal terror and shock of beauty that close "Sour Grapes" into a natural phenomenon. "Lifeless in appearance," as it is summarily put midway through the poem, "sluggish / dazed spring approaches," and the approach clearly comes as the external accomplishment of an earlier, more personal moment:

> and leaves me—with shrinking heart
> and startled, empty eyes—peering out
> into a cold world.
>
> .   .   .   .
>
> And coldly the birch leaves are opening one by one.
> Coldly I observe them and wait for the end.
> And it ends.
> > (from "Portrait of the Author")
>
> By the road to the contagious hospital
> under the surge of the blue
> mottled clouds driven from the
> northeast—a cold wind. Beyond, the
> waste of broad, muddy fields
> brown with dried weeds, standing and fallen
>
> patches of standing water
> the scattering of tall trees
> > (from "Spring and All")

The echoing phrases "cold world" and "cold wind" draw special attention to the dense network of dental stops (d's and t's, even more emphasized by the spondees of the latter passage) that these moments share and that so effectively arrests any incidental melodiousness in both of them. And the single word "cold" helps suggest a similarity between the stunned repetition of that word in the earlier poem and the similar effect of the repeated words and low vowels in the later poem's "standing and fallen / patches" and "standing water / the scattering."

Such effects do not, however, lead to any further sense of paralysis in the new sequence. As "One by one objects are defined," the opening poem of "Spring and All" declares the trauma as "the stark dignity of / entrance," and the immediately succeeding poem, "The Pot of Flowers" (originally "The Pot of Primroses"), retrieves from "Sour Grapes" its brighter complement to aesthetic shock. Everywhere the poem's brilliant illumination of color and prominently active verbals contrast with the drabness of "Spring and All" the poem and the stasis of its predominantly prepositional phrasing:

> red where in whorls
> petal lays its glow upon petal
> round flamegreen throats
>
> petals radiant with transpiercing light
> contending
>   above
>
> the leaves
> reaching up their modest green
> from the pot's rim

Were it not for the wild confusion of motion and shape, the botanical excitement here, with its suggestion of ecstatic transport, might even approach the more disciplined sort of "The Crimson Cyclamen." But as it is, the excitement more accurately completes the tension that "Spring and All" the section inherits from "Sour Grapes," for it reveals that tension for what it really is: an essential if precarious recovery from the reclusive mood of "Al Que Quiere."[2]

This retrospective function is perhaps clearer in the "Longer Poems" counterpart to "Spring and All" since the single female figure of "The Waitress" quite obviously reconceives the Beautiful Thing of "Paterson: Episode 17" in the transporting terms of the intervening "The Crimson Cyclamen." But in the opening landscape of "Spring and All," there is as well a parallel reappearance of the terrene figures of aesthetic communion from "Al Que Quiere," and they are quite plainly cast in the struggling, traumatic terms of the intervening "Sour Grapes." Thus, the entire present section inherits both a immediate lyrical tension (from the ending of "Sour Grapes" alone) and a more remote thematic and lyrical history from the whole of the preceding sequences; and it is ultimately this entire complex that the third and fourth poems of "Spring and All" bring to bear upon the special sense of a public aesthetic issue that will dominate the rest of the present sequence.

Confirming the restored spirit and the terrene motif of the opening two poems, "The Farmer" is a portrait of a firmly resolved "farmer in deep thought" (actually "the artist figure of / the farmer—composing"), imagining his spring-drenched fields already planted and harvested. Then "Flight to the City" repeats this sense of resolve, only now as a lover's desire to adorn a larger, urban skyscape. Together, the heroic figure of the third poem and the great task of the fourth define a clear sense of determination to renew aesthetically the world in general.

Against this noble ambition drag certain established realities as a group of five poems enact a basic reluctance of spirit that goes back to "Al Que Quiere." "Black Winds" expresses a somewhat misanthropic disillusionment with the aesthetic capacities of men in general, and "To Have Done Nothing" counters with a rather facile note of reproach for a failure of will. "The Rose (The rose is obsolete)" retreats to a fortifying but perhaps too rarefied meditation upon the geometry of roses that is very similar to "The Crimson Cyclamen" in its exactitude and its etherealness. Then, as though slowly teased out into the public arena, "At The Faucet of June" at least toys with the possibility of an aesthetic arousal even in the products of mass production and in the face of a potent philistinism. And finally, "Young Love" appears to reevaluate the original impulse for the group with a deep sense of regret over a lost sexual and aesthetic opportunity.

All the while, of course, the poems carry out the basic diatribe of the section. Even "The Rose (The rose is obsolete)" starts out with a sarcastic cultural complaint: "The rose is obsolete." And honored in "Young Love" is the man with enough imaginative courage to destroy "the city": "Clean is he alone / after whom stream / the broken pieces of the city— / flying apart at his approaches." So too does the next group of poems continue this polemical edge. "The Eyeglasses," for instance, promotes "the favorable / distortion of eyeglasses" as though it were a consumer product ("in the most practical frame of / brown celluloid") rather than a principal of aesthetic clarity, and "The Right of Way" truculently challenges "Why bother where I went?" as it affirms the "supreme importance" of a stray street scene's aesthetic composition.

At the same time, both of these latter poems establish a lyrical shift from the reluctance of the previous group to the deliberate if tentative evangelical spirit that follows. Both poems display a certain confidence in the public importance of the aesthetic dimensions (color, shape, texture, arrangement, etc.) they promote, and the poem that follows, "Composition," appears to offer its "red paper box" as nothing less than an aesthetic cure-all. Finally, "The Agonized Spire" raises the aesthetic effects of a modern bridge to a consecrational intensity, much as "The Waitress" will later do for the aesthetic charms of its title subject.

The nearly inspirational zeal that builds here, however, leads only to a greater disappointment as the next three poems follow with a simple but thorough astonishment over the comparative impoverishment of imagination in most folks. With something like the facile manner of "To Have Done Nothing," "Death the Barber" plays out the entropic idiocy at the heart of a barber's theory that sleep is a nightly slice of death. Then there is the scornful confusion of religion and cinema in "Light Becomes Darkness," and the ultimately pathetic disbelief in her own imminent death by a desperately ill woman in "To an Old Jaundiced Woman."

The outcome of this astonishment in turn seems to be a general irritation. "Shoot It, Jimmy!" begins with the manic impatience of a jazz musician for the bogus "sheet stuff" that substitutes for real rhythm. Then "To Elsie" breaks out into an angry diatribe against the aesthetic impoverishment of America's sexual and cultural traditions. And then with both an anger for their debasement and a love for their fundamental vitality, "Horned Purple" curses the young "Dirty satyrs, . . .vulgarity raised to the last power," who lewdly wear lilac sprigs in spring.

After this comes the sharply contrasting sexual tenderness of "The Sea" with its metaphor of an embracing ocean and the unabashedly rocking rhythms of lines like "ula lu la lu." The contrast is made even more pointed by the resemblance of the poem's three-line stanzas to those of "To Elsie" and the entirely different effect achieved by them:

> The blazing secrecy of noon is undone
> and and and
> the broken sand is the sound of love—

The middle line, which in "To Elsie" serves to tease stray phrases of delight out of the otherwise angry diatribe that enjambs the lines with the rushing syntax of discourse, here serves to rhythmically accent the strophe. The triple stress of the repeated "and's" makes explicit the embedded sexual tension that resides in the single extra stress of "is" in the surrounding, otherwise iambic lines. And the and/sand rhyme further helps to define the middle line as part of the sexual excitement rendered in the b, s, and n alliteration and in the slanted end-rhymes of the first and third lines. In short, a fundamental pleasure pervades the poem, even as it complains, characteristically for the section, that "lips too few / assume the new—marruu."

It is a pleasure that the following four poems, in a common two-line stanza that slows and suspends poetic effects in a way similar to the three-line stanza of "The Sea," extend to more strictly aesthetic moments. Following the last line of "The Sea" ("so two—") with what appears as a punning extension of logic (i.,e.: so too, "so much depends"), "The Red Wheelbarrow" creates a hopeful primacy of aesthetic possibility in the visual play of color and texture in the deliberately humble subject of its title, and then "Quietness" parabolically notes the paradisiacal serenity that a "Gipsy" enjoys in some common foliage. "Rigamarole" develops this ideal more fully in a rhapsody of color, sound, and texture that attends a moonlight scene of orchard and yard, and then "The Avenue of Poplars" returns to the "Gipsy" figure, literally embracing it in a visionary transport over some overhead leaves noticed in a casual automobile ride.

Even here, at this nearly transcendental moment, there still emerges a promotional dimension to the ecstasies of the single sensibility. "He who has kissed / a leaf // need look no further" pronounces the speaker in the middle of his special sort of Whitmania. The context of a *public* aesthetic agenda—an agenda for the generic "He"—is simply never omitted throughout the section, and it is this same context that finally rises to the visionary, even evangelical, intensity of this last group of poems with the adversarial intensity of the next two. With the quick rudeness of a curse and the unrelenting insincerity of an advertisement, "Rapid Transit" counters the profound and personal basis to the preceding aesthetic awareness with the easy cliché of a brochure description for a day trip to Pelham Bay. And "At the Ball Game" reveals the dangerous violence that lies just underneath the idle imagination of the spectators, lacking as they do any really disciplined aesthetic direction. Together, the two poems oppose considerable elements of scorn, danger, intimidation, and recalcitrance to the missionary zeal that ultimately resides in the aesthetic conviction of the five poems before them. The world is clearly not yet ready for aesthetic salvation.

This essential standoff of aesthetic temperaments is repeated by the section's last two poems in terms that recall both the very private botanical examination of beauty in "Sour Grapes" and the reclusive spirit of "Al Que Quiere." "The Hermaphroditic Telephones" first withdraws the sequence from its thread of logical discourse by employing an extremely abstruse figure—the phones of the title—and displacing the figure with the sheer profusion of color in some spring anemones. Beauty is thus established as an unimpeachable and irreducibly aesthetic fact before "The Wildflower" finally merges the floral figure of beauty with a female figure of aesthetic possibility in an appeal to some single exotic exception to the usual aesthetic deprivation of the world:

> black-eyed susan
> rich orange
> round the purple core
>
> the white daisy
> is not
> enough
>
> Crowds are white
> as farmers
> who live poorly
>
> But you
> are rich
> in savagery—
>
> Arab
> Indian
> dark woman

The speaker might as well have asked, as he does in "The Waitress," to "Speak to me of her! // —and nobody else and nothing else." Indeed, "The Wildflower" brings to the fore as the final word of the section the same aesthetically motivating image of female beauty that runs throughout both the present section (in poems like "Flight to the City," "Young Love," "To an Old Jaundiced Woman," and "To Elsie") and the later longer poem. And as in all those poems, that image is involved with a compelling sense of inadequacy that renders the appeal here more a measure of desperation than hope. There is the plain admission that ""the white daisy / is not / enough," and the overstatement of "Arab / Indian / dark woman" establishes its own fanciful, too wishful character more than any real exotic identity. So we emerge from "Spring and All" with something like an unsatisfied sense of inefficacious beauty—not perhaps as strong as in the closing lines of "The Waitress," with its litany of impossibilities, but discernable nonetheless. And as that sense in "Longer Poems" later leads to the sober reappraisal of "The Flower," so too does it lead here to the retrenchment of aesthetic ambition in "The Descent of Winter."

"The Descent of Winter" and "The Flower" did in fact share the same broad lyrical moment of distress that formed the climax of *Collected Poems 1921–1931:* the former was the fourth and antepenultimate section of that book while the latter was the immediately succeeding, fifth section. And contiguous as they were, they naturally shared many of the same lyrical elements. Both, for instance, have as their impulse an essentially depressed sensibility, preoccupied with its own personal limitations. The claustrophobic sense of dislocation and dispossession that in "9/29" initiates "The Descent of Winter" resembles in more literal and immediate terms the myopic view of a broader biographical deprivation that opens "The Flower":

> My bed is narrow
> in a small room
> at sea
>
> The numbers are on
> the wall
> Arabic I
>
> Berth No. 2
> was empty above me
> the steward
>
> took it apart
> and removed
> it
>
> only the number
> remains
> • 2 •

("9/29")

> A petal colorless and without form
> the oblong towers lie
>
> beyond the low hill and northward the great
> bridge stanchions,
>
> small in the distance, have appeared,
> pinkish and incomplete—
>
> It is the city,
> approaching over the river. Nothing
>
> of it is mine, but visibly
> for all that it is a petal of a flower—my own.
>   (from "The Flower")

Similarly, there is in the Bolshevik sympathies of both "11/2 A Morning Imagination of Russia" and the four stanzas upon "Madam Lenine. . .benefactress" in "The Flower" a common strain of social discontent that helps turn the initial sense of retreat towards some sort of modest aesthetic counteraction. And then that counter action itself is expressed in the closing notes of both sequence and poem—in the sequence as the defiant repudiation of public success in favor of personal aesthetic integrity ("I make really very little money. / What of it?"); in the poem as the interpolated lampoon of professional ambition that falls within a modest and personal aesthetic agenda ("I plan— . . . —to write").

Despite this basic resemblance, however, there was one affect which "The Descent of Winter" did not share with "The Flower" in *Collected Poems 1921–1931:* the disabusing candor that, in the person of a forthright "naked woman, about 38," forms the "heart (the stamens, pistil, / etc.)" of the reappraisal in the later longer poem. But *The Complete Collected Poems 1906–1938* restores "The Descent of Winter" to its originally larger 1928 state, and in so doing, it completes the correspondence of lyrical character between sequence and poem. Immediately following the cloistered state of "9/29" in the restored version there is a rather blunt self-criticism in "9/30":

> There are no perfect waves—
> Your writings are a sea
> full of misspellings and
> faulty sentences. Level. Troubled

And toward the end of the section, just after the climactic "11/2 A Morning Imagination of Russia," there is a similar note of self-reproach in the also restored entry for "11/8." "O river of my heart polluted / and defamed," the speaker cries out to the heart he likens to a befouled river—"That river will be clean / before ever you will be."

The sheer invective in these two notes goes far beyond both the woman's later pitiless but nonetheless friendly reception to the speaker's confession of public failure and her merely jaded cynicism about the purity of his aesthetic motives. It was probably for their harshness that the two entries were excluded from the 1934 arrangement of "The Descent of Winter"—perhaps in deference to the basically amiable tension between mother and son that ultimately drives the entirety of *Collected Poems 1921–1931*. But included as they are in *The Complete Collected Poems 1906–1938*, they suggest something of both the difference between the two volumes and the way the further additions from the original arrangement for "The Descent of Winter" more exactly address that difference.

The 1934 arrangement, for instance, was an essentially successful episode for the section's sensibility (cf. Part 1, Chapter 3, earlier in this study). After the initial distress of "9/29," "10/10," and "10/21 (the orange flames)," it rather rapidly worked its way up through the recovery of aesthetic spirit in "10/22 (And hunters still return)," "10/28 (On hot days)," and "10/29" before it concluded on the cautious victory of "11/12 A Morning Imagination of Russia" and the small defiance of "11/28."

To some extent, the 1938 restorations amount to little more than lyrical redundancy to this overall movement. The early entries, for example, tend to prolong the initial moment of distress in the section. Following the besiegement of "9/29," there is now the self-laceration of "9/30" (already noted) and a disturbing sense of witness in the "10/9" portrait of a privy "little blackboy." And the new "10/22 (that brilliant field)," with its pining for the fleeting remnants of summer bloom, extends into a bit of melancholy the depressive infatuation with fire in "10/21 (In the dead weeds a rubbish heap)."

By the same token, the increase here in lyrical "weight" is immediately balanced by the middle restorations, which proportionately strengthen the succeeding sense of recovery, first with a luminous transfiguration of a beechtree in "10/28 (in this strong light)"; then with the "ethereal" onomatopoetic music of an elevated train in "10/30"; and finally with the self-assertions of both a boldly colored dahlia and an importunate old woman.

So the section arrives at its climax—"11/12 A Morning Imagination of Russia"—very much in the same way it did in 1934. But the original arrangement is not so unequivocally successful after "A Morning Imagination of Russia." It includes, for example, the harsh moral self-reproach of "11/8" as one of the additional five entries between "A Morning Imagination. . ." and "11/28," and it challenges the attractiveness of the aesthetic principle declared in "11/28" by adding this entry for "12/15" as the last word:

> What an image in the face of Almighty God is she
> her hands in her slicker pockets, head bowed,
> Tam pulled down, flat backed, lanky legged,
> loose feet kicking the pebbles as she goes

The first line's insinuation of a profanity within the expression of astonishment adds to the woman's eccentric gait a suggestion of both ugliness and purely willful defiance. So that suddenly we are not so clear whether the sequence ends with a small note of personal integrity or of perverse resistance.

The other closing poems exert a similar effect as they tend to inflect not so much the promise of the revolutionary newness in "A Morning Imagination. . ." but the equal measure of uncertainty in it. Note for instance how the episode in "11/7" of a woman's last minute panic in an otherwise graceful death strongly seizes the closing lines of "A Morning Imagination. . .":

> We have little now but
> we have that. We are convalescents. Very
> feeble. Our hands shake. We need a
> transfusion. No one will give it to us,
> they are afraid of infection. I do not
> blame them. We have paid heavily. But we
> have gotten—touch. The eyes and the ears
> down on it. Close.

11/7
> We must listen. Before
> she died she told them—
> I always liked to be well dressed
> I wanted to look nice—
>
> So she asked them to dress
> her well. They curled her hair . . .
>
> Now she fought
> She didn't want to go
> She didn't want to!

The final enumeration of the senses in "A Morning Imagination . . ." and the pseudocommand to come "Close" make a specially strong link to the "listen" in the first line of "11/7" and indeed to the imminent extinction of senses which the anecdote involves. And then the deep self-skepticism in "11/8" undermines the small confidence of "A Morning Imagination. . ." on an even more personal, moral basis before "11/10" directly challenges its naive revolutionary optimism by first adducing (somewhat derisively) the inveterate aesthetic and sexual shams of the bourgeoisie and then threatening the sterner revolutionary attitude of a graffiti artist:

> and in chalk crudely
> upon the railroad bridge support
> a woman rampant
> brandishing two rolling pins

"11/20" then advances the disapproval here into something close to scorn as it appears to repeat the disturbing witness-figure of "10/9" by holding up in mock superiority the developmental capacities of an idiot goatherd. Finally "11/22" (entered as "10/22 (and hunters still return)" in *Collected Poems 1921–31*) helps ease back to the diminished self-satisfaction of "11/28" with the partially humiliating, partially venerable procession of empty-handed hunters returning through the municipal precincts.

Such an interlude reveals a more thoroughly shaken dimension to "The Descent of Winter" than was present in its 1934 version, and it signals as well just how much in touch with its new context the 1938 sequence is. Note for instance that prominent in the restorations and especially in this final interlude of recrimination and self-doubt is the same sort of female figure that throughout "Spring and All" was so involved with the developing sense of personal and public inadequacy. The equation of a passionately colored flower and a "dark" woman in the additional entry for "11/2" especially harkens back to the similar conflation of the two in "Black-Eyed Susan," that wishful appeal to an impossible woman.[3] Only now the elusive mystique previously imagined for the woman yields to the brusque public importunity of a tousled old woman looking for directions:

> Dahlias—
> What a red
> and yellow and white
> mirror to the sun, round
> and petaled

      is this she holds?
        with a red face
    all in black
        and grey hair
        sticking out
    from under the bonnet brim
    Is this Washington Avenue Mr. please
        or do I have to
    cross the track?

The new poem answers the earlier moment with a disenchanting element of effrontery that is typical of the generally greater sense of personal siege throughout "The Descent of Winter." The old woman's question, appearing as it does to resume for the third time the identically phrased "What . . . is this" begun in the second line, literally usurps the interrogative rhythms of the poem, and its sudden directness jolts the poem out of its ambiguity of reference as well as its general confusion of color.

Of course, this mild bit of effrontery suggests the basis for the fuller disabusing boldness that so distinguishes the "The Flower" as the later counterpart to "The Descent of Winter." The sternly censuring graffito of a "woman rampant" in "11/10" even over-states that element of bold female judgment a bit. At the same time, the venereal woman who appears earlier in that same entry seems to inherit the same sort of defilement as that suffered by the earlier Beautiful Thing and the more immediately preceding Elsie. Only here again, the woman's part is laced with a distinctive feistiness that extends even to the previously submissive relationship of patient to doctor. A single prominent rhyme underscores the monosyllabic line that carries the greatest burden of impudent sarcasm in the answer to the doctor's implicitly foolish question:

      —Wore my bathing suit
      wet
      four hours after sundown.
      That's how. Yea?
      Easy to get
      hard to get rid of.

It is finally this same fundamental estrangement from the female figure and the especially subverted beauty it represents that the last entry restates in considerably more problematic terms. Echoing the "What" phrasing of "11/2 (Dahlias)" and recasting the "Dahlia" of that entry into the sullen image of an ill-tempered old woman, "12/15" appears to involve a sort of transference. The aggressiveness that characterizes the previous female figures here gives way to a sullenness that in its withdrawal might better typify the initially depressed central sensibility of the sequence. Instead of a "woman rampant," we witness the gestures of a sulking old woman: a hunching down, a peevish kicking of stones—even an outright scowl is suggested by the profane "image in the face" with which she flouts God himself. Beneath the anger, the notes of a simple personal discontent prepare perfectly for the old woman whose personal depression instigates the succeeding and seventh sequence, "Collected Poems 1934."

10

A Better Record than "Longer Poems": "Collected Poems 1934," "An Early Martyr," "Adam & Eve and The City," and "Recent Verse"

Although Williams made significant changes to the "Poems" sequence of *Collected Poems 1921–1931* as he fashioned it into the "Collected Poems 1934" of *The Complete Collected Poems 1906–1938,* the basic elements of the sequence remained the same, and they fit their new context quite neatly. The initial tension of the sequence, for instance—that between a sad old woman and a happier, solicitous companion (probably her son)—seems very much a specific expression and even development of the general aesthetic dispositions evolved in "The Descent of Winter." The old woman's incorrigible nostalgia for the lost aesthetic paradise of her youth particularizes the very unreferenced depression that opens "The Descent of Winter." And the speaking companion's answering optimism reduces to a more plausible sentiment the revolutionary counternote in "11/2 A Morning Imagination of Russia" of that sequence. Finally, the basic estrangement between the woman and the speaking son makes intimately familiar the preceding sequence's broad and even caricatured sense of male/female estrangement.

In a similar way, the overall relationship between "Collected Poems 1934" and "The Descent of Winter" quite accurately parallels that between their respective counterparts in "Longer Poems." Just as the hyperactive "Romance Modern" later follows the retrenchment of "The Flower," "Collected Poems 1934" appears to struggle against the general sense of self-constraint developed in "The Descent of Winter." Only of course, as in all the sequences of the book, the keynotes here parallel the later longer poem in a more dispersed and less intense fashion. Instead of the impulsive vandalism that ditches a car, there is an irrepressible aesthetic optimism that flippantly challenges the old woman's sad disposition in "Brilliant Sad Sun" or that proudly owns up to some household mischief in "This Is Just to Say." Instead of the delirious romanticism of the mountain landscape, there is the calmer druidic enchantment with the forest of "The Source." And instead of passionate ejaculations of love and jealousy, there are the affectionate statements of filial love and maternal displeasure in "Birds and Flowers."

Despite the essential resemblance, however, there were other significant lyrical disjunctions between the original "Poems" sequence and the new context of *The Complete Collected Poems 1906–1938*. Most obviously, the adolescent strain in "Romance Modern" that ultimately parodies itself into the silly futility of a suicide pact with the landscape-lover had little correspondence with the genuine sense of reconciliation that concluded the original arrangement for "Poems" of 1934. Yet that element of futility, of a lyrical false start, seems important to the overall lyrical position of the new volume as it seeks desperately to counteract rather than simply accept the excessively diminished sense of self and ambition that is the net result of "The Descent of Winter." Thus it probably was that Williams made for the 1938 volume a few changes in the original arrangement of "Poems" that add a substantial element of stalemate.

He moved, for example, the strong northern counternote of "Young Sycamore" from out of its medial position between the opening three poems of geriatric depression and the fifth through seventh poems of broader cultural aesthetic malaise. The effect is to consolidate in the first six poems the now less challenged tropical elements of personal, aesthetic, and cultural fatigue that dominate them. At the same time, Williams consolidated the immediately succeeding poems into a just as clearly defined unit of the opposing northern vigor. Leading off with "Young Sycamore" as now the seventh poem of the group, Williams eliminated the transitional mixture of lazy southern pleasure and northern hardships in the original eighth poem ("The Sun Bathers"); eliminated the complicated probing of the northern spirit and vision of beauty in the original tenth poem ("Struggle of Wings"); and wound up with a something more like a schema than a sequence: there is the keynote of northern vigor in "Young Sycamore"; an illustrative northern seascape in "The Cod Head"; an illustrative northern skyscape in "New England" (formerly "Down-town"); and an illustrative northern landscape in "Winter."

This kind of simplified lyrical blocking reduces the subtle dynamism of the original opening tensions to a more simply contentious state, one that makes of the son's aesthetic optimism more a simple gainsaying to the constraints of the old woman's depression than an interrelated and persuasive answer to it. And a similar change is evident in the signal effect Williams creates in one of the two new poems he adds to the old arrangement. Just after the graceful acrobatics of the cat in "Poem (As the cat)," as the section is poised for the winning reformulation of its opening terms and tensions— as it readies for the triumph of aesthetic optimism over depression—there now comes a poem entitled "Sluggishly." The title alone appears to mock the image of the cat's passage in "Poem (As the cat)" and thus to renew the negative, contentious outlook that had been substantively left behind in the opening six poems. And the poem itself caricatures the impending repossession of the tropic realm in the succeeding poem, "The Jungle," by prefacing it with a cynical ultimatum that renews the sense of clearly, even vehemently, opposite temperaments in the sequence:

SLUGGISHLY

or with a rush
the river flows—

and none
is unaffected—

Think:
the clear stream

boiling at
the boat's wake

or—
    a stench
your choice is—

And respond?

              crapulous
—having eaten

fouling
the water grass

The syntactic parsing that leaves "a stench" and "your choice is" in apposition adds an insult to this proposition and helps make the succeeding challenge "And respond?" almost a demand for satisfaction, with the outdented "crapulous" an attendant and especially provocative invective. Clearly this is no precursor to gentle rapprochement between mother and son. It is instead an impatient exacerbation of their tension, similar in spirit to the bristling "blind emotions" of "Romance Modern" that drive the overtures of love in that poem ultimately to the exacerbated jealousy of its suicide wish.

Yet this single note clearly does not entirely defeat the basic success of the remaining poems from the original collection. With only two other lyrically insignificant changes (the addition of the further domestic exotica in "Between Walls" after "The Jungle," and the transposition of the genial "Interests of 1926" with the austere "The Attic Which Is Desire" in more direct transition to the strange delight of "This Is Just To Say"), the final group still eventually works its lyrical way to the happier resolution of "Birds and Flowers." But a rather large alteration right after that poem does manage to deflect the sequence's conclusion from a purely happy note to a partially thwarted one, one more like the self-defeating suicide wish that closes "Romance Modern."

Removing the hopeful afterbeat of "Full Moon" and incorporating it within "Della Primavera Transportata Al Morale," Williams adds another poem to that sequence ("The Wind Increases"), shuffles it around a bit, and makes the entire, newly formulated sequence the final poem for "Collected Poems 1934." Considering that "Primavera," the 1934 version of this final sequence, had as a separate section followed "Poems" in the 1934 *Collected Poems 1921–1931* anyway, this addition seems hardly surprising. But the original effect of that succession was to help broaden—and test— the generous aesthetic spirit into which "Poems" had grown. In the 1938 arrangement, however, there is exactly the opposite effect.

"Full Moon," for example, that hopeful afterbeat that signaled an extension of the spirit in "Birds and Flowers," now arrives after the happy jaunt of "April," and in so doing, it interrupts the passage from the somewhat transcendental epiphany at the end of that poem to the angry, clearly impending denunciation of "The Trees." Now, as the closing lines of "April" slowly insinuate into the platonic mediation on "the forms / of the emotions" a physical ferocity of "lashing branches," there follows not the fully and immediately angry trees that "being trees / thrash and scream" but the "Blessed moon / noon / of night" instead. The interposition of this fully romantic note places a special emphasis upon it: the hopeful, expectant note is revealed as a sort of *naiveté,* ridiculously holding out against the bitter disappointment with the real world that is the inevitable corollary to a transcendental enchantment with the ideal one.

This revision, then, is an important one, for it introduces an element of futility early on in the Primavera sequence and alerts us to larger but similar shifts in lyrical alignments throughout. The super gracious "The House," for example, which used to provide some relief from the guilty, brooding "Rain" before passing into the disturbingly rude "Death (He's dead)," has been removed to the first half of the sequence, where along with the love talk of "The Bird's Companion" and a new poem entitled "The Wind Increases," it consolidates the more tender, solicitous notes, much as those same sorts of notes are blocked out in the revision to "Poems." This assignment leaves the three succeeding poems (the ironic "The Sea-Elephant," the brooding "Rain," and the rude "Death (He's dead)") to answer those notes with something like the definitiveness of the last word. The cheerful optimism that governs the earlier groups is essentially parodied, even ridiculed as a quintessential naiveté. Note for instance the similarity in these lines from "The Wind Increases" and "The Sea-Elephant":

> The trees
> the tulip's bright
> tips
> sidle and
> toss—
>
> Loose your love
> to flow
>
> Blow!
>
> (from "The Wind Increases")

> Swing—ride
> walk
> on wires—toss balls
> stoop and
>
> contort yourselves—
> But I
> am love. I am
> from the sea—
>
> Blouaugh!
>
> (from "The Sea-Elephant")

The grotesque animal's antics, his "tossings" and his blowing, are a direct mockery of the romantic injunctions in the earlier poem. And the excited spirit that motivates those injunctions is thus overwhelmed by the bitterness that governs the performance of the sea-animal. Similarly, when the tree and sea-elephant motifs reappear in "Rain," they appear swamped in the guilty brooding of that poem, and they confirm the lyrical balance of the sequence to be on the side of a futile self-pity:

> The trees
> are become
> beasts fresh risen
> from
>   the sea—
> water
>
> trickles
> from the crevices of
> their hides—
>
> So my life is spent
>   to keep out love

The other poems of aesthetic cheer meet similar fates and in almost schematic order. Just as the fourth poem ("The Wind Increases") is subverted by the seventh ("The Sea-Elephant"), the gentle reassurance of the fifth poem ("The Bird's Companion") is subverted by the guilty brooding of the eighth ("Rain"), and the gracious sixth ("The House") is subverted by the inexplicably rude ninth ("Death"). Thus at the close of the sequence, there is left in "The Botticellian Trees" only the delicate, refined reformulation of the tree motif that closed the 1934 arrangement as well. But its formal refinement no longer seems to answer solely the sprawling cheerfulness of "April" in a purely corrective way. After the onslaught of the immediately preceding chord, especially the reinforced and unnerving bluntness of "Death (He's dead)," there is implied as well an inevitable association of the poem's affectations with a discredited romantic idealism:

> by the rain and sun—
> The strict simple
>
> principles of
> straight branches

> are being modified
> by pinched out
>
> ifs of color, devout
> conditions
>
> the smiles of love—
> .   .   .   .

Although the ellipsis that serves as the last line in this passage might well suggest a speechless serenity, it might also be a cue for the "Blouaugh!" that has previously attended the projection of such natural principles of love as trees. Much as there is for the affected romanticism in "Romance Modern," there is ultimately some doubt about the silly geniality and the finally highly stylized approach to beauty that in "Della Primavera Transportata Al Morale" comes to substitute for the aesthetic optimism developed in the preceding variation of the old "Poems."

In this sense, then, "Collected Poems 1934" has been transformed from the persuasive aesthetic answer to an old woman's intractable depression that it was in 1934 into a less successful, fitful reaction against the sense of personal limitation evoked in "The Descent of Winter." And it is this new character that the later "Romance Modern" restates in perhaps more shrill terms as it too kicks against the personal aesthetic retrenchment of "The Flower." But despite this essential similarity between sequence and longer poem, there are some rather clear and striking differences, differences that suggest much about the lyrical logic of the volume as a whole.

In the first place, there is the clear distinction between the adolescent and adult temperaments that respectively dominate the two parts. The sensibility that despite all its frustration seeks always seriously and tenderly to redeem the oppressive aesthetic legacy of the old woman in "Collected Poems 1934"—this sensibility is fundamentally more mature than the rambunctious speaker who conspires like a child (or a prisoner) in the back seat of an automobile and then "Punch[es] the steersman!" in a break for the "gnome"-animated world of the mountain forest. Compare, for instance, these passages:

> The slope of the heavy woods
> pales and disappears
> in the wall of mist that hides

the edge above whose peak
last night the moon—

But it is morning and a new light
marks other things
a pasture which begins

where silhouettes of scrub
and balsams stand uncertainly

On whose green three maples

are distinctly pressed
beside a red barn

with new shingles in the old
all cancelled by

A triple elm's inverted
lichen mottled
triple thighs from which

wisps of twigs
droop with sharp leaves

Which shake in the crotch
brushing the stained bark
fitfully
            (from "The Source, I")

I would sit separate weighing a
small red handful: the dirt of these parts,
sliding mists sheeting the alders
against the touch of fingers creeping
to mine. All stuff of the blind emotions.
But—stirred, the eye seizes
for the first time—The eye awake!—
anything, a dirt bank with green stars
of scrawny weed flattened upon it under
a weight of air—For the first time!—
or a yawning depth: Big!
            (from "Romance Modern")

The lines from "The Source" are all aesthetic caution and dis-
crimination. Aside from its general visual precision in the notation
of botanical species, number, and color, there is something of a

surveyor's eye in this animist northern answer to the old woman's memories of a tropical paradise that so beset the section. The very mist which opens the poem is involved in an act of reference, of navigation, as the speaker locates the previous night's position of the moon. And there is a studied plotting of natural landmarks as boundaries, as points where "a pasture . . . begins" and where lines of sight intersect or are "cancelled." The lines from "Romance Modern" on the other hand are indeed nearly "blind" by comparison. The initial preoccupation with a vague tactile sensation gives way to an equally impulsive visual seizure of "anything," of some undefined "scrawny weed" as the only point of reference in a frenzy of excitement. Of course, the poem ultimately trails off into a dizzying visual blur that smacks of mania: "River and mountain, light and rain—or / rain, rock, light, trees—divided: / rain-light counter rocks—trees or / trees counter rain-light-rocks or—."

This relationship between sequence and longer poem reverses the one that has thus far characterized the volume. Just how deliberate this sort of contrast is can be best inferred by one of the two poems from the 1934 "Poems" that Williams omitted from the 1938 "Collected Poems 1934." More than any other in the gathering, "Struggle of Wings" most exactly reflects the mood and manner of "Romance Modern." Full of infatuation with the reflective enchantment of light on winter landscape, it too grows comically rambunctious as it portrays the birth of "Poesy" in a farcical vein similar to the juvenile mentality that fantasizes ditching the car in the later poem:

> Roundclouds occluding patches of the
> sky rival steam bluntly towering,
> slowspinning billows which rival
> the resting snow, which rivals the sun
>
> .   .   .   .
>
> It is a baby!
> Now it is very clear (*) they're keeping the child
> (naked in the air) warm and safe between them.
> The eyes of the birds are fixed in
>
> a bestial ecstasy. They strive together panting.
> It is an antithesis of logic, very
> theoretical. To his face the baby claps
> the bearded face of Socrates . . .
>
> Ho, ho! he's dropped it. It was a mask.

Presumably, however, this poem was excluded precisely because it was *too* similar to "Romance Modern," and it would have undermined the changing relationship between the sectional sequences and the longer poems that the volume clearly begins to develop at this point in its organization. The simple chronology of "Longer Poems," for instance, reveals that "Romance Modern" marks the first time that a longer poem antedates its corresponding sequence. It therefore represents work from a presumably less developed period of Williams's career, and it in fact initiates a trend along these lines that continues throughout the remainder of the volume. Thus, at the very end of the book, Williams's earliest long poem, "The Wanderer," is set parallel to the sequence that contains his most recent shorter work—much of which contains the first steps towards *Paterson,* his fully mature and greatest long work.

This inversion of poetic stages provides a basis for evaluating the "development" of the entire volume—the sort of "development" to which Williams himself would someday refer in his review of Sandburg's *Collected Poems.* Just as the restatement in the more accomplished "Morning" or "An Elegy for D. H. Lawrence" helps to validate the basic intent of the sometimes clumsy early sections like "The Tempers" and "Transitional," so too does the counterpointing of the earlier, perhaps broader expression in a longer poem like "Romance Modern" (and in all the remaining longer poems) help to reveal in the chronologically more recent and poetically more mature sections like "Collected Poems 1934" the authentic presence of Williams's earliest poetic gestures. Thus, the *perfections,* not just the noble attempts, provide throughout the volume a baseline against which we may judge the worth or promise of all of Williams's work.

With the close of "Collected Poems 1934," *The Complete Collected Poems* of 1938 leaves behind all traces of its predecessor, *Collected Poems 1921–1931,* and in so doing, it leaves behind the intimate (probably familial) quarrel that ultimately impelled the earlier collection. Advancing the broader, more worldly orientation of "Della Primavera Transportata al Morale," the succeeding and eighth section, "An Early Martyr," throws the volume back into the sort of public domain it left when it moved from the cultural diatribe of "Spring and All" and into first the more private agony of "The Descent of Winter" and then the familial/aesthetic tension of "Collected Poems 1934." The opening and title poem of the new section lampoons a criminal justice system that defeats with the worst sort of euphemistic arrogance the preeminently honest and revolutionary spirit of a notorious shoplifter. Denying this transgressor the opportunity he so desires for the public justification of a trial, the courts have remanded him to a mental hospital and finally to exile from the state—all in the interest of his mental health.

There is plenty of pure social satire here, of course, and in fact a strain of social realism does express itself throughout the section. Its climactic poem, "The Yachts," turns at its end from a literal harbor scene into a shocking vision of human carnage that redefines the entire episode as a sort of allegory about the cruel side of modern capitalism. And the chummy final poem of the section, "A Poem for Norman Macleod," gloats over a transformation of certain social values: "noble has been / changed to no bull // After that / has sickered down / slumming will / be done on Park Ave."

But the primary affect in all these moments is really more than a simple matter of social disposition. It is part of a fundamental eschewal of conventional sentiment that forms a corrective to the perhaps too buoyant optimism of "Collected Poems 1934," an optimism that finally showed itself to be profoundly naive. In "A Poem for Norman Macleod," for example, the posture of a social subversion is dominated by the fuller and refreshingly "vulgar" anecdote about an apocryphal Indian ("Chief / One Horn") who instructs a "constipated / prospector" about the easy availability of natural laxatives in a nearby balsam tree that the prospector stupidly ignores. And before there is expressed any social insight in "The Yachts," there is a general skepticism that attends the performance and capability of the boats themselves.

Such features make the entire section and its social complaints more of a response to the lyrical conditions of the volume's special stage of development rather than the historical conditions of the depression during which the arrangement was originally created. Note especially how as the opening poem establishes a skeptical irreverence for the cant of established authority, it directly addresses the same elements of naive futility that closed the preceding section:

> They "cured" him all
> right
> But the set-up
> he fought against
> Remains—
> and his youthful deed
> Signalizing
> the romantic period

> Of a revolt
> he served well
> Is still good—
>
> Let him be
> a factory whistle
> That keeps blaring—
> Sense, sense, sense!
> so long as there's
> A mind to remember
> and a voice to
> carry it on—

Although there is a generic similarity here between the thief's fatuously noble intent and the son's naive aesthetic optimism in "Collected Poems 1934," the "romantic period / Of a revolt" honored in this passage perhaps better describes the landscape antics of "Romance Modern" than it does that poem's counterpart in the preceding sequence. And indeed there is in this passage much that resembles equally well the essential character and terms of the longer poem "Paterson" that follows those landscape antics. The "Sense, sense, sense!" for instance, that so urges itself anticipates the equal urgency of the fundamental "solution" to the predicament outlined in "Paterson:"

> They walk incommunicado, the
> equation is beyond solution, yet
> its sense is clear—that they live
> his thought is listed in the Telephone
> Directory—

And the "factory whistle" itself that suddenly replaces the terms and tone of a traditional encomium with a shriller note of modern industrial and political reality anticipates the way that same sort of reality counters the diffused landscape effects that "Paterson" seems to inherit from "Romance Modern":

> in a recoil of spray and rainbow mists—
> —Say it, no ideas but in things—
> and factories, crystallized from its force,

From "mists" to "factories": the abrupt change in realms of experience is underscored by the interjection of an aesthetic injunction that becomes the refrain of the poem—"no ideas but the facts," as the final line rephrases it. And it is a series of such "facts," like those of the hapless paraplegic Jacob, that form the principal achievement of "Paterson" as they rigorously defeat every impulse to sentiment. And it is this same sort of achievement that distinguishes the entire section of "An Early Martyr."

Take, for instance, the testimony of the rape victim in "The Raper From Passenack." The normal measure of pity we might accord this woman is everywhere prohibited, as in this early passage where she perversely defies medical attention in sheer abreaction to the violation she has suffered:

> . . . But if I get a
> veneral infection out of this
> I won't be treated.
>
> I refuse. You'll find me dead in bed
> first. Why not? That's
> the way she spoke,

Then there is the even more disturbing ruthlessness of "The Dead Baby," who has departed this life like no cherub but instead has gone "to heaven, blindly / by force of the facts." Pathos has given way to the business-like efficiency of a funeral director preparing a household to receive its corpse:

> Sweep the house
> under the feet of the curious
> holiday seekers—
> sweep under the table and the bed
> the baby is dead—

The discernable scorn for the self-indulgent condolence givers; the prominent repetition of grammatical imperatives; and the syncopated play of babble-like b's and d's together with the tacky, doggerel-like rhyme of bed/dead—such touches deflect our pity and prepare for the ultimate objectivity of the final stanza, when the baby is finally rendered into the purest sort of aesthetic fact:

> Hurry up! any minute
> they will be bringing it
> from the hospital—
> a white model of our lives
> a curiosity—
> surrounded by fresh flowers

All of these "facts" are of course part of the larger "sense" that both sequence and its corresponding longer poem seek to establish as a communal truth. In "Paterson," it is explicitly identified with the "wit" that one must "drive" into the cheap aesthetic artifacts that constitute the common substitute for a true aesthetic solution to human dilemmas. In "An Early Martyr," that sense expresses itself as a similar but more implicit attempt to retrieve common pleasures from the realm of the tawdry, even the shoddy, by placing those things on a superior aesthetic base.

"To a Mexican Pig-Bank," for example, reveals an admirable fineness of construction and purity of color in a gaudy souvenir. "To a Poor Old Woman" savors with epicurean deliberation a passing woman's casual "munching" of plums out of a bag. And "Proletarian Portrait" manages to make an act of aesthetic attention out of a woman's preoccupation with some shoddy shoes:

> A big young bareheaded woman
> in an apron
>
> Her hair slicked back standing
> on the street
>
> One stockinged foot toeing
> the sidewalk
>
> Her shoe in her hand. Looking
> intently into it
>
> She pulls out the paper insole
> to find the nail
>
> That has been hurting her

The possible social suggestions of the details here—the husky stature of the peasant-like woman, her uncoiffured hair, the cheapness of her shoes—are largely denied by a stanza structure that emphasizes the details in general as separate items of absorbing visual attention. Each short second line in the first three stanzas, for instance, brings the rhythms of its stanza up short and jerks the poem out of its surface discourse while at the same time, the odd off-rhymes (the feminine rhyme of woman/apron, the alliteration of standing/street, the consonance of the velar stops that end toeing and sidewalk) subtly accent the isolated phrases of those lines. Thus, the apron, street, and sidewalk all gain an imagistic prominence and invite a broader visual perspective for the poem, a perspective that defines in a special way the "Looking" that is so emphasized by the poem's single unequivocally syntactical use of capitalization. And within the purely pictorial context of this "portrait," the minor "proletarian" pain of the woman's poorly cobbled footwear that is finally established in the truncated last stanza signals an intensity of simple concentration more than it implies some symbolic Marxist interpretation of her predicament.

The overall movement of the sequence as a whole plays out in larger terms something similar to this miniature and specifically aesthetic victory over a generally devalued life. After "An Early Martyr" rescues the futile revolutionary naiveté of its hero with a more savvy aesthetic approach to his defeat, two poems follow that secure that aesthetic orientation with some purely natural subjects. "Flowers By the Sea" first contemplates the sublime transformations of floral shape, color, and movement occasioned by the background of a heaving ocean, and then "The Locust Tree in Flower" partitions a budding branch into its most delectable and promising parts. "Item" then returns the section to the same realm of social oppression hinted at in "An Early Martyr," only now it is conceived of as more directly brutal by an imaginative capacity that transforms a newspaper footnote into a grisly episode of assault:

> This, with a face
> like a mashed blood-orange
> that suddenly
>
> would get eyes
> and look and scream
> War! War!

The true horror that is realized here by virtue of its *aesthetic* facts literally drives out from the sequence any incidental sentiment that may have attended the opening poem's tribute to the noble thief, and its dramatic impact prepares as well for the next poem's ridding of sentiment from a less gruesome scene of social dispossession. "View of a Lake" studies three shanty children with a disciplined attention to the facts (rather than the pity) of their surroundings that is mirrored in the children's own staunch, even military-like gaze toward the water. And then the next three poems all set out the more pleasurable expressions of this sort of disciplined attention. Whimsically addressing a trinket as though it were a human audience, "To a Mexican Pig Bank" carefully subsumes the souvenir's potential revolutionary symbolism within a painstaking attention to the miniature details of its happily decorative design. "To A Poor Old Woman" then notices as an exception-ally fulfilling act in itself a woman's sensory attention to her plums, regardless of her incidental economic impoverishment. And "Late for Summer Weather" flaunts the carefree gaiety affected by a pair of poorly dressed loafers-about-town.

Building upon the invigoration of these three poems, the follow-ing four poems turn the aesthetic attention to some harsher sub-jects. The woman who was so intensely and happily involved with her plums in "To a Poor Old Woman" is complemented by the young woman in "Proletarian Portrait," who is equally involved with a smarting shoe. Then "Tree and Sky" paints a stark, even menacing landscape and prepares for the pitiless testimony of "The Raper from Passenack," a testimony that is the most factually at-tentive instance of abused womanhood in the sequence. Then, as if to underscore that fact, "Invocation and Conclusion" sarcastically sums up that oppressive predicament with some simple numerical facts about another woman's pre-pubescent marriage and sexual exploitation.

The overall effect of these preceding seven poems is to extract and equate, by virtue of a single aesthetic attention, both the simple pleasures and extreme distresses of this socially defective world. All the facts become a redeeming sort of beauty, whatever they may be as social reality. And so it is that "The Yachts" at once bristles with an aesthetic excitement at the sheer visual brilliance of a regatta even as it intuits the larger social implications about these capitalist dreadnaughts. Indeed, the climax of the poem is at once a moment of social insight and an ecstasy of the visual imagination. It is a supreme sort of symbolic vision:

> until the horror of the race dawns staggering the mind,
> the whole sea become an entanglement of watery bodies
> lost to the world bearing what they cannot hold. Broken,

"The Yachts" brings the sequence most fully into possession of its own aesthetic values, and the last poems apply that sense of command rigorously. "Hymn to Love Ended" shrewdly devalues the "extremes of passion" that, once overcome, give rise to the more rigorous achievements of great art. And "Sunday" raises to the station of worship the attentive gathering of the sabbath day's routine facts—things like the vivid sounds of cookery and snippets of casual conversation. And almost conversely, "The Catholic Bells" desanctifies a peeling church belfry by celebrating not its call to worship but its aesthetic accent to the stray joys and afflictions of the parishioners' lives. And finally "The Dead Baby" recovers even infant death from its vague sadness and places it on a firm, factual, and aesthetic footing:

> Hurry up! any minute
>   they will be bringing it
>   from the hospital—
> a white model of our lives
>   a curiosity—
> surrounded by fresh flowers

This is, in somewhat more daring terms, exactly the same sort of audaciously aesthetic reconception of life, especially of life's tragedy, that will later inform the spectacle of hapless Jacob near the end of "Paterson." And it is ultimately to both achievements that the final poem—"A Poem for Norman Macleod"—alludes when, with a deliberate eschewal of grandeur and pretension, it refers to an accomplished revolution of definition: "noble has been / changed to no bull." The very triteness of the pun and the subsequent buffonery of the Chief One Horn anecdote confidently affirm for a final time the factually accurate character of this revolution—just as the finally brisk images in the "actual, florid detail of cheap carpet" attend in "Paterson" the final statement of its factual aesthetic principle: "no ideas beside the facts." It is precisely these last and overall elements of an honest, even blunt acceptance of things as they truly are that mark for the volume at large the ascendancy of a truly adult aesthetic.[1]

Just how lyrically important the ascendancy of that aesthetic is for the volume is made immediately clear in the following, ninth sequence, "Adam & Eve and the City." Like "March," the ninth longer poem to which the sequence corresponds, "Adam & Eve and the City" constitutes a mobilization for a specifically poetic campaign against an aesthetically enfeebled world, only the campaign here is more of a sage's than a warrior's. Instead of a motivating desire "to write poetry" that in the later longer poem combines great cultural traditions with the elemental vigor of a blustery northern spring and then fashions them all into a sort of aesthetic battle-cry, there runs throughout the sequence an explicit wish "to write" that gathers into a quieter inspiration the personal legacies of two primordial parent-figures ("Adam" and "Eve") and the subtler elemental renewal in a spring presided over by the author of relativity theory ("St. Francis Einstein of the Daffodils").

The poems of the sequence, in other words, express a distinctly more mature sensibility, for they involve awakenings as equally profound as those of "March" but in a far more sedate frame of response; they in fact make "March" seem positively overstated in comparison. The difference extends and makes even more prominent the inverted relationship between sequence and longer poem that was first expressed between "Collected Poems 1934" and "Romance Modern." And it reflects just how thoroughly "Adam & Eve and the City" is a response to the distinctly adult spirit that emerges in "An Early Martyr."

Thus, rather than beginning and ending with ferocious notes like a spring sky "closing in black / and sudden, with fierce jaws" and Winds! / lean, serious as a virgin" enjoined to "Fling yourselves upon / their empty roses—cut savagely!," the opening and closing notes of "Adam & Eve and the City" are full of a quieter aesthetic determination that more accurately completes the eschewal of grandeur announced in "A Poem for Norman Macleod." The reposeful moment of bird song at dusk that opens the sequence, for example, while not particularly aggressive, does immediately prompt the expression of an artistic sincerity intent upon a fully adequate response to the bird's song:

> Singing across the orchard
> before night, answered
> from the depths
> of the wood, inversely
> and in a lower key—
>
> First I tried to write
> conventionally praising you
> but found it no more
> than my own thoughts
> that I was giving. No.
>
> What can I say?
>   Vistas
> of delight waking suddenly
> before a cheated world.

And it is an imagined foreglimpse of harvest bounty that completes the "tired workman's" respite in "Cancion," the final poem of the sequence, and makes of his restful moment an act of planning and resolution:

> The tired workman
> Takes his ease
> When his stiff beard's all frosted over
> Thinking of blazing
> August's corn
> And the brimming wine-cribs of October.

A similar sort of subtle strength is marshalled in the three central poems of the sequence. Whereas the male principle of power in "March" is equated with imperial Babylonian grandeur, it is revealed in "Adam" in the understated terms of a male parental legacy. Instead of gorgeous cavalcades in basreliefs that commemorate kingly victories, there is the stoic display of a father's chauvanistic British demeanor that disdains even the mortal menace of domestic "duty":

> Naked on a raft
> he could see the barracudas
> waiting to castrate him
> so the saying went—
> Circumstances take longer—
>
> But being an Englishman
> though he had not lived in England
> *desde que avia cinco años*
> he never turned back
> but kept a cold eye always
> on the inevitable end
> never wincing—never to unbend—
> God's handyman
> going quietly into hell's mouth
> for a paper of reference—
> fetching water to posterity
> a British passport
> always in his pocket—
> muleback over Costa Rica
> eating patés of black ants
>
> And the Latin ladies admired him

The male accomplishment that is recovered here is a supreme sort of adult fortitude and steadiness of vision that is at once a personal, cultural and aesthetic trait. The insidious "circumstances" of family responsibility; the inhospitability of foreign tropical climes; the vividness of some "patés of black ants"—all yield to the unblinking "cold eye." For all its quietness, there is a kind of victory in this march "into hell's mouth." It is, in the terms of the poem itself, the most realistic victory available to man "driven— / out of Paradise—to taste / the death that duty brings."

Similarly, it is a distinctly adult fate that forms the female legacy in "Eve." Instead of Fra Angelico's delicate virgin who so plainly enjoys the favor of a divine Annunciation, there is the recalcitrant old matriarch who hangs onto life with a bone-crushing grasp:

> Might He not take
> that wasted carcass, crippled
> and deformed, that ruined face
> sightless, deafened—
> the color gone—that seems
> always listening, watching, waiting
> ashamed only
> of that single and last
> degradation—
> No. Never. Defenseless
> still you would keep
> every accoutrement
> which He has loaned
> till it shall be torn from
> your grasp, a final grip
> from those fingers
> which cannot hold a knife
> to cut the meat but which
> in a hypnotic ecstasy
> can so wrench a hand held out
> to you that our bones
> crack under the unwonted pressure—

It is a powerful resistance to death and sensory disability that the speaker (the son) extracts from out of the embarrassing eccentricities of the old woman's behavior and that he earlier identifies as the old woman's "fertile darkness / in which passion mates— / reflecting / the lightnings of creation." And it is the creative power to which he dedicates his own aesthetic plan for salvation, his determination to "write a book about you— / making you live (in a book!)."

The net effect of this quieter, more thoughtful sort of inspiration is to release more fully the plainly aesthetic beauty that is the proper corollary achievement to aesthetic motivation. Zeal, in other words, does not become, as it tends to in "March," an end unto itself. And so it is that in the succeeding poem to "Adam" and "Eve" there is discovered in nature not the simple, physically ravishing and upstaging vigor of the March winds but a spring of quieter and more profound elemental arousal. Presided over by the beneficent patron saint of relativity himself, "St. Francis Einstein of the Daffodils" introduces a promised land in which a refreshing floral beauty is everywhere discovered by disturbances in the space-time continuum. "'Sweet land' / at last!" the poem opens before it proclaims its unique sort of liberation:

> freedom
> for the daffodils!
> —in a tearing wind
> that shakes
> the tufted orchards—
> Einstein, tall as a violet
> in the lattice-arbor corner
> is tall as
> a blossomy peartree
>
> O Samos, Samos
> dead and buried. Lesbia
> a black cat in the freshturned
> garden. All dead.
> All flesh they sung
> is rotten
> Sing of it no longer—
> Side by side young and old
> take the sun together
> maples, green and red
> yellowbells
> and the vermilion quinceflower
> together—

The disjunction in the physical size of the similes for Einstein's height; the bending of a grided space in the arbor image; the confusion of an ancient poet with a recently interred cat (poisoned, it is implied in the following stanza, by a "old negro" in need of fertilizer)—the only true clarity that remains through all these distortions are the exactly identified botanical species and their vivid colors. These aesthetic elements have become the new measure of the world, actually overcoming the temporal death that could only be defied in "Adam" and "Eve" and vindicating in that success the earlier, less certain struggle to do the same in the volume's fourth sequence, "Sour Grapes."[2] In this sense, the poem's final affect of a subtle refreshment borne of winds more changeable than forceful represents as well a really rather powerful aesthetics:

> Sring days
> swift and mutable
> winds blowing four ways
> hot and cold
> shaking the flowers
> Now the northeast wind
> moving in fogs leaves the grass
> cold and dripping. The night
> is dark. But in the night
> the southeast wind approaches.
> The owner of the orchard
> lies in bed
> with open windows
> and throws off his covers
> one by one

The inverted half-rhymes of "flowers" and "wind" with "windows" and "covers" make a special point of the transfer from the simple violent "shaking" of the flowers to the gradual, literally somnolent gestures of refreshment for a single human individual, the "owner of the orchard." And that final emphasis, along with its Edenic associations, also substantially completes the sort of archetypal dimensions that "Adam" and "Eve" establish and that function much as the broader cultural traditions do in the later "March." The real fulfillment of that dimension, however, occurs in the penultimate poem of the section, "Perpetuum Mobile: The City," where issues of cultural reexamination and aesthetic achievement are made identical to a sense of personal growth and individual wisdom:

> PERPETUUM MOBILE:
> THE CITY
> —a dream
> we dreamed
> each
> separately
> we two
>
> of love
> and of
> desire—

that fused
in the night—

in the distance
          over
the meadows
          by day
impossible—
          The city
disappeared
          when
we arrived—

          A dream
a little false
toward which
          now
we stand
          and stare
transfixed—

all at once
          in the east
rising!

          All white!

          small
as a flower—

a locust cluster
a shad bush
          blossoming

Gathering up the key themes and motifs of the sequence—the disappointing but illuminating fates of marital partners in "Adam" and "Eve," the floral renewal of "St. Francis Einstein of the Daffodils," and inspirational impact of all three poems—this poem represents as the culminating note of the sequence not a resignation but a highly buoyant determination to rigorously penetrate the shams of both personal and cultural ambitions—to "cut savagely" "their empty roses," as "March" would put it. Armored car guards privately indistinguishable from thieves; a black man enduring the tonsorial tedium of a hair weaving; the repulsive waste of food in a too affluent world—such things become punctuated with an ironic refrain of "For love!" that echoes the discredited motive of the

personal "dream / a little false" which is identified with the city
and which is bravely and painfully abandoned at the poem's
conclusion:

> Tearful city
>   on a summer's day
> the hard grey
>   dwindling
> in a wall of
>   rain—
>
>   farewell!

It is this unique sort of bravery that serves as the real goal of
the entire sequence as it proceeds poem by poem. "To a Wood
Thrush," for example, the pseudo-ode that prompts the sequence,
involves at once an aesthetic challenge in the bird-song, a personally difficult concession of past failure, and a culturally larger corresponding sense of "a cheated world." From this insecure
beginning, the next three poems survey the casual expressions of
the strength that in "Adam," "Eve," and "St. Francis Einstein of
the Daffodils" will more deliberately address the opening note.
"Fine Work with Pitch and Copper" notes the distinctively male
respect for labor and craftsmanship that pervades even the lunch
hour of some common roofers; "Young Woman at a Window (She
sits with)" is a madonna and child, the mother tearfully sad in her
pose as she affords her child an excellent view of things, "his nose /
pressed / to the glass"; and "The Rose (First the warmth)" draws
the excitement of aesthetic precision in an unfolding flower.

Two more poems then prepare for the more disturbing aspects
of the paternal and maternal fates that will follow. There is an
infatuation with the mechanical obedience of an automaton in "A
Chinese Toy" that anticipates the oppressive "duty" in the life of
"Adam"; and there is another automaton in "La Belle Dame de
Tous Les Jours," only this time grotesque, like the trance-inclined
old woman in "Eve."

Both of these sets of poems are an indirect approach to the more
difficult personal assessment made of the parent figures, and in
their very indirection they seem comparatively timid when the
sequence finally arrives at the three poems that form its heart. In
a similar way, the two poems that follow that core, "The Death of
See" and "To an Elder Poet," anticipate the artistic self-assessment
of "Perpetuum Mobile: The City" with first a farcical obituary of
a poet's murder/suicide pact and then a somewhat glib spurning

of artistic incapicitation. The nervous facileness of both poems functions not only to further translate the aesthetic issue of the section into an explicitly poetic one, but also to add a greater lyrical pressure and impact to the bold candor of the larger poem to follow.

Williams created this basic movement towards personal and aesthetic confidence without much change in the basic ordering for *Adam & Eve & the City.* He merely transposed "A Chinese Toy" and "La Belle Dame de Tous Les Jours"—apparently only to observe the order of male and female principles in the preceding and following sets of poems—and moved "Perpetuum Mobile: The City" out of its place as the final poem for "Cancion," a change that better uses the brevity of the latter as an afterbeat. The excisions he made, however, were more substantial. A single long poem, "The Crimson Cylcamen," which brought to a richer focus the motif of floral beauty from "St. Francis Einstein of the Daffodils," was assigned to the fourth position of "Longer Poems," where it counterpoints the preliminary attempt at an aesthetic definition of the world in "Sour Grapes." And the set of "Translations from the Spanish" to which "Cancion" originally belonged was, except for that single poem, entirely dropped from the Williams canon forever. (The set was apparently an attempt to align more fully the sometimes depressing tropical heritages of the parental figures with the more uplifting lyrical strains of the floral beauty in the section.)

The remaining excision, however, was of a four-part poem entitled "From the Poem 'Patterson'" [sic]. Originally following "The Death of See" and "To An Elder Poet," this conspicuous fragment suggested itself as a representative excerpt from some larger, perhaps alternative poetic world. The sordid affair of "The Death of See" was answered with the most wholesome, happy, and forthright of courtings; and the anxious threat of poetic incapicitation in "To an Elder Poet" was replaced with a happy promise of poetic blessing:

> Your lovely hands
> Your lovely tender hands!
> Reflections of what grace
> what heavenly joy
>
> predicted for the world
> in knowing you—

blest, as am I, and humbled
by such ecstasy.

Of course, the very wholesomeness of the poem probably ac-
counted for its removal from "Adam and Eve and the City," for it
seems a bit out of immediate keeping with the very adult emotional
sophistication toward which the section grows. But unlike the
"Translations from the Spanish," however, the Paterson piece was
retained in *The Complete Collected Poems 1906–1938.*

Retitled "Unnamed: From 'Paterson,'" the poem heads a group
of four identically subtitled fragments ("At the Bar . . ." "Graph
for Action . . ." "Breakfast . . ." and "To Greet a Letter-Carrier
. . .") that precedes the very last poem of the volume's tenth sequence and section, "Recent Verse." There the entire group consolidates the sexual wholesomeness of "Unnamed" and associates it
with an idiomatic usage that redeems with its friendly spirit some
coarse public behaviors. Note for instance how the sexual potency
commonly associated with clams becomes retrieved from its lewd
ignorance by the happy vigor of the raillery in "At the Bar . . .":

Hi, open up a dozen.

Wha'cha tryin' to do—
charge ya batteries?

Make it two.
                    Easy girl!

You'll blow a fuse if
ya keep that up.

A similar sort of chummy ribaldry works in the next two poems
as well. Some orchestrated flatulence in "Graph for Action . . ."
adds real comic charm to the otherwise preposterous cavil over
the complimentary close in some correspondence:

Don't say, "humbly".
"Respectfully", yes
but not "humbly".

And the Committee
both farted
and that settled it.

The scatology of "Breakfast . . ." becomes part of a humorous bequest, the last lines employing the standard phrasing from most wills:

> Twenty sparrows
> on
>
> a scattered
> turd:
>
> Share and share
> alike.

And the greedy complaint of "To Greet a Letter Carrier" is purely a pretext for the friendly hail the speaker so clearly relishes:

> Why'n't you bring me
> a good letter? One with
> lots of money in it.
> I could make use of that.
> Atta boy! Atta boy!

These spare idiomatic expressions of a popular sensibility are at the heart of "Recent Verse" and of its special achievement as the final primary sequence of the volume. Like the Paterson that so embodies a debased "modernity" and so motivates the aesthetic mission in "The Wanderer: A Rococo Study," these Paterson fragments are equally tied in the sequence to a modernity with an overwhelming need for aesthetic deliverance. Yet unlike the longer poem's Paterson, the fragments everywhere display the evidence of not just dedication to the cause but of its preliminary success as well.

Compare for instance the essential charm of the above fragments with the unrelieved squabbling and brutality of the Paterson strikers in "The Wanderer":

> It sank deep into the blood, that I rose upon
> The tense air enjoying the dusty fight!
> Heavy drink where the low, sloping foreheads
> The flat skulls with the unkept black or blond hair

And then compare the privileged familiarity with Paterson's inhabitants that is so surely injected by the idiomatic accuracy of the fragments with the futility of this histrionic address from the

speaker of "The Wanderer" as he responds to his muse's call for
a new recognition of a subtler beauty:

> "Waken! my people, to the boughs green
> With ripening fruit within you!
> Waken to the myriad cinquefoil
> In the waving grass of your minds!
> Waken to the silent phoebe nest
> Under the eaves of your spirit!"
>   .   .   .   .
>
> But my voice was a seed in the wind.

The difference persists in either a lyrical or poetic fashion
throughout every other parallel keynote, and it reveals "The Wanderer" to be nothing less than a romantic melodrama, painfully at
odds with its own modern agenda. There is everywhere in the
longer poem the overwhelming presence of the supernatural, particularly in the metamorphosing crone who serves as the poem's
muse. More like some Mephistopheles than a Calliope, she con-
jures vast panoramas of the world and then empowers the speaker
of "The Wanderer" to reveal in them her own aesthetic body—
"the subtle," as the speaker calls it. But in "Recent Verse," the
muse figure is restrained to the single firm appearance of a modern
window shopper in "Weasel Snout" who brings things to wondrous
if simple beauty—to "daintiness"—merely by admiring them:

> Staring she
> kindles
> the street windows
>
> to daintiness—
> Under
> her driving looks
>
> gems plainly
> colored blue and
> red and
>
> green grow
> fabulous again—She
> is the modern marvel
>
> the ray from
> whose bulbous eyes
> starts

>through glass walls
>to animate
>dead things—

The isolation of the stones and their color in the third stanza secures the primacy of their aesthetic character and effectively precludes any possibility of irony in the following stanza's blunt reference to the woman as "the modern marvel." Yet there is little that is marvelous about her aspect in the usual sense of the word. She is in fact remarkably nondescript. Aside from the "driving looks" and "bulbous eyes" that establish the intensity of her attention, her only distinctive feature is that of the title: "Weasel Snout." And the very failure of the conspicuous ignominy in that title to materialize is itself the really special achievement of the poem's moment, for it effectively disarms any traditional notion of what constitutes the mean and what the precious. Recall, on the other hand, the radically different way a similar phrase functions in "The Strike" segment of "The Wanderer":

>Faces all knoted up like burls on oaks,
>Grasping, fox-snouted, thick-lipped
>Sagging breasts and protruding stomachs,
>Rasping voices, filthy habits with the hands.
>Nowhere you! Everywhere the electric!

"Fox-snouted"—the animal trait entirely confirms a fundamentally depraved state. Of course, it is exactly this depraved state to which the muse dedicates the transformational enegeries of both herself and her aesthetic charge. But it is a depraved state that nonetheless asserts its insuperable features everywhere throughout the long poem—from the parade of spectrous hollow men of "Broadway" to the brutes in the bread line of "The Strike" to the foul Passaic River itself in "St. James Grove." The features mount like so many special effects from a gothic—or perhaps, as the poem's subtitle has it, "rococo"—imagination. And it is against such excess that the quiet and complete effacement of the sordid in "Weasel Snout" is ultimately to be measured.

So too ought we to note how the melodrama of the youth's heroic personalization in "The Wanderer" is expressed in "Recent Verse" as the diffused presence of children who consistently embody the central lyrical principal affirmed by both poetic units—aesthetic refreshment and renewal. In the longer poem, that principle is over and over again established with literally dramatic statement. The speaker asks his muse to "Grant me power to catch something of this day's / Air and sun into your service! / That these toilers after peace and after pleasure / May turn to you, worshippers at all hours!" And the muse responds with an injunction to reveal her beauty in the natural refreshment of a pure mountain landscape, in the "air's clear coolness" and the "richness of greenery." Yet finally the speaker can only accomplish a quixotic call to the world, and the glimpse of his childhood terrain that asserts a renewal is belied by an overweening sense of personal nostalgia:

> . . . the Hackensack
> So quite that seemed so broad formerly:
> The crawling trains, the cedar swamp on the one side—
> All so old, so familiar—so new now

The moments of natural refreshment and renewal in "Recent Verse," however, are far more successful, fused as they are with a human presence of anonymous children who suggest only their present youth rather than some speaker's nostalgic memory. In "The Sun," for instance, the physical immediacy of a breaking dawn and beach surf seamlessly leads to the equally exuberant immediacy of children's play:

> burned wood washed
> clean—
> The slovenly bearded
> rocks hiss—
>
> Obscene refuse
> charms
> this modern shore—
> Listen!
>
> it is a sea-snail
> singing—
> Relax, relent—
> the sun has climbed
>
> the sand is
> drying—Lie
> by the broken boat—
> the eel-grass
>
> bends
> and is released
> again—Go down, go
> down past knowledge

shelly lace—
among the rot
of children
screaming

their delight—
logged
in the penetrable
nothingness

whose heavy body
opens
to their leaps
without a wound—

Literally, the children are at the center of the poem's own stated aesthetics—"down past knowledge" and into the concrete world of sensory refreshment. Yet the children themselves are almost transparent. Through their only vaguely defined image come their sounds: the sibilants of their "screaming" and of the fanciful "shelly lace" into which they transform abstract "knowledge"; the assonance of their "rot" that completes the phonetic passage from that "knowledge" to the punning "logged"[3] and finally to the newly substantiated "body" of atmosphere; and the other echo of their "rot," the one with the only other "r" words in the poem—the hissing "rocks" that most define the visual reference for the poem's sibilance and the sea-snail's song of "Relax, relent" that most defines the poem's lyrical burden; and finally their "delight" that repeats the prominent "sprung" rhyme of "drying—Lie," which itself translates the surging rhythm of the sea into the assumption of an easeful pose. All these sound effects merge the presence of the children into the overall effects of the refreshing sea, and the joyous human spirit they represent becomes identical with an accomplished natural fact.

Finally, there is apparent a similar difference between sequence and longer poem even in the darker components to their respective inspirations. The sinister element in the old woman's possession of the speaker's will in "The Wanderer" is almost a grotesque thing. Her terms are demonic and her manner wicked: "A little wistfully yet in a voice clear cut: 'Good is my over lip and evil / My underlip to you henceforth: / For I have taken your soul between my two hands.'" And the clearly satanic baptismal rite she performs in the poem's final segment is consecrated with the literal filth of the river and with a profound sadness, a sadness of "mourning" that grows out of the clear awareness of damnation in "the wandering."

But in "Recent Verse," such gothic elements are expressed in the more profoundly unnerving terms of the poem "These" that follows the brighter gestures of a recovered culture in the Paterson fragments. The final note of the sequence plunges into a realm of mental despair—

> to an empty, windswept place
> without sun, stars or moon
> but a peculiar light as of thought
>
> that spins a dark fire—
> whirling upon itself until,
> in the cold, it kindles
> to make a man aware of nothing
> that he knows, not loneliness
> itself. . .

There is modern psychology suggested here, especially in the ensuing nervous recognition of the despair as a necessary element in the creative process, and the final sadness in the poem is induced by memory's own capacity for a super-awareness of temporal transience rather than by some primeval curse:

> Hide it away somewhere
> out of the mind, let it get roots
> and grow, unrelated to jealous
>
> ears and eyes—for itself.
> In this mine they come to dig—all.
> Is this the counterfoil to sweetest
>
> music? The source of poetry that
> seeing the clock has stopped, says,
> The clock has stopped
>
> that ticked yesterday so well?
> and hears the sound of lakewater
> splashing—that is now stone.

This more accurate assessment of modern aesthetic psychology—like all the other more accurate assessments of the modern aesthetic predicament—most immediately fulfills the greater sense of specifically contemporary insight that emerges in "Adam & Eve

and The City" (particularly in "St. Francis Einstein of the Daffodils" and "Perpetuum Mobile: The City") as part of that sequence's
fortifying recovery of personal tradition. But it also brings to accomplishment much of the overall volume's impulses. Take, for
instance, the first three poems of the section, the first one of which
is "Classic Scene:"

> A power-house
> in the shape of
> a red brick chair
> 90 feet high
>
> on the seat of which
> sit the figures
> of two metal
> stacks—aluminum—
>
> commanding an area
> of squalid shacks
> side by side—
> from one of which
>
> buff smoke
> streams while under
> a grey sky
> the other remains
>
> passive today—

The scene almost explicitly extends the reevaluation of the urban
landscape begun in "Perpetuum Mobile: The City," but it does so
with more portentous effect. There is vestigial idolatry revealed
in the enthroned colossi, oppressiveness in the arrangement of
service sheds, and an anxious propitiation in the volcanic suggestions of the last lines. The two poems that follow each do something
quite similar. "Autumn" creates some strong suggestions of ritual
interment and propitiation out of the ground breaking ceremonies
for a road project. And "The Term" involves some distinctively
sacrificial dimensions to the automotive trampling of some wind-
blown packing paper. And there is always the same portentous cast
to these elements as there is to the industrial deities of "Classic
Scene." The modern world is, in other words, revealed as a profoundly superstitious one, enslaved to new gods of a more insidious
sort than those of the ancients. The revelation reaches all the way
back to the volume's original impulse toward classicism in "The

Tempers," and it corrects the naive attempt of that section to reinstall that tradition with the insidious reality of its actual transformed presence.

The remainder of the poems summon up and correct other volume keynotes as well. As it counters the portentous classicism with its own, most unpretentious of figures, "Weasel Snout" recalls the strict factual basis finally established for modern beauty in "An Early Martyr"; the old woman herself especially recalls the two women who in "To a Poor Old Woman" and "Proletarian Portrait" of that earlier sequence serve as such excellent representatives of the sequence as a whole. So too when the next two poems ("bringing today / out of yesterday" as the first puts it) introduce the natural isometric force of first an upheaving, gale-force storm ("Advent of Today") and then the ensuing seaside calm and clearing ("The Sun"), the rhythm recalls in more successful terms the difficult struggle in "Sour Grapes" with intensities of natural beauty. And the equivalent aesthetic beauty that both "A Bastard Peace" and "The Poor" perceive in impoverished, industrial, settings recalls in the same way the defeated attachment to those realms in "Al Que Quiere" and "Spring and All."

Similarly, the blissful sense of an aesthetic retirement from a profoundly confused world in "To A Dead Journalist" and "Africa" replays with greater contentment some of the sulking withdrawal in "The Descent of Winter," while "Lovely Ad" and "The Defective Record" revise with almost amusement the angry social indictment of "Spring and All." Then "Middle" finally repeats the aesthetic optimism of "Collected Poems 1934" only without any discrediting element of naiveté. There is only the eminently sensible decision of a doctor to refresh his spirit with a walk through town:

> of this profusion
> a robin flies carrying
> food on its tongue
> and a flag
>
> red white and
> blue hangs
> motionless. Return
> from the sick
>
> wean the mind
> again from among
> the foilage also of
> infection. There

is a brass band at
the monument
and the children
that paraded

the blistering streets
are giving lustily
to the memory
of our war dead.

Remain and listen or
use up the time
perhaps
among the side streets

watching the elms
and rhododendrons the
peonies and
changeless laurels.

Ultimately, this hearty, immensely wholesome jaunt represents as well a poetic embarkation even more profound than the heroic launching of "The Wanderer." For it is out of this happy passage through town that the key "Paterson" fragments of "Recent Verse" arise, and it is those fragments that, spare as they are, so perfectly embody the sense of a work-in-progress, of truly "recent verse," and that so perfectly clarify the lyrical characters of the sequence's medial poems as profoundly suggestive notes—suggestions of the fuller corrections that yet needed to be done, and would be done in *Paterson*.

Part III

The Collected Earlier Poems and
The Collected Later Poems

11

"Much More to It Than I Thought Would Be Involved": Some Problems with the Texts

The Complete Collected Poems 1906–1938 was really an outstanding achievement for Williams, one with which he was greatly pleased. After looking at some proofs for the book in early August 1938, he wrote James Laughlin that "Floss and I have been having an orgy over the damned thing. It has a decided build-up when one reads it through that is something new to us" (Williams and Laughlin 34). And two days latter Flossie Williams as well wrote to Laughlin that "the manuscript of Bill's book reads most interestingly and develops as one reads it consecutively into quiet a chunk of living. It gave me a start the other night as I was reading it" (Letter 8-3-38). It was an effect that Williams apparently sought to consolidate even further by making some last minute changes in ordering and headings, changes which he insisted Laughlin not "veto," regardless of their cost (Williams and Laughlin 34).

But the sort of careful attention that Williams gave to *The Complete Collected Poems 1906–1938* and the kind of great satisfaction he took in it never really attended his final volumes of collected poetry, the 1950 *Collected Later Poems* and the 1951 *Collected Earlier Poems*. As James Laughlin recalls,

> CEP and CLP were put together in very haphazard fashion. Bill turned over to his friend Kitty Hoagland all the poems he could find around the house. She typed them up, he made some corrections, then she did most of the arranging. The chronology is not good and "The Rose" section was at first left out. He had kept no copies of many poems he had sent to magazines and no search was made. (Laughlin)

Of course it seems astonishing that Williams could be so indifferent to the books by which posterity would come to know almost all his poetry outside of *Paterson* as to leave their configurations entirely to Kitty Hoagland! But it is difficult to dismiss Laughlin's memory as altogether faulty. Although Laughlin himself concedes—and manuscript evidence shows—that Williams certainly saw and never objected to the final scripts for the two collections, the greater part of biographical and textual evidence suggests that Williams was anything but in command of their preparation.[1]

Despite having approved the typescripts for *The Collected Later Poems,* for instance, Williams was profoundly disappointed—and entirely surprised—at his actual advance copy of the book. He reported to Laughlin on December 18, 1950, that he was "absolutely crushed" at Babette Deutsch's discovery of numerous outright omissions in the book, an accident he two days later (December 20) attributed to his own careless attention to the galleys and then three more days later (December 23) to "the little bitch" who must have "lost the originals, then, not having noticed the lack, gone on with the typing" (Letters).

Something had clearly gone wrong in Williams's supervision of the book's preparation, and the only remedy available to him at this late stage of production was to have all the omitted poems bunched together under the collective title of "The Rose" and have them included in future bindings as the volume's last section; already bound books would have it simply stuffed into their back covers. Of course, none of this suggests that Kitty Hoagland was responsible for anything more than a few omissions. But a number of other circumstances attending the publication of the book make a deeper involvement on her part—perhaps even in its arrangement, as Laughlin recalls—a very plausible notion.

Hoagland was, to begin with, no mere typist to Williams. She was a genuine literary friend from whose original research Williams had borrowed much material for the historical matter of *Paterson,* Book I (Mariani 464; Whittemore 290-291), and to whom Williams had turned over a short story of his ("Life Along the Passaic") for dramatization upon a local Rutherford stage (*Paris Review* 139; Whittemore 291). Williams himself referred to her in *I Wanted to Write a Poem* as the

> very devoted friend and patient, an educated woman, who took the manuscript [of *The Build-Up*] as I wrote it—at tremendous speed—and transposed [sic] my sometimes illegible writing to the neatly typed page. . . .very possibly the results were distorted because of illegible writing transcribed by a second party. (87)

Whether the "distortions" in *The Build-Up* were intentional or not, Williams clearly tolerated them, perhaps even welcomed them, if we can judge from his affectionate regard for their source. Indeed, according to Reed Whittemore, Williams's first biographer, Hoagland herself claimed a really rather radical editorial role in Book I of *Paterson* (Whittemore 291). There is also in the Williams-Hoagland correspondence at the University of Virginia a carbon of a three-page list of poems that Mrs. Hoagland prepared for Williams, presumably at his invitation, as the suggested contents for his 1949 *Selected Poems* (Williams and Hoagland). And although the ninety poems that eventually constituted that volume include only forty of the one hundred and fifty poems Mrs. Hoagland proposed, the list suggests the type of substantive privilege she may have typically enjoyed in the preparation of Williams's books.

It is not, therefore, entirely implausible that Williams would have entrusted to Mrs. Hoagland real editorial duties in his last two volumes of collected poetry. Moreover, such a delegation may have been a powerfully attractive thing for Williams at the time, for during 1950 and 1951, Williams was preoccupied with things other than his own past poetry.

He was, in the first place, quite enamored of the increasing notoriety that the first three parts of *Paterson* had gained him, and in his retirement he was eagerly assuming a hectic schedule of reading and speaking engagements, book reviews, and essays.[2] Even more important, however, Williams was quite preoccupied throughout 1950 with completing the fourth part of *Paterson,* the work that was really the most explicit and complete fulfillment of his ambitions for major lyrical form.

At the same time, he was equally preoccupied with a more practical ambition for commercial literary success, the exciting possibility for which had finally emerged with David McDowell's offer of a five thousand dollar advance on three books to be published within the next two years by Random House. Driven by ambition and contractual deadlines, Williams spent much of 1950 and most of 1951 putting together his *Collected Stories* (the first Random House book) and actually writing his autobiography and *The Build-Up,* the second and third Random House books. He also spent a few months recovering from a stroke that (at the end of March, 1951) followed four months of obsessive work on the autobiography.

In addition to the substantial demand of these projects upon Williams's attention, there was also the personal estrangement that had developed between Williams and his old publisher, James Laughlin, an estrangement that may well have temporarily dampened Williams's enthusiasm for his own productions at New Directions. Indeed, it was Williams's rather bitter dissatisfaction with

Laughlin's failure to promote aggressively his previous books that had led Williams to deal with McDowell (a former protégé of Laughlin) in the first place. Laughlin in turn felt utterly betrayed by Williams, although he so desperately wanted to retain him as an author that he countered McDowell's offer with his own respectably competitive one of two hundred and fifty dollars per month in perpetuity. But Williams refused, and things grew rancorous; Williams actually hired an attorney to handle his affairs with New Directions.

When a settlement was finally reached, it assigned the remainder of *Paterson* and probably other future poetry to New Directions and left the more lucrative prose projects with Random House. (In fact, however, Williams's next two books of poetry— *The Desert Music* and *Journey to Love*—were placed with McDowell as well.)

Williams and Laughlin would be reasonably reconciled by the year's end, but their squabble made it quite clear where Williams's priorities lay just then—with the popular success that Random House could bring him through its greater resources in distribution and promotion.[3] Indeed, on February 17, just a week or so after Williams had put Laughlin on notice that he was negotiating with Random House, he wrote that although he fully intended to give the new collected poems to Laughlin, he was "particularly anxious to get the short stories [a Random House project] in print again, all of them" (Williams and Laughlin 185). Just then, Laughlin probably wanted these last two volumes of collected poetry more than Williams himself,[4] and in the absence of his own enthusiasm, both Williams and Laughlin may have welcomed a surrogate attention from Kitty Hoagland, especially as it became increasingly clear to Williams that he was overtaxing himself with his multiple projects.

Note for example how Williams very subtly but radically diminished the plans for his last "Collected" work. In the same 17 February letter that declared his special interest in preparing the collected stories, he could still be struck with enough inspiration about the poetry to announce that he "had a hell of a good idea for the *Collected,* something I've been searching for for quite a while. It's new and shd work out to good advantage. You'll see."[5] Yet as the increasingly hectic year passed, Williams began to complain of some unexpected overwork.

"All I'm doing now," he wrote to Laughlin on 27 March, "is trying to get my scripts for the short stories and the poems in order. It is a man's size job, much more to it than I thought would be involved" (Letters). By 10 May, he promised Laughlin that he was "fully engaged with the new Collected" but he cautions that "the new arrangement has to be studied right down to the last word. I'm coming along but it's a bit slow" (Letters). On 16 May and apparently in response to Laughlin's prodding, he declares that "I want to bring the script of the Collected in to you personally" and that he is "in the midst of completing that now," but he also once again explains that "it is more of a job than I anticipated" (Letters).

By 29 August, Williams was on the verge of executing the formal contract with Laughlin that he (Williams) had been demanding, and he finally promises to actually deliver a finished script in exchange: "The minute everything [is] signed he [Williams's attorney, James Murray] will deliver to you the full and carefully checked script of the Collected Later Poems; it will be far better to bring this out first and the earlier volume later— as I have revised and perfected it" (Letters).

"The Collected Later Poems"—judging from the defensive explanation he gave for delivering this volume first, Williams apparently had abruptly changed plans when the time actually came for him to deliver the "Collected" with which he had teased Laughlin throughout the course of their summer's contractual negotiations.[6] No doubt the "man size job" of putting the entire "Collected" or even just the much bulkier *Collected Earlier Poems* together had proven impossible for Williams to handle, so when the time came to actually produce something, he settled upon delivering only the more slender script for *The Collected Later Poems.* Indeed, one wonders just how honest Williams was being when he referred to that script as "full and carefully checked." He would, after all, also declare in a later letter, dated "Yom Kippur, 1950," that despite exhaustion, he was eager to return the page proofs for the book and would "stay up all night for it" (Letters). Yet just three months later he would confess to "haste in correcting the galleys" when the volume's omissions were finally brought to his attention.

The relationship between Williams and Laughlin was, in other words, apparently complicated by all the bluff and feints that normally attend wary business deals. And so it is difficult to tell just how much real attention Williams did in fact give to any aspect of *The Collected Later Poems,* from its simple contents to its lyrical arrangement.

By the same token, however, *The Collected Earlier Poems* should have benefited from the lesson of its earlier companion volume. But even in the final preparation of that book, there was another, quite unexpected sort of interference: Williams's stroke of 28 March 1951. Given the severity of the stroke, it is surely amazing that during the following four weeks, Williams was able to both finish revising the last third of the *Autobiography* for Mc-Dowell (Mariani 631) *and* send off to Laughlin a complete script for *The Collected Earlier Poems* (Williams and Laughlin 202–4).

Yet somehow he did, assuring Laughlin moreover on 21 May that "there is no such omission in the case of the Earlier Collected" (Williams and Laughlin 203). Perhaps there were no such omissions, but measured against the competitive demands of the *Autobiography* and the at least partial incapicitation of his stroke, Williams's implied claim to genuine diligence and thoroughness seems almost as preposterous as the notion that Williams would have substantially left the book's arrangement to Kitty Hoagland.

Ultimately, such circumstantial considerations shed a strange light on even the direct manuscript evidence of Williams's personal involvement in the preparation of his own books. None of the evidence in the final typescript for *The Collected Later Poems,* for instance, eliminates with any real certainty the possibility that Hoagland was responsible for the substantive arrangement of that volume.[7] The relatively few proof corrections that are scattered throughout the script in Williams's own hand prove only that he approved (and carelessly at that) the final versions of the individual poems; nothing indicates that he himself originated either the organization or the sectioning of the book as a whole.

Indeed, the original section titles seem suspiciously more like the result of a typist's convenience than an author's thoughtful lyrical or thematic intention: sections representing previously published groupings were simply named as they originally were, and newly created sections were simply named after their individual lead poems. Thus, the title pages of the typescript could propose something so uninventive as "INCOGNITO etc" for one new section and "BALLAD OF FAITH etc" for another.

The etceteras seemed to bother even Laughlin, who scratched them and proposed his own uncertain alternative of "and Other Poems (?)." He was also bothered by another feature of the typescript—the placement of the "Author's Introduction" after the title page for "The Wedge." Thinking that the introduction belonged to the whole book rather than to just the lead section, Laughlin made a note on the title page to check with Williams on the matter. And Williams did in fact answer Laughlin's queries, along with others about acknowledgements and copyrights, in a letter dated 10 September 1950: the introduction belonged only to "The Wedge," and Laughlin's alternative phrasing was acceptable (Letters). But the answers and the letter in general are more telling in their tone than in their substance, for they suggest a basic indifference more than any serious attention on Williams's part.

About the "Author's Introduction," Williams was of course definitive; it had always belonged to just "The Wedge." But about Laughlin's alternative phrasing for the section titles, he was amiably apathetic: "it might be better as you suggest to say, 'and other poems' instead of 'etc' where that occurs in some of the half-titles."[8] And he was the same on a number of other points Laughlin had raised:

> #7, no use bothering with dates, the dates when the various groupments appeared. However, the total list of the poems as you have them is a chronological one. It isn't important.

> #8, you might indicate somewhere on the jacket that this is work covering a 10 year span, 1940 to 1950, 55 to 65 of my age. Even that means little. You've always done a good job on covers, suit yourself.

> I hope I can keep kicking along until all my committments [sic] have been completed. It looks like a heavy schedule but I ain't discouraged. And I'm NOT interested in prizes, so don't let that bother you.

Small points as they may have been, the character of Williams's reaction both to them and to any ambition for the volume's special success lends support to the notion that he may have been indifferent as well to the very fundamentals of organization and titling in *The Collected Later Poems*. It is, on the other hand, almost absolutely certain that he himself named and ordered at least the overall sections of *The Collected Earlier Poems*. Inserted throughout the final and otherwise continuously paginated typescript for that volume are Williams's own handwritten and numbered (in Roman numerals) title pages for the individual parts. (The pagination *may* be in Williams's hand as well.) Yet even here, his involvement may have only resulted in yet another major production blunder.

As originally written, the title pages indicate the following sequence for the sections and longer poems:[9]

(I) The Wanderer
(II) The Tempers
(III) March
(III^B) History
(IV) Al Que Quiere
(V) Fish
(V^B) Romance Moderne

(VI) Sour Grapes
(VII) Paterson
(VIII) The Flower
(IX) Spring and All
(X) Struggle of Wings
(XI) Descent of Winter
(XII) Impromptu: The Suckers
(XIII) Collected Poems: 1934
(XIV) An Early Martyr
(XV) Della Primavera Transportata al Morale
(XVI) An Elegy for D. H. Lawrence
(XVII) Adam & Eve and the City
(XVIII) Morning
(XIX) The Crimson Cyclamen
(XX) Recent Verse
(XXI) The Drunkard

Reflecting as it does a primarily chronological ordering, the sequence differs from the printed version in its placement of "An Early Martyr" and "Della Primavera Transportata al Morale." In the printed version, those sections are reversed and then placed much earlier in the book—between "History" and "Al Que Quiere," parts IIIB and IV. The difference results from Williams's own directions on two of the title pages.

On the title page for "An Early Martyr" he wrote "(To follow Section XV & renumber the pages accordingly)," and thus the sections were intended to be transposed, probably in order to better observe both chronology and perhaps even the strong lyrical connection between "Collected Poems: 1934" and "Primavera" that had been established in *The Complete Collected Poems 1906–1938,* where the two parts were actually merged. But then on the title page to "Della Primavera Transportata al Morale" he wrote "*Note:* Place this section (XV) before section IV and renumber the pages accordingly."

In all probability, Williams actually meant simply to repeat his previous order for transposition—to place XV before *XIV,* not IV. Laughlin (or a copy editor) apparently recognized just such an intention, and the typescript was in fact reorganized and repaginated accordingly, in which state it still remains. But when the book was finally printed, William's *literal* directions were somehow followed, and the two later sections (1930 and 1935) were placed before the much earlier (1917) "Al Que Quiere."

If Williams did simply mis-write his Roman numeral, no doubt his recent stroke played a part in the error. The aftereffects of the stroke might also have combined with a basic lack of concern for the book's production to prevent Williams from noticing the confusion in the galleys. On the other hand, it is perfectly possible that Williams meant exactly what he wrote, for he never did register any complaint about the final outcome. As with much of *The Collected Later Poems,* there is no really convincing evidence one way or the other. Thus, with the exception of the omissions from *The Collected Later Poems,* we must ultimately assume Williams to hold responsibility for the arrangements of the books—whether or not he actually authored or really approved of those arrangements— and it is ultimately to the actual texts of those books that we must turn for the facts of their lyrical and structural accomplishment.

12

The Collected Earlier Poems:
An Inferior Successor

Given the really impressive achievement of *The Complete Collected Poems 1906–1938* and Williams's own satisfaction with it, it is curious that Williams should have been interested in producing a new *Collected Earlier Poems* at all. Indeed, as has already been noted, the first two typescripts for the volume were simply repetitions of the 1938 edition. Yet by the time of the third and final typescript, Williams had somehow (perhaps with stroke-impaired judgment) settled upon *The Collected Earlier Poems* as we know it, and the product testifies to nothing so much as the wisdom of a popular old saying: "If it ain't broke, don't fix it." On its own literary merits (and without regard to the production difficulties discussed earlier), the new volume seems more like a bungled recast of the 1938 volume than a genuine revision of it.

Violating an otherwise clear respect for chronology throughout most of the new volume, two previously contiguous sections— "Della Primavera Trasportata Al Morale" (1928; separated out again from "Collected Poems 1934") and the 1936 "An Early Martyr"—are in the 1951 volume inexplicably placed between the much earlier "The Tempers" (1913) (which here subsumes "Transitional" as well) and "Al Que Quiere" (1917). Since the only change to the actual substance of the transferred sequences is the addition of some six, lyrically inconsequential poems to "An Early Martyr," the result of this shuffle is to place two sections full of emotional and social sophistication right smack between two full of innocent sexual, literary, and social idealism.[1] The larger effect is to render the two earlier sections as almost comically fatuous episodes and thus to belittle along with those episodes the profound desire for aesthetic growth that had previously served as the overall volume's fundamental motivation. It all seems a dubious effect, to say the least.

So does the very conspicuous irregularity that the relocation of sequences creates in the volume's placement of its longer poems, which except for the stretch from "Della . . ." to "Al Que Quiere," are routinely interspersed *between* sections. This anomaly, however, seems quite in keeping with the equally nonsensical revisions to the order and actual roll of longer poems. Instead of simply juxtaposing the superbly matched longer poems and sequences of *Complete Collected Poems 1906–1938,* for instance, *The Collected Earlier Poems* takes the previously final sequence, "The Wanderer," and places it at the head of the volume, directly before "The Tempers."

The intent is clearly thematic, recognizing as it does the episode of poetic embarkation that the longer poem constitutes. But in a more substantive way, the placement only creates a deep thematic confusion, for "The Wanderer" involves a profound (if flawed) discovery of and commitment to "modernity," and it seems absolutely bizarre to move from these things to the classical fawning of "The Tempers."

So too do the confusions continue in the selection and arrangement of the longer poems that succeed "The Tempers." Retrieving the old long poem "History" from the original *Al Que Quiere, The Collected Earlier Poems* partners with it "March" and then places them both right on the heels of "The Tempers." The ostensible logic here is again more thematic than anything else, resting as it does in the antiquity that as a subject dominates all three poetic units, yet even here the relative enamorment with and positive use of the ancient world and its legacy fail to recognize the fundamental difficulties confronted within those realms in the preceding sequence.

Lyrically, the arrangement makes even less sense, despite the fact that all the poems were composed within the space of a few years and perhaps a single stage of Williams's emotional life. The ruthless aesthetic vigor of "March" and the rather successful, sensuously sophisticated necromancy of "History" are quite out of keeping with the frustrated adolescent dreaminess that (in the poems previously grouped as "Transitional") closes "The Tempers." On the other hand, the long poems are to some extent a preparation for the happier spirit of the lead poem in the ensuing "Della Primavera Trasportata al Morale." But they entirely fail to anticipate the disturbing self-doubt that concludes that sequence in its last few poems.

A similar defect is noticeable in the paired placement of "Paterson" and "The Flower" between "Sour Grapes" and "Spring and

All," the fifth and sixth sequences. Both longer poems clearly share a measure of localism in their themes, but the supremely tough aesthetic certitude that reclaims the tawdry social reality of "Paterson" forms an implausible precedent to the personal and artistic retrenchment that flinches from that same reality in "The Flower." And taken together, the two moments seems a pointlessly erratic recovery from the personal aesthetic terror that evolves out of "Sour Grapes," just as they form an equally incomprehensible preparation for the public aesthetic struggle with an unregenerate world that follows in "Spring and All."

In a similar way, a richly evocative memory of the Scandinavian sea's enormous abundance in "Fish" is joined to the hyperactive mountain episode of "Romance Moderne," apparently on the common basis of the surface naturalism in both poems. Yet they are radically discontinuous lyrically. The former poem is deeply nostalgic and peaceful while the latter is thoroughly fantastic and manic. Even more importantly, the poems together fail to convey effectively the lyrical passage between the two sequences they separate. After the irascibility and deliberate solitude that end the preceding "Al Que Quiere," for instance, the sublime memory of "Fish" introduces far too quickly an entirely too contented episode. And while the manic "Romance Moderne" does indeed anticipate the hyper state of aesthetic terror that concludes the ensuing "Sour Grapes," it more immediately contradicts the far more temperate and adult state that opens the sequence.

It is the same everywhere throughout the volume: lyrical disjunctions from sequence to poem to sequence. Of course, part of the overall problem here is the basic placement itself of longer poems *between* sections. Instead of allowing the poems to speak retrospectively to the larger lyrical accomplishments of a whole set of preceding sequences (as did the final "Longer Poems" in *The Complete Collected 1906–1938*), this new arrangement forces the poems to perform within a serial sort of lyrical continuity and to narrowly address the most immediately contiguous lyrical elements within the sequences. Combined with the poor lyrical matches among the various poetic units, the entire scheme is enough to obscure any kind of lyrical coherence in the volume at all.

Given the lyrically ineffective organization of the entire volume, it is no surprise that the one section in it that truly reconceives a part of Williams's canon does so along thematic lines. "The Drunkard" is an original arrangement of twenty-five poems from a variety of sources. Some were either previously uncollected or entirely unpublished; some were taken from two earlier volumes (*An Early Martyr* and *The Clouds*) and the 1941 New Directions "Poet of the Month" pamphlet *The Broken Span* (an arrangement that is further dismembered in *The Collected Later Poems*); and two poems— "Paterson: Episode 17," and "The Waitress"—served as longer poems in the *The Complete Collected Poems 1906–1938*. Yet despite its diversity of sources, the section displays a very prominent unity of theme.

Take, for instance, the similarity of the rhetorical intent and idea in the opening and closing of the section. As the first and title poem of the group, "The Drunkard" establishes as something of a keynote Williams's personal justification of his aesthetic values to his mother. The poem is prefaced by an explanation of its recent recovery from a 1923 letter that Williams had sent to her, and included in the explanation is this excerpt from the letter itself:

> Here is a poem to set beside some of my 'incomprehensible' latter work. I think you will like this one. It seems the sort of thing that I am going to do. Art is a curious command. We must do what we are bidden to do and can go only so far as the light permits. I am always earnest as you, if anyone, must know. But no doubt I puzzle you—as I do myself. Plenty of love from your son. W.

The statement highlights the declarative nature of the ensuing poem itself and reveals the figure of the bum in it to be not so much an imagistic portrait as an embodiment of some very abstract ideas:

> You drunken
> tottering
> bum
>
> by Christ
> in spite of all
> your filth
>
> and sordidness
> I envy
> you
>
> It is the very face
> of love
> itself

        abandoned
        in that powerless
        commital

        to despair

Aside from some generic details like "drunken" and "filth," there is little that is visual here, so that the real impression of the poem is not the physical repulsiveness of the tramp himself, but the strength of the speaker's conviction about the bum's ethical and aesthetic value. The profane oath taking of "by Christ"; the intensive usage of "very face / of love / itself"; the utter seriousness of the final and starkly isolated "to despair"—these elements emerge to define the poem.

    It is that same steadfast commitment to the idea of what Stevens called the "anti-poetic" that at the end of the section reappears within the more discursive, academic idiom of "The Phoenix and The Tortoise." Contending with Kenneth Rexroth's objection to surrealism (and specifically to the surrealist Nicholas Calas) as mere freak-fetishism, the speaker exerts his full scholastic strength in a barrage of interpretation, supposition, conditional clauses, conclusions, and supporting quotation:

        the six-legged cow, the legless woman

        for each presents a social concept
        seeking approval, a pioneer society
        and a modern asserting the norm
        by stress of the Minotaur.

        It's a legitimate manoeuvre,
        perhaps it is all art
        and Barnum our one genius (in the arts

        . . . .

               . . . If so,

        in spite of Rexroth, Barnum
        our Aeschylus, we
        should show ourselves
        more courteous to Calas the Greek

        . . . .

"If, in a study such as this, in which the ideas of the writer are discussed, we stop short at questions concerning form, it is because forms—and I hope this appears clearly in everything I have so far said—are for us tightly bound up with ideas and feelings . . . and when ideas are erroneous and when feelings are untrue, then conformity bursts out and appears in form."

Clearly there is a certain development in the terms of the aesthetic issue at hand here, but the surrealist monstrosities that this speaker finally embraces as "details of / The Greatest Show on Earth—if / the mind survive and I be an American"—are in principle identical to the repulsive derelict that is embraced in "The Drunkard." It is an equation that the final prose quotation helps point up by recalling the similarly elucidating use of a prose preface in the earlier poem. And again, it is the conviction itself rather than some visual image or emotional state that defines the moment here. Except for the quick notation of just some two monstrosities, the poem is all rationalization, a polemic within a rather well defined aesthetic debate, replete with specific personalities, positions, and texts.

The basic frame of the section is, in other words, more thematic than lyric. And it is an emphasis repeated throughout the interior poems of the arrangement. Again and again, the same sort of "point" is made with a remarkable lack of affective variety. There is the serious devotion to a local river and some immigrant "Polack" thieves upon its bank in "The Marriage Ritual." There is the sure assertion of "the godly" in some meadow grass upon a cinder-bank in "The Province." There is the literally cocky endorsement of "the gutter, where everything comes / from, the manure heap" as the source of the "marvelous" in "Fragment." There is a heartfelt patriotism pledged in "The United States." There is the righteous diminishment of foreign exoticism in favor of the aesthetic localism manifest in the "Passic's dignity" of "The Men." There is the axiomatic statement of "disorder (a chaos)" as a fructuous thing in "Descent." And there is the unflappable rebuttal to a detractor's mockery of the speaker's life in "You Have Pissed Your Life." The baseline of self-assertion reads like a credo of Williams's most notable ideas on the "anti-poetic," the local, and the American idiom.

Even the section's two former "longer poems" are caught up in the dominant thematic current of the gathering. The rich and subtle lyrical states of those poems that had been so emphasized in the 1938 arrangement are here bracketed by far less dimensional elements. Coming immediately upon the heels of the declaration in "The Drunkard," for instance, much of the confusion in the response to the Beautiful Thing of "Paterson: Episode 17" becomes overshadowed by the simple compassion in the poem for this downtrodden woman, a quality that more accurately echoes the simple feeling expressed for the downtrodden man in the preceding poem. And then intervening between "Paterson: Episode 17" and "The Waitress" is not the meditational discipline of "The Crimson Cyclamen" but the simpler sadness of "The Last Words of My English Grandmother," so that "The Waitress" loses its special significance as a lyrically rehabilitated response to the same sort of female beauty that lies at the center of "Paterson: Episode 17." Instead, there lingers the pathos of the grandmother poem, and the entire set of three poems—"Paterson: Episode 17," "The Last Words of My English Grandmother," and "The Waitress"—come off like a thematic trio, merely illustrating the essential position of "The Drunkard" with similar statements of affection for three variously abused women.

What makes all this ineffective for the lyrical design of the volume as a whole is that the really disturbing elements—the violent assault upon Beautiful Thing, the angry loss of self-determination for an dying old woman, the demeaning necessities of employment for the waitress—these things are taken as simple absolutes within a calm and ultimately inexplicable empathy. And that calm empathy, while it clarifies Williams's aesthetic and social values that developed over the years, also obscures the real labor in the development of those positions—the labor that is fundamentally manifest in the chronologically and lyrically superior arrangement of 1938.

13

The Collected Later Poems:
A More Uniform Record

It is perhaps a bit unfair to judge *The Collected Earlier Poems* of 1951 according to the standards of its predecessor volume, *The Complete Collected Poems 1906–1938*. But the accomplishment of that early book—its lyrical coherence, its poetic organization—is just so strong that it is impossible not to.

The Collected Later Poems, on the other hand, suffers from the shadow of no such precedent; the works it includes are collected here for the first time. Nor does *The Collected Later Poems* face the same difficult task as did its companion volumes, for it includes only a single decade's work, and it is, moreover, work from a mature and poetically stable period of Williams's art—the 1940s, when he was writing *Paterson* as well. But by the same token, there are in *The Collected Later Poems* none of the specific sources of large scale poetic and lyrical articulation that inform the other volumes. There is nothing like the large growth from the awkward classicism of "The Tempers" to the spare and incisive gestures of modernity in "Recent Verse." There is instead a generally equivalent poetic accomplishment and emotional disposition throughout the book.

"The Wedge," for instance, the 1944 collection that opens *The Collected Later Poems,* bears an essential resemblance in feeling, idiom, technique, sensibility, and aesthetic values to the 1949 grouping "Two Pendants: for the Ears" that closes the book. Throughout both sections there is an easy and confident aesthetic vitiation of some major human scourges. In "The Wedge," the scourge is the natural force of violent upheaval and conflagration into which Williams translates the military violence that so wracked the world in World War II. In "Two Pendants: for the Ears," the scourge is the impending loss of an elderly mother that comes to typify the anxious prospect of all individual human death. Yet despite the objective distress of these profound plights, the poems of both sections almost axiomatically transform them into the source of an aesthetic joy bred from the most casual language attesting to the most common of beauties.

Note, for instance, how some post-holiday languour in "Burning the Christmas Greens" (from "The Wedge") is entirely disarmed by an accurate eye for the aesthetic brilliance in the very incineration of the season's adornments:

> were walking there. All this!
> and it seemed gentle and good
> to us. Their time past,
> relief! The room bare. We
>
> stuffed the dead grate
> with them upon the half burnt out
> log's smoldering eye, opening
> red and closing under them
>
> .   .   .   .
>
> and quick in the contracting
> tunnel of the grate
> appeared a world! Black
> mountains, black and red—as
>
> yet uncolored—and ash white,
> an infant landscape of shimmering
> ash and flame and we, in
> that instant, lost,
>
> breathless to be witnesses,
> as if we stood
> ourselves refreshed among
> the shining fauna of that fire.

There is such a casual movement to the anecdotal rhythms here that it is easy not to notice just how carefully achieved is the transition from the nostalgic distraction of the first stanza to the alert immediacy of the second, a transition that makes the poem's final refreshment in "the shining fauna of that fire" seem a nearly inescapable lyrical conclusion. Notice how the surprising exclamation "relief!" so symmetrically yet unobtrusively answers the repining "All this!" diagonally across the first stanza; how the emphatic assonance of "relief!" and "We" in that same stanza's last line jolts the embedded phrase "The room bare" away from its usually disconsolate associations; how at the same time that phrase reaches back to redefine as precursors of joy the pensive phrases that it echoes (the parallel "Their time past" and the rhyming preterit "were walking there" that floats the beginning of the stanza). Then notice in the next stanza how in a similar way the words "grate" and "eye" stand out from the balanced network of assonance among the other stressed words—how the long a and i sounds of the words distinguish themselves from the short u of "stuffed" and "under"; from the short e of "dead" and "red"; the short o of "upon" and "log's"; the back o of "smoldering," "opening," and "closing"— from all the sounds that establish a sense of post-holiday malaise, so that the two distinctive words and their images very effectively dominate that malaise and prepare for the rapt visual attention that fixes itself upon the newly fueled fire later in the poem.

Along with this sort of unimpeachable poetic expertise, there is also in "Burning the Christmas Greens" a remarkable measure of sheer stability—even complacency—in the broader lyrical intelligence that governs the entire poem. There is simply never any question of the poem's values or its ultimate lyrical target. Indeed, it opens with three stanzas that very much appear to be a précis of what is to follow:

> Their time past, pulled down
> cracked and flung to the fire
> —go up in a roar
>
> All recognition lost, burnt clean
> clean in the flame, the green
> dispersed, a living red,
> flame red, red as blood wakes
> on the ash—
>
> and ebbs to a steady burning
> the rekindled bed become
> a landscape of flame
>
> At the winter's midnight
> we went to the trees . . .

This almost frighteningly efficient attachment to purgation resonates throughout the entire poem and makes all its lyrical moments but a preparation for a inevitable return of the opening note. (Recall, for instance, how the later phrase "time past" in the previously cited stanza will echo the same phrase from the poem's ruthless first line.) So that in terms of both poetic and lyrical development, there is much less open structure here, much less intrinsic tension forward beyond the immediate poem and towards a further resolution. Things seem quite under control.[1]

They seem equally so at the very end of the volume. Note for instance how the following excerpts from the title poem of "Two Pendants: for the Ears" establish on a broader scale a similar pattern. An unequivical statement of lyrical disposition is followed first by an essential poetic rhythm established within the difficulty at hand, then by an efficient transformation of that rhythm into the vehicle for an unimpeachable joy. First the son's public determination not to sentimentalize his mother's passing:

> How can you weep for her? I
> cannot, I her son—though
> I could weep for her without
> compromising the covenent
>
> She will go alone.

Then a bit later the upsetting exchange of an inauspicious hospital visit:

> Elena is dying.
> In her delirium she said
> a terrible thing:
>
> Who are you? NOW!
> I, I, I, I stammered. I
> am your son.
>
> Don't go. I am unhappy.
>
> About what? I said
>
> About what is what.
>
> The woman (who was watching)
> added:
> She thinks I'm her father.

Then finally, at the end of the poem, the same sorts of elements from that exchange—the shock and urgency of the mother's question; the play of nonplus in her failures of recognition and her echolalic answers; the pathos of her plea not to be left; the distressing news of the other woman's reportage—these elements reappear, realigned with a moment of unshakeable cheer:

Elena is dying

> The canary, I said, comes and sits
> on our table in the morning
> at breakfast, I mean walks about
> on the table with us there
> and pecks at the table-cloth

He must

be a smart little bird

Good-bye!

Now it is the delightful news of a hungry and fearless canary that is set against the factual refrain of the woman's approaching death, and it is the son's blithe and aesthetically attentive reportage of that trivial event that comes to possess something like the urgency and nonplus of the earlier episode. Echoing his own stammer of "I, I, I, I," the son repeats himself in and out of dialogue with an insistent "I said" and "I mean," then efficiently departs from a now clear headed, even ironical old woman. The temporary disconcertion of the earlier delirium has, in other words, been effectively worked into a happy and salutary aesthetic outlook that simply precludes the usual (and useless) sentimentalities of filial devotion.

This kind of basic poetic, aesthetic, and lyrical success characterizes the volume from beginning to end, and as a result the arrangement of the book never approaches anything like the dynamism of the 1938 collection. Yet there is *The Collected Later Poems* a discernible change in at least the specific terms and surface spirit of its success: the focus upon elemental landscapes and powers in "Burning the Christmas Greens" differs fundamentally from the unique family circumstances of "Two Pendants: for the Ears"; and despite a common efficiency in the aesthetic perspectives of the two poems, there is an equal (if not profound) distinction between the impatient disposal of outdated holiday ornaments and the essentially solicitous regard for the recovery of an elderly mother's health. These sorts of differences reflect the volume's overall movement away from what amounts to a tendentious expression of an aesthetic ideology and toward the simply confident expression of a special aesthetic identity.

As it is measured in the discrete stages of the volumes ten separately titled units, that movement runs something like this.[2] "The Wedge" opens the volume with a vigorous, almost zealous promotion of the *principle* of violence and upheaval as forces of aesthetic renewal: everything from a volcanic eruption to the blatant language of an immigrant to the combat of warfare itself is delightedly embraced as an effective way to awaken a chronically insensible world to the possibilities of new beauty. Then "The Clouds" brings a similar orientation to bear upon the aesthetic materialism that it proposes as the ultimate reality: an essentially constant pleasure in the beauties of the physical world becomes inseparable from a corollary denunciation of the perceptual obfuscations allegedly produced by religious spiritualism. Together, these two opening sections constitute over half the volume, and if for no other reason than sheer bulk, they pose the major themes for the entire volume—aesthetic renovation and aesthetic materialism—and place them within the equally dominant framework of a happy but essentially tendentious and philosophic spirit.

These are, in short, the major facts of the volume, and it is to them that the remainder of the book—if it is to cohere at all—needs must address itself. The first four succeeding units do so with considerable fidelity but also with greater lyrical focus and variety. "Ballad of Faith" repeats the theme of aesthetic materialism by *satirically* (rather than simply tendentiously) distinguishing it from such ersatz substitutes as simple consumerism and political secularism; it also grows just a bit less shrill in the proclamation of its aesthetic truth. "All That Is Perfect in Woman," on the other hand intensifies the theme of an aesthetically fructuous violence with an almost perversely thrilling glimpse of the slaughter in a world at war. Then "The Rat" restrains the boldness of that theme by translating the violence into such milder subversions of the civil order as a healthy social irreverence and a vital sexual curiosity. Finally, "Choral: The Pink Church" raises the pitch yet again by elevating aesthetic materialism into an episode of sexual initiation that amounts to nothing less than a sublime gospel of fleshly salvation.

The overall effect of the greater lyrical accent in these sections is two-fold: it adds some kind of lyrical variety, at least in pitch, to the basic sense of absolute conviction that governs "The Wedge" and "The Clouds"; and in so doing, it obscures a bit the fundamentally tendentious basis upon which both the themes and that sense of self-satisfied conviction ultimately rest.

The last four units, however, more effectively erode that tendentiousness itself as the easy assertions of an a priori aesthetic philosophy give way to the more difficult conclusions of a personal artistic appraisal. "Incognito" dramatically wrenches the volume out of its automatic complacency with at least some measure of outright if only fleeting self-doubt. The major themes and motifs of the volume come to appear as states of artistic sensibility undergoing self-appraisal: fructuous violence appears in a number of poems as the momentary agitation of a reflective and finally hopeful mind; and a superior corporeal reality reveals itself in, among other things, the remembered image of a woman's suddenly exposed breast that signals a tranquil close to introspective questions about poetic goals.

The aesthetic conclusions, in other words, remain the same, as does the finally self-assured sensibility. But such moments do signal the emergence in the volume of a much less *tendentious* sensibility, one that is far more emotionally open to even the established anathemas of the earlier units. The much bashed spiritualism of "The Clouds," for instance, is now appreciated as the pathetically desperate attempt to the speaker's feeble mother to hold on to a reality of any kind. And the mother herself, viewed with great sympathy and compassion, comes finally to replace the too easily anonymous opponents of correct aesthetic thought that were previously condemned so routinely.

In this same emotionally open and tolerant spirit, the speaker of "The Birth of Venus" troubles himself to refine the notion of a renewing violence in order to eliminate from it the objectively disturbing traces of literal bloodletting that retrospectively seem more a product of tendentious overstatement than of true ghoulishness. "An April of small waves—deadly as all slaughter" comes to replace war as the best arousal of a stagnant world. And the more benign spirit behind that replacement leads as well to the broad and happy call for artistic and aesthetic fellowship that in "14 New Poems (1950)" comes to replace the rather pervasive censure of bad art in the earlier units of the volume. And finally, the very personal basis for this change in spirit leads in "Two Pendants: for the Ears" to a complete translation of the volume's two major themes from out of the abstract positions of aesthetic philosophy and into the specific aesthetic legacies bequeathed by a muse-mother to her poet-son. In sum, the efficient transformation of the world's difficulties into its aesthetic pleasures becomes compelling testimony more than convincing truth per se.

Nothing in all this has changed the essential thematic or lyrical substance of the volume. The same aesthetic upheaval and coporeal beauty so relished by "The Wedge" and "The Clouds" are relished as well by "Incognito" and "Two Pendants: for the Ears." And with just a brief exception in "Incognito," it is a uniformly confident mood that governs the entire book. Nor has there ever really evolved any significant forward momentum to the collection; no clear lyrical tension has evolved to demand resolution. Yet a change has occurred: a tendentious and theoretically minded spirit has given way to a more tolerant, personal one, and an aesethetic philosophy has given way to an aesthetic identity. It is almost as though the later sections were deliberately assembled to correct a single flaw in Williams's poetic record of the forties without having to meddle with the original text of the two major collections for that period. All in all, however, *The Collected Later Poems* does not redefine that record in any fully lyrical way profound enough to merit much regard for (or further examination of) the book as an extended sequence in its own right.

Conclusion: "They Say I'm Not Profound"

"They say I'm not profound" complained a line from Williams's 1945 poem "Aigeltinger," and what they probably meant of course was that Williams's poetry lacked both great ideas and large-scale form. Fortunately, *Paterson* pretty much silenced such criticism, although it still manages to voice itself every now and then.[1] But in 1945, the year before *Paterson I* appeared, Williams was still insecure enough to be very much upset by the charge. He would, for instance, almost rant at length over the issue of his form and meaning in a 25 July letter to Norman Macleod:

> My poetry appears to most as formless, to the neo-orthodox as an offense to be safely ignored. The God-damned fools. . . .So that when I say, and some well-meaning critic attacks my intelligence for saying it, that art has nothing to do with metaphysics—I am aiming at the very core of the whole matter. Art is some sort of an honest answer, the forms of art, the discovery of the new in art forms—but to mix that with metaphysics is the prime intellectual offense of my day. But who will understand that?
>
> The first part of *Paterson* begins my detailed reply of which I want only to live to complete the full four parts—but already I have been informed that *Paterson* will not be accepted because of its formlessness, because I have not organized it into some neo-classical *recognizable* context. Christ! Are there no intelligent men left in the world? (*Selected Letters* 238–239)

Given Williams's level of frustration with the critics and his determination to make *Paterson* his definitive answer to them, it is not surprising that he was so thankful for Macleod's offer to dedicate an upcoming number of *Briarcliff Quarterly* to him. A critical retrospective would help him succeed with the sequence. "I need help to hold it [*Paterson*], and to tame it—a little," he would confess right after bemoaning the lack of a patron for the work's eventual publication. "That's why I want," he continued, "if I can get it, coherence in any aggolmerate that you would publish touching me. I want a transfixing light through the whole. But not too blinding a glare, just a candle light" (*Selected Letters* 239).

Presumably, the "whole" was Williams's achievement to date and the "candle light" of coherence for it would enlighten both Williams and the rest of the world just enough so that he could better manage the great task of *Paterson* and the world could be more disposed to receive it. As Williams put it in the opening of his letter, it all really amounted to an important opportunity to vindicate his poetic record:

> What I'd most appreciate would be to have the whole coherent, if possible, lucid. For I know that whatever my life has been it has been single in purpose, simple in design and constantly directed to one end of discovery, if possible, of some purpose in being alive, in being a thinking person and in being an active force. The purpose in my "composit" [sic] is never clear or has never been made clear. Oh well, that's to be found by the critic, not me. I know my own difficult answer and it is not to be put into words—but work.
>
> Poetry, an art, is what answer I have. (*Selected Letters* 238)

In fact, Williams's "composit" work had already given something of its own answer. The volumes of collected poetry he had put together during 1930s really did succeed in establishing a coherent structure and a profound meaning for the whole of his poetic record, but the coherence and profundity were not of the conventionally recognizable sort. They were instead the features of the work's constituent lyrical identities as those identities were aligned together within the single and simple design of his poetic life—within his passionate desire to establish the supremacy of a generally aesthetic and specifically poetic perception of life.

So, for instance, in gathering together Williams's tacit lyrical sequences of the 1920s (*Spring and All,* "Della Primaverra Transportata al Morale," and "The Descent of Winter"), *Collected Poems 1921–1931* revised them, added to them a longer poem and two new lyrical groupings, and then arranged the whole bunch to reveal in their composite a single and hard-won triumph of aesthetic optimism over an archetypal old woman's depressive imagination. So too did *The Complete Collected Poems 1906–1938* revise and arrange the groupings for Williams's originally separate volumes of verse in order to vindicate every stage and broad lyrical moment of his work as part of a continuous and profound poetic dedication to the modern age.

In both instances, the result of such comprehensive alignment was the creation of a new and unique lyrical sequence on a major scale—the creation of a super-sequence—that not only redefined Williams's poetic record but also animated its considerable bulk with something quite like the compelling dynamics of a single lyric poem. Unfortunately, these great "collecteds" of the 1930s never really gained any recognition as distinctive works in and of themselves, and even as simple compilations of Williams's work they were superseded in the early 1950s by collections that never really accomplished what they could have as the final word on the greater bulk of his poetic canon. Marred by production blunders and perhaps even by third-party interference, both *The Collected Later Poems* and *The Collected Earlier Poems* tend only to obscure with thematic tendentiousness and lyrical redundancy the large scale structural articulation in poetic and lyrical development that was so evidenced by the earlier collections.

By 1950 and 1951, however, such issues were probably less important in Williams's mind. Finally completed and generally acclaimed, *Paterson* had come to serve as the basis upon which Williams's reputation would be built. Yet surely it ought not to eclipse the equally impressive accomplishment of Williams's first two "composit" poetic works. Indeed, although the texts of Williams's individual poems have now taken definitive shape in the scholarly editions of Litz and MacGowan, it is hard not to wish as well for a simple reprint of those other works—Williams's original and long lost attempts "to gain 'profundity.'"

Appendix A: Tables of Contents for the Volumes of Collected Poetry

COLLECTED POEMS, 1921–1931 (1934)

POEMS

All the Fancy Things
Hemmed in Males
Brilliant Sad Sun
Young Sycamore
It Is a Living Coral
To
This Florida: 1924
The Sun Bathers
The Cod Head
Struggle of Wings
Down-town
Winter
The Waitress
The Bull
In the 'Sconset Bus
Poem (As the cat)
The Jungle
The Lily
On Gay Wallpaper
The Source
Nantucket
The Winds
Lines on Receiving The Dial's Award
The Red Lily
The Attic Which Is Desire:
Interests of 1926
This Is Just to Say
Birds and Flowers
Full Moon

DELLA PRIMAVERA TRANSPORTATA AL MORALE

April (the beginning)
The Trees

The Birds' Companion
The Sea-Elephant
Rain
The House
Death (He's dead)
The Botticellian Trees

SPRING AND ALL

Flight to the City
At the Faucet of June
The Pot of Primroses
The Eyeglasses
Composition
Light Becomes Darkness
The Red Wheelbarrow
Rapid Transit
The Avenue of Poplars
At the Ball Game
Rigamarole
To Elsie

THE DESCENT OF WINTER

9/29   (My bed is narrow)
10/10 (Monday)
10/21 (the orange flames)
10/22 (and hunters still return)
10/28 (On hot days)
10/29 (The justice of poverty)
11/1   (The moon, the dried weeds)
11/2   A Morning Imagination of Russia
11/28 (I make very little money)

THE FLOWER

The Flower (A petal, colorless and without form)

(PRIOR TO 1921)

At Night
To Mark Anthony in Heaven
Transitional
Man in a Room
A Coronal
Sicilian Emigrant's Song

The Revelation
Portrait of a Lady

THE COMPLETE COLLECTED POEMS, 1906–1938 (1938)

THE TEMPERS, 1913

Peace on Earth
Postlude
First Praise
Homage
The Fool's Song
From "The Birth of Venus," Song
Immortal
Mezzo Forte
Crude Lament
An After Song
The Ordeal
Appeal
Fire Spirit
The Death of Franco of Cologne: His Prophecy of Beethoven
Portent
Ad Infinitum
Contemporania
Hic Jacet
Con Brio
To Wish Myself Courage

TRANSITIONAL, 1915

To Mark Anthony in Heaven
Transitional
Sicilian Emigrant's Song
Le Médecin Malgré Lui
Man in a Room
A Coronal
The Revelation
Portrait of a Lady

AL QUE QUIERE (TO HIM WHO WANTS IT), 1917

Sub Terra
Spring Song (Having died)
The Shadow
Pastoral (When I was younger)
Chickory and Daisies
Metric Figure (There is a bird in the poplars)

Pastoral (The little sparrows)
Love Song (Daisies are broken)
Gulls
Winter Sunset
In Harbor
Tract
Apology
Promenade
Libertad! Igualidad! Fraternidad!
Summer Song (Wanderer moon)
The Young Housewife
Love Song (Sweep the house clean)
Dawn
Hero
Drink
El Hombre
Winter Quiet
A Prelude
Trees
Canthara
M.B.
Good Night
Keller Gegen Dom
Danse Russe
Mujer
Portrait of a Woman in Bed
Virtue
Smell!
The Ogre
Sympathetic Portrait of a Child
Riposte
K. McB.
The Old Men
Spring Strains
A Portrait in Greys
Pastoral (If I say have heard voices)
January Morning
To a Solitary Disciple
Ballet
Dedication for a Plot of Ground
Conquest
Love Song (I lie here thinking of you)

SOUR GRAPES, 1921

The Late Singer
A Celebration
April (If you had come away with me)

At Night
Berket and the Stars
A Goodnight
Overture to a Dance of Locomotives
The Desolate Field
Willow Poem
Approach of Winter
January
Blizzard
Complaint
To Waken an Old Lady
Winter Trees
The Dark Day
Spring Storm
Thursday
The Cold Night
Time the Hangman
To a Friend
The Gentle Man
The Soughing Wind
Spring
Play
Lines
The Poor (By constantly tormenting them)
Complete Destruction
Memory of April
Daisy
Primrose
Queen-Ann's-Lace
Great Mullen
Epitaph
Waiting
The Hunter
Arrival
To a Friend Concerning Several Ladies
The Disputants
The Birds
Youth and Beauty
The Thinker
The Tulip Bed
Spouts
The Widow's Lament in Springtime
The Nightingales
Blueflags
Light Hearted William
The Lonely Street

Portrait of the Author
The Great Figure

SPRING AND ALL, 1923

(Poems numbered but titleless; original—and later restored—
titles in brackets.)

   I. [Spring and All]
   II. [The Pot of Flowers]
   III. [The Farmer]
   IV. [Flight to the City]
   V. [The Black Winds]
   VI. [To Have Done Nothing]
   VII. [The Rose (The rose is obsolete)]
   VIII. [At the Faucet of June]
   IX. [Young Love]
   X. [The Eyeglasses]
   XI. [The Right of Way]
   XII. [Composition]
   XIII. [The Agonized Spires]
   XIV. [Death the Barber]
   XV. [Light Becomes Darkness]
   XVI. [To an Old Jaundiced Woman]
   XVII. [Shoot it Jimmy!]
   XVIII. [To Elsie]
   XIX. [Horned Purple]
   XX. [The Sea]
   XXI. [The Red Wheelbarrow]
   XXII. [Quietness]
   XXIII. [Rigamarole]
   XXIV. [The Avenue of Poplars]
   XXV. [Rapid Transit]
   XXVI. [At the Ball Game]
   XXVII. [The Hermaphroditic Telephones]
   XXVIII. [The Wildflower]

THE DESCENT OF WINTER

9/29 (My bed is narrow)
9/30 (There are no perfect waves)
10/9 (and there's a little blackboy)
10/10 (Monday)
10/21 (In the dead weeds a rubbish heap)
10/22 (that brilliant field)
10/28 (On hot days)
10/28 (in this strong light)

10/29 (The justice of poverty)
10/30 (To freight cars in the air)
11/1 (The moon, the dried weeds)
11/2 (Dahlias)
11/2 A Morning Imagination of Russia
11/7 (We must listen. Before)
11/8 (O river of my heart polluted)
11/10 (The shell flowers)
11/20 (Even idiots grow old)
11/22 (and hunters still return)
11/28 (I make really very little money)
12/15 (What an image in the face of Almighty God is she)

COLLECTED POEMS, 1934

All the Fancy Things
Hemmed in Males
Brilliant Sad Sun
It Is a Living Coral
To
This Florida: 1924
Young Sycamore
The Cod Head
New England
Winter
The Bull
In the 'Sconset Bus
Poem (As the cat)
Sluggishly
The Jungle
Between Walls
The Lily
On Gay Wallpaper
The Source
Nantucket
The Winds
Lines on Receiving The Dial's Award
The Red Lily
Interests of 1926
The Attic Which Is Desire:
This is Just to Say
Birds and Flowers
Della Primavera Transportata al Morale
    1. April (the beginning—or)
    2. Full Moon
    3. The Trees
    4. The Wind Increases

5. The Birds' Companion
6. The House
7. The Sea-Elephant
8. Rain
9. Death (He's dead)
10. The Botticellian Trees

AN EARLY MARTYR, 1935

An Early Martyr
Flowers by the Sea
The Locust Tree in Flower
Item
View of a Lake
To a Mexican Pig-Bank
To a Poor Old Woman
Late for Summer Weather
Proletarian Portrait
Tree and Sky
The Raper from Passenack
Invocation and Conclusion
The Yachts
Hymn to Love Ended
Sunday
The Catholic Bells
The Dead Baby
A Poem for Norman Macleod

ADAM & EVE AND THE CITY, 1936

To a Wood Thrush
Fine Work with Pitch and Copper
Young Woman at a Window (She sits with)
The Rose (First the warmth, variability)
A Chinese Toy
La Belle Dame de Tous les Jours
Adam
Eve
St. Francis Einstein of the Daffodils
The Death of See
To an Elder Poet
Perpetuum Mobile: The City
Cancion

RECENT VERSE (1938)

Classic Scene
Autumn

The Term
Weasel Snout
Advent of Today
The Sun
A Bastard Peace
The Poor (It's the anarchy of poverty)
To a Dead Journalist
Africa
Lovely Ad
The Defective Record
Middle
Unnamed: From "Paterson"
   1. Your lovely hands.
   2. When I saw
   3. I bought a new
   4. Better than flowers
At the Bar: From "Paterson"
Graph for Action: From "Paterson"
Breakfast: From "Paterson"
To Greet a Letter-Carrier: From "Paterson"
These

LONGER POEMS, 1910–1938

Morning
An Elegy for D. H. Lawrence
Paterson: Episode 17
The Crimson Cyclamen
The Waitress
The Flower (A petal, colorless and without form)
Romance Modern
Paterson
March
The Wanderer

THE COLLECTED EARLIER POEMS (1951)

THE WANDERER

The Wanderer

THE TEMPERS

Peace on Earth
Postlude
First Praise

Homage
The Fool's Song
From "The Birth of Venus," Song
Immortal
Mezzo Forte
Crude Lament
An After Song
The Ordeal
Appeal
Fire Spirit
The Death of Franco of Cologne: His Prophecy of Beethoven
Portent
Ad Infinitum
Contemporania
Hic Jacet
Con Brio
To Wish Myself Courage
To Mark Anthony in Heaven
Transitional
Sicilian Emigrant's Song
Le Médecin Malgré Lui
Man in a Room
A Coronal
The Revelation
Portrait of a Lady

MARCH—HISTORY

March

HISTORY

History

DELLA PRIMAVERA TRASPORTATA AL MORALE

Della Primavera Trasportata al Morale (April/the beginning—or)
Full Moon
The Trees
The Wind Increases
The Bird's Companion
The House
The Sea-Elephant
Rain

Death (He's dead)
The Botticellian Trees

AN EARLY MARTYR

An Early Martyr
Flowers by the Sea
Wild Orchard
Winter
The Flowers Alone
Sea-Trout and Butterfish
A Portrait of the Times
The Locust Tree in Flower (Among/of/green)
The Locust Tree in Flower (Among/the/leaves/bright)
Item
View of a Lake
To a Mexican Pig-Bank
To a Poor Old Woman
Late for Summer Weather
Proletarian Portrait
Tree and Sky
The Raper from Passenack
Invocation and Conclusion
The Yachts
Hymn to Love Ended
Sunday
The Catholic Bells
The Dead Baby
A Poem for Norman Macleod

AL QUE QUIERE (TO HIM WHO WANTS IT)

Sub Terra
Spring Song (Having died)
The Shadow
Pastoral (When I was younger)
Chicory and Daisies
Metric Figure (There is a bird in the poplars)
Pastoral (The little sparrows)
Love Song (Daisies are broken)
Gulls
Winter Sunset
In Harbor
Tract
Apology
Promenade
Libertad! Igualidad! Fraternidad!

Summer Song (Wanderer moon)
The Young Housewife
Love Song (Sweep the house clean)
Dawn
Hero
Drink
El Hombre
Winter Quiet
A Prelude
Trees
Canthara
M. B.
Good Night
Keller Gegen Dom
Danse Russe
Mujer
Portrait of a Woman in Bed
Virtue
Smell!
The Ogre
Sympathetic Portrait of a Child
Riposte
K. McB.
The Old Men
Spring Strains
A Portrait in Greys
Pastoral (If I say I have heard voices)
January Morning
To a Solitary Disciple
Ballet
Dedication for a Plot of Ground
Conquest
First Version, 1915
Love Song (I lie here thinking of you)

FISH—ROMANCE MODERNE

Fish
Romance Moderne

SOUR GRAPES

The Late Singer
A Celebration
April (If you had come away with me)
At Night
Berket and the Stars

A Goodnight
Overture to a Dance of Locomotives
The Desolate Field
Willow Poem
Approach of Winter
January
Blizzard
Complaint
To Waken an Old Lady
Winter Trees
The Dark Day
Spring Storm
Thursday
The Cold Night
To Be Closely Written On A Small Piece Of Paper Which Folded
    Into A Tight Lozenge Will Fit Any Girl's Locket
The Young Laundryman
Time the Hangman
To a Friend
The Gentle Man
The Soughing Wind
Spring
Play
Lines
The Poor (By constantly tormenting them)
Complete Destruction
Memory of April
Daisy
Primrose
Queen-Anne's-Lace
Great Mullen
Epitaph
Waiting
The Hunter
Arrival
To a Friend Concerning Several Ladies
The Disputants
The Birds
Youth and Beauty
The Thinker
The Tulip Bed
Spouts
The Widow's Lament in Springtime
The Nightingales
Blueflags
Lighthearted William

The Lonely Street
Portrait of the Author
The Great Figure

PATERSON—THE FLOWER

Paterson (Before the grass is out the people are out)
The Flower (A petal, colorless)

SPRING AND ALL

       I. Spring and All
      II. The Pot of Flowers
     III. The Farmer
     IV. Flight to the City
      V. The Black Winds
     VI. To Have Done Nothing
    VII. The Rose (The rose is obsolete)
   VIII. At the Faucet of June
     IX. Young Love
      X. The Eyeglasses
     XI. The Right of Way
    XII. Composition
   XIII. The Agonized Spires
   XIV. Death the Barber
    XV. Light Becomes Darkness
   XVI. To an Old Jaundiced Woman
  XVII. Shoot it Jimmy!
 XVIII. To Elsie
   XIX. Horned Purple
    XX. The Sea
   XXI. The Red Wheelbarrow
  XXII. Quietness
 XXIII. Rigamarole
 XXIV. The Avenue of Poplars
  XXV. Rapid Transit
 XXVI. At the Ball Game
XXVII. The Hermaphroditic Telephones
XXVIII. The Wildflower

STRUGGLE OF WINGS

Struggle of Wings

THE DESCENT OF WINTER

9/29 (My bed is narrow)
9/30 (There are no perfect waves)

10/9   (and there's a little blackboy)
10/10 (Monday)
10/21 (In the dead weeds a rubbish heap)
10/22 (that brilliant field)
10/28 (On hot days)
10/28 (In this strong light)
10/29 (The justice of poverty)
10/30 (To freight cars in the air)
11/1   (The moon, the dried weeds)
11/2   (Dahlias)
11/2   A Morning Imagination of Russia
11/7   (We must listen)
11/8   (O river of my heart polluted)
11/10 (The shell flowers)
11/20 (Even idiots grow old)
11/22 (and hunters still return)
11/28 (I make really very little money)
12/15 (What an image in the face of Almighty God is she)

IMPROMPTU: THE SUCKERS

Impromptu: The Suckers

COLLECTED POEMS 1934

All the Fancy Things
Hemmed-in Males
Brilliant Sad Sun
It Is a Living Coral
To
This Florida: 1924
Young Sycamore
The Cod Head
New England
The Bull
In the 'Sconset Bus
Poem (as the cat)
Sluggishly
The Jungle
Between Walls
The Lily
On Gay Wallpaper
The Source
Nantucket
The Winds
Lines on Receiving The Dial's Award: 1927
The Red Lily

Interests of 1926
The Attic Which Is Desire
This Is Just to Say
Birds and Flowers

AN ELEGY FOR D. H. LAWRENCE

An Elegy for D. H. Lawrence

ADAM AND EVE AND THE CITY

To a Wood Thrush
Fine Work with Pitch and Copper
Young Woman at a Window (She sits with)
The Rose (First the warmth)
A Chinese Toy
La Belle Dame de Tous les Jours
Adam
Eve
St. Francis Einstein of the Daffodils
The Death of See
To an Elder Poet
Perpetuum Mobile: The City
Cancion

MORNING—THE CRIMSON CYCLAMEN

Morning
The Crimson Cyclamen

RECENT VERSE 1938

Classic Scene
Autumn
The Term
Weasel Snout
Advent of Today
The Sun
A Bastard Peace
The Poor (It's the anarchy of poverty)
To a Dead Journalist
Africa
Lovely Ad
4th of July
The Defective Record
Middle
A Fond Farewell

The Unknown
Porous
The Petunia
The Graceful Bastion
The Return to Work
The Deceptrices
Detail (Her milk don't seem to)
Detail (Doc, I bin lookin' for you)
Detail (Hey!)
Detail (I had a misfortune in September)
Their Most Prized Possession—
Unnamed: From "Paterson"
At the Bar
Graph for Action
Breakfast
To Greet a Letter-Carrier
These

THE DRUNKARD

The Drunkard
Paterson: Episode 17
The Last Words of My English Grandmother
The Waitress
A Marriage Ritual
The Swaggering Gait
The Predicter of Famine
Illegitimate Things
The Province
The Brilliance
Fragment (My God, Bill, what have you done)
The Yellow Season
Mistrust of the Beloved
Passer Domesticus
The United States
The Sun Bathers
Sparrow Among Dry Leaves
The Men
Song (The black-winged gull)
Descent
You Have Pissed Your Life
Moon and Stars
The Girl (The wall, as I watched, came neck-high)

Simplex Sigilum Veri
The Phoenix and the Tortoise

The Collected Later Poems (1950)

THE WEDGE

Author's Introduction
A Sort of Song
Catastrophic Birth
Paterson: The Falls
The Dance (In Brueghel's great picture, The Kermess)
Writer's Prologue to a Play in Verse
Burning the Christmas Greens
In Chains
In Sisterly Fashion
The World Narrowed to a Point
The Observer
A Flowing River
The Hounded Lovers
The Cure
To All Gentleness
Three Sonnets
St. Valentine
The Young Cat and the Chrysanthemums
The Poem
[The Rose (The stillness of the rose)]*
Rumba! Rumba!
A Plea for Mercy
Figueras Castle
Eternity
The Hard Listener
The Controversy
Perfection
These Purists
Fertile
A Vision of Labor: 1931
The Last Turn
The End of the Parade
The A, B & C of It
The Thoughtful Lover

---

*Accidentally omitted and later gathered together into a new final section entitled "The Rose."

The Aftermath
[The Semblables]*
The Storm
The Forgotten City
The Yellow Chimney
The Bare Tree
Raleigh Was Right
The Monstrous Marriage
Sometimes It Turns Dry and the Leaves Fall before They are
    Beautiful
Sparrows Among Dry Leaves
Prelude to Winter
Silence
Another Year
A Cold Front
Against the Sky
An Address
The Gentle Rejoinder
To Ford Maddox Ford in Heaven

THE CLOUDS

Aigeltinger
Franklin Square
Labrador
The Apparition
The Light Shall Not Enter
A Woman in Front of a Bank
The Night Rider
Chanson
The Birdsong
[The Visit]*
[The Quality of Heaven]*
To a Lovely Old Bitch
The Bitter World of Spring
Lament
A History of Love
When Structure Fails Rhyme Attempts to Come to the Rescue
Education a Failure
The Banner Bearer
The Goat
Two Deliberate Exercises
    1. Lesson from a Pupil Recital
    2. Voyages
The Mirrors
His Daughter
Design for November

The Manoeuvre
The Horse
Hard Times
Dish of Fruit
The Motor-Barge
Russia
The Act
The Savage Beast
The Well Disciplined Bargeman
Raindrops on a Briar
[Ol' Bunk's Band]*
Suzanne
Navajo
Graph
The Testament of Perpetual Change
The Flower (This too I love)
For a Low Voice
The Words Lying Idle
[Lear]*
Picture of a Nude in a Machine Shop
[The Brilliance]*
[A Unison]*
[The Semblables]*
The Hurricane
[The Province]*
The Mind's Games
The Stylist
Note to Music: Brahm's 1st Piano Concerto
[The Injury]*
The Red-Wing Blackbird
A Place (Any Place) to Transcend All Places
The Old House
The Thing
The Mind Hesitant
Tragic Detail
Philomena Andronico
The Woodpecker
The Girl (with big breasts)
The Clouds

BALLAD OF FAITH

Ballad of Faith
And Who Do You Think "They" Are?
The Non-Entity
Childe Harold to the Round Tower Came

Io Baccho!
The Centenarian

ALL THAT IS PERFECT IN WOMAN

All That Is Perfect in Woman

THE RAT

The Rat
Jingle
Every Day
The Unfrocked Priest
For G. B. S., Old
The Words, the Words, the Words
Lustspiel
April Is the Saddest Month
To Be Hungry Is to Be Great
The Complexity
A Note
Drugstore Library
The R R Bums

CHORAL: THE PINK CHURCH

Choral: the Pink Church

INCOGNITO

Incognito
3 A.M. / The Girl with the Honey Colored Hair
A Crystal Maze
New Mexico
Seafarer
The Sound of Waves
Venus over the Desert
Mists over the River
"I Would Not Change for Thine"
The Pause
Mama
The Love Charm
Approach to a City
Song (If I)
A Rosebush in an Unlikely Garden
The Lion
An Eternity

The Three Graces
The Horse Show

THE BIRTH OF VENUS

The Birth of Venus

14 NEW POEMS (1950)

May 1st Tomorrow
Après le Bain
Spring Is Here Again, Sir
The Hard Core of Beauty
Tolstoy
Cuchulain
Twelve Line Poem
Nun's Song
Turkey in the Straw
Another Old Woman
Wide Awake, Full of Love
Song (Pluck the florets from)
Song (Russia! Russia! you might say)
Convivo

TWO PENDANTS: FOR THE EARS

The Lesson
Two Pendants: for the Ears
To Close

THE ROSE

The Rose (The stillness of the rose)
The Visit
Ol' Bunk's Band
Lear
A Unison
The Quality of Heaven
The Province
The Injury
The Brilliance
The Semblables

Appendix B: Short-Title Tables of the Sectional Arrangements for the Volumes of Collected Poetry

The Earlier Sections

Order of previous publication*	in *CP 21–31*	in *CCP 06–38*	in *CEP*
Tempers	Poems	The Tempers	The Wanderer
Al Que Quiere	Primavera	Transitional*	The Tempers
Sour Grapes	Spring & All	Al Que Quiere	March•History
Spring & All	Descent of Winter	Sour Grapes	Primavera
Descent of Winter	The Flower	Spring & All	Early Martyr
Primavera (w. Flower)	Prior To 1921	Descent of Winter	Al Que Quiere
		Poems/Primavera	Fish•Romance
Early Martyr		Early Martyr	Sour Grapes
Adam & Eve		Adam & Eve	Paterson•Flower
		Recent Verse	Spring & All
		Longer Poems	Struggle of Wings
			Descent of Winter
			Impromptu
			Poems
			Elegy for DHL
			Adam & Eve
			Morning•Cyclamen
			Recent Verse
			The Drunkard
*For sections published separately as either volumes or distinct sequences		*Retitled version of Prior to 1921	

312

The Later Sections

Order of previous publication*	CLP
The Wedge	The Wedge
The Clouds	The Clouds
The Pink Church	Ballad of Faith
Fourteen New Poems	All Perfect in Woman
	The Rat
	Pink Church*
	Incognito
	Birth of Venus
	Fourteen New Poems
	Two Pendants
	The Rose†
*For sections published separately as either volumes or distinct sequences	*Title poem only
	†Added after first printing

Appendix C: Short-Title, Number-Referenced Tables of Successive Arrangements for Individual Sections

The Tempers

The Tempers (1913) ⟶	in *CP 21–31* ⟶	in *CCP 06–38* ⟶	in *CEP*
1. Peace on Earth	Not	1.	Same as in *CCP 06–38*
2. Postlude	included	2.	except for addition of
3. First Praise		3.	poems from previously
4. Homage		4.	separate "Transitional"
5. The Fool's Song		5.	
6. From "Venus," Song		6.	
7. Immortal		7.	
8. Mezzo Forte		8.	
9. An After Song		10.	
10. Crude Lament		9.	
11. The Ordeal		11.	
12. The Death of Franco		New. Appeal	
13. Portent		New. Fire Spirit	
14. Con Brio		12.	
15. Ad Infinitum		13.	
16. Translations		15.	
17. Hic Jacet		18.	
18. Contemporania		17.	
19. To Wish Myself		14.	
		19.	
			New. To Mark Anthony
			New. Transitional
			New. Sicilian
			New. Le Medecin
			New. Man in a Room
			New. A Coronal
			New. The Revelation
			New. Portrait

Note: Only sections comprising more than just one or two longer poems, and published as distinct sequences or groups more than once, are included in this appendix.

Prior to 1921/Transitional, 1915

1913 to 1923 ⟶	"Prior to" in CP 21–31 ⟶	"Transitional" in CCP 06–38 ⟶	in CEP
Poems published individually in separate periodicals	1. At Night 2. Mark Anthony 3. Transitional 4. Man in a Room 5. A Coronal 6. Sicilian 7. Revelation 8. Portrait	2. 3. 6. New. Le Medecin 4. 5. 7. 8.	Same as in CCP 06–38 except untitled and appended to "The Tempers"

Al Que Quiere

Al Que Quiere (1917) ⟶	in CP 21–31 ⟶	in CCP 06–38 ⟶	in CEP
1. Sub Terra	Not	1.	Same as in CCP 06–38
2. Pastoral (When)	included	New. Spring Song	except for addition of a
3. Chickory		New. The Shadow	single poem
4. Metric Figure		2.	
5. Woman Walking		3.	
6. Gulls		4.	
7. Appeal		11.	
8. In Harbor		12.	
9. Winter Sunset		6.	
10. Apology		9.	
11. Pastoral (The little)		8.	
12. Love Song (Daisies)		14.	
13. M. B.		10.	
14. Tract		15.	
15. Promenade		18.	
16. El Hombre		21.	
17. Hero		New. Housewife	
18. Libertad!		22.	
19. Canthara		27.	
20. Mujer		17.	
21. Summer Song		New. Drink	
22. Love Song (Sweep)		16.	
23. Foreign		26.	
24. A Prelude		24.	
25. History		43.	
26. Winter Ouiet		19.	
27. Dawn		13.	
28. Good Night		28.	
29. Dance Russe		34.	
30. Portrait Woman Bed		29.	
31. Virtue		20.	
32. Conquest		30.	
33. Portrait Man Heart		31.	

Al Que Quiere *(continued)*

Al Que Quiere (1917)→ in *CP 21–31*→in *CCP 06–38* ————————→ in *CEP*			
34. Keller Gegen Dom	35.		
35. Smell!	38.		
36. Ballet	37.		
37. Sympathetic Portrait	39.		
38. The Ogre	50.		
39. Riposte	40.		
40. The Old Men	42.		
41. Pastoral (If I say)	44.		
42. Spring Strains	41.		
43. Trees	47.		
44. Portrait in Greys	48.		
45. Invitation	36.		
46. Divertimento	49.		
47. January Morning	32.	32.	
48. To Solitary Disciple	51.	New. First Version: 1915	
49. Dedication for Plot		51.	
50. K. McB.			
51. Love Song (I lie)			
52. The Wanderer			

7: to "Tempers"   7: to "Tempers"
52: to "Longer Poems" 25: to "March•History"
                       52: to "Wanderer"

5:		5:	
23:		23:	
25:	omitted	33:	omitted
33:		45:	
45:		46:	
46:			

Sour Grapes

Sour Grapes (1921) → in *CP 21–31*→in *CCP 06–38* ————————→ in *CEP*			
1. The Late Singer	Not	1.	Same as in *CCP 06–38*
2. March	included	4.	except for addition of two
3. Berket & Stars		5.	poems
4. A Celebration		New. At Night	
5. April (If you)		3.	
6. A Goodnight		6.	
7. Overture to Dance		7.	
8. Romance Moderne		9.	
9. Desolate Field		10.	
10. Willow Poem		11.	
11. Approach of Winter		12.	
12. January		13.	
13. Blizzard		16.	

Sour Grapes *(continued)*

Sour Grapes (1921) → in CP 21–31 → in CCP 06–38 →			in CEP
14. To Waken Old Lady	14.		
15. Winter Trees	15.		
16. Complaint	21.		
17. The Cold Night	18.		
18. Spring Storm	20.		
19. The Delicasies	17.	17.	
20. Thursday	22.	New. To Be Closely	
21. The Dark Day	23.	New. Young Laundryman	
22. Time & Hangman	24.	22.	
23. To a Friend (Well,)	25.		
24. The Gentle Man	26.		
25. The Soughing Wind	27.		
26. Spring	28.		
27. Play	29.		
28. Lines	30.		
29. The Poor (tormenting)	31.		
30. Complete Destruction	33.		
31. Memory of April	34.		
32. Epitaph	35.		
33. Daisy	36.		
34. Primrose	32.		
35. Queen-Ann's-Lace	37.		
36. Great Mullen	38.		
37. Waiting	39.		
38. The Hunter	40.		
39. Arrival	43.		
40. Concerning Ladies	45.		
41. Youth and Beauty	41.		
42. The Thinker	42.		
43. The Disputants	44.		
44. The Tulip Bed	47.		
45. The Birds	49.		
46. The Nightingales	46.		
47. Spouts	48.		
48. Blueflags	50.		
49. Widow's Lament	52.		
50. Light Hearted Will	51.		
51. Portrait of Author	53.		
52. The Lonely Street			
53. The Great Figure			
	2, 8: to "Longer Poems"	2: to "March•History"	
		8: to "Fish•Romance Mod"	
	19: omitted	19: omitted	

Spring and All

Spring & All (1923) → in CP 21–31 → in CCP 06–38 → in CEP			
1. Spring & All	4.	Same as in	Same as in CCP
2. Pot of Flowers	8.	original except	06–38
3. The Farmer	2.	for one trans-	
4. Flight to City	10.	position and	
5. Black Winds	12.	one addition	
6. To Have Done	15.		
7. The Rose (obsolete)	22.		
8. At the Faucet	25.		
9. Young Love	24.		
10. The Eyeglasses	26.		
11. Right of Way	23.		
12. Composition	18.		
13. Agonized Spires			
14. Death the Barber			
15. Light Becomes Dark			
16. To Jaundiced Woman			
17. Shoot it Jimmy!			
18. To Elsie			
19. Horned Purple			
20. The Sea			
21. Quietness		22.	
22. Red Wheelbarrow		21.	
23. Rigamarole			
24. Avenue Poplars			
25. Rapid Transit		26.	
26. At Ball Game		New. Hermaphroditic	
27. The Wildflower		27.	
	All others omitted		

Descent of Winter

"Descent of W" (1928) → in CP 21–31 → in CCP 06–38 → in CEP			
1. 9/27	2.	Same as in 1928	Same as in CCP 06–38
2. 9/29	5.	original except for	
3. 9/30	7.	omission of	
4. 10/9	31. 10/22*	opening poem and	
5. 10/10	12.	all prose	
6. 10/13*	15.		
7. 10/21	18.		
8. 10/22	20. Morning		
9. 10/23*	33.		
10. 10/27*			
11. 10/28*			
12. 10/28 (hot)			

Descent of Winter *(continued)*

"Descent of W" (1928) →	in *CP 21–31* →	in *CCP 06–38* →	in *CEP*
13. 10/28*			
14. 10/28 (strong)			
15. 10/29			
16. 10/30			
17. 11/1*			
18. 11/1			
19. 11/2 (Dahlias)			
20. 11/2 Morning			
21. 11/6*			
22. 11/7			
23. 11/8			
24. 11/8*			
25. 11/10			
26. 11/11*			
27. 11/13*			
28. 11/16*			
29. 11/13*			
30. 11/20			
31. 11/22			
32. 11/24*			
33. 11/28			
34. 12/2*			
35. 12/9*			
36. 12/15			
37. 12/18*			

| *prose | *originally dated 11/22 All other entries omitted | 1, 6, 9, 10, 11: 13, 17, 21, 24, 26, 27: 28, 29, 32, 34, 35, 37: ⎫⎬⎭ omitted | |

Della Primavera Transportata al Morale

no title (1930) →	"Primavera" in *CP 21–31* →	"Della . . ."* in *CCP 06–38* →	"Della . . ."
1. Della . . .*	1. April	1.	Same as in *CCP*
2. The Trees	2.	New. Full Moon	*06–38* except that it
3. The Wind Increases	New. Bird's Comp.	2.	is treated again as a
4. Sea-Elephant	4.	3.	separate section
5. Rain	5.	2'. (Birds' Comp)	
6. The Flower	New. House	5'. (House)	
	New. Death	4.	
	New. Botticellian	5.	
		5". (Death)	
		5'''. (Botticellian)	
*An incomplete version of "April"	6: to "The Flower" 3: omitted	*Appended to "Collected Poems, 1934"	

Collected Poems, 1934

1922–1932 →	"Poems" in *CP 21–31* →	"CP, 1934" in *CCP 06–38* →	in *CEP*
Poems either	1. All Fancy	1.	Same as in CCP 06–38
not pub-	2. Hemmed in	2.	except that Primavera
lished before	3. Brilliant Sad	3.	sequence is separate
or published	4. Young Sycamore	5.	again
individually	5. Living Coral	6.	
in separate	6. To	7.	
periodicals	7. Florida: 1924	4.	
	8. Sun Bathers	9.	
	9. Cod Head	11.	
	10. Struggle Wings	12.	
	11. Down-town	14.	
	12. Winter	15.	
	13. Waitress	16.	
	14. The Bull	New. Sluggishly	
	15. 'Sconset Bus	17.	
	16. Poem (As cat)	New. Walls	
	17. The Jungle	18.	
	18. The Lilly	19.	
	19. Gay Wallpaper	20.	
	20. Source, I–II	21.	
	21. Nantucket	22.	
	22. The Winds	23.	
	23. Receiving Dial	24.	
	24. Red Lily	26.	
	25. Attic Desire	25.	
	26. Interests 1926	27.	
	27. Just to Say	28.	
	28. Birds/Flowers	New. Della	
	29. Full Moon	Primavera*	

*entire sequence   8, 13: to "The Drunkard"
  appended   10: to "Struggle of Wings"
13: to "Longer Poems"   12: to "Early Martyr"
11: retitled New England
8, 10: omitted

An Early Martyr

An Early Martyr (1935) ⟶	in *CCP 06–38* ⟶	in *CEP*
1. An Early Martyr	1.	1.
2. Flowers by the Sea	2.	2.
3. Item	4.	New. Wild Orchard
4. Locust Tree (green)	3.	New. Winter
5. View of a Lake	5.	New. Flowers Alone
6. To Mexican Pig Bank	6.	New. Sea-Trout
7. To Poor Old Woman	7.	New. Portrait of Times
8. Sadness of the Sea	9.	4.
9. Late for Summer Weather	10.	New. Locust Tree (leaves)
10. Proletarian Portrait	11.	3.
11. Tree and Sky	12.	5.
12. Raper from Passenack	13.	6.
13. Invocation & Conclusion	16.	7.
14. Genesis	18.	9.
15. Solstice	20.	10.
16. The Yachts	21.	11.
17. Young Romance	24.	12.
18. Hymn to Love Ended	29.	13.
19. Elegy to D. H. Lawrence		16.
20. Sunday		18.
21. Catholic Bells		20.
22. The Auto Ride		21.
23. Simplex Sigilium Veri		24.
24. The Dead Baby		29.
25. The Immemorial Winds		
26. The Farmer		
27. The Wind Increases		
28. To Be Hungry		
29. A Poem for Norman Macleod		
30. You Have Pissed Your Life		

19: to "Longer Poems"	
17, 22: } reassigned to	
25, 26: } "Spring & All"	19: to "An Elegy for DHL"
27: reassigned to	17, 22: } reassigned to
"Primavera"	25, 26: } "Spring & All"
8, 14, 15: } omitted	27: reassigned to "Primavera"
23, 28, 30: }	23, 30: to "The Drunkard"
	28: to "The Rat" in CLP
	8, 14, 15: omitted

Adam and Eve & City

Adam and Eve & The City (1936) →	in CCP 06–38 →	in CEP
1. To a Wood Thrush	1.	Same as in CCP 06-38
2. Fine Work in Pitch	2.	
3. Young Woman at Window	3.	
4. The Rose (First the)	4.	
5. La Belle Dame de Tous	6.	
6. A Chinese Toy	5.	
7. Adam	7.	
8. Eve	8.	
9. St. Francis Einstein	9.	
10. Death of See	10.	
11. To Elder Poet	11.	
12. From "Patterson" [sic]	19.	
13. Crimson Cyclamen	14.	
Translations:		
14. Cancion		
15. Stir your fields		
16. The dawn is upon		
17. Tears that still		
18. Poplars of the		
19. Perpetuum Mobile: City		
	12: to "Recent Verse"	12: to "Recent Verse"
	13: to "Longer Poems"	13: to "Morning-Crimson"
	15, 16: 17, 18: } omitted	15, 16: 17, 18: } omitted

Recent Verse, 1938

1935 to 1938 →	in CCP 06–38 →	in CEP
Poems either not published before or published individually in separate periodicals	1. Classic Scene	1.
	2. Autumn	2.
	3. The Term	3.
	4. Weasel Snout	4.
	5. Advent of Today	5.
	6. The Sun	6.
	7. Bastard Peace	7.
	8. The Poor (anarchy)	8.
	9. To Dead Journalist	9.
	10. Africa	10.
	11. Lovely Ad	11.
	12. Defective Record	New. 4th of July
	13. Middle	12.
	14. Unnamed	13.
	15. At the Bar	New. Fond Farewell
	16. Graph for Action	New. The Unknown

Recent Verse, 1938 *(continued)*

1935 to 1938 ⟶	in *CCP 06–38* ⟶	in *CEP*
	17. Breakfast	New. Porous
	18. To Greet a Letter	New. Petunia
	19. These	New. Graceful Bastion
		New. Return to Work
		New. Deceptrices
		New. Detail (Her milk)
		New. Detail (Doc, I)
		New. Detail (Hey!)
		New. Detail (I had a)
		New. Their Most Prized
		14.
		15.
		16.
		17.
		18.
		19.

The Wedge

The Wedge (1944) ⟶	in *CLP*
1. Author's Intro.*	1.
2. Sort of Song	2.
3. Catastrophic Birth	3.
4. Paterson: The Falls	4.
5. The Dance (In Brueghel's)	5.
6. Writer's Prologue to Play	6.
7. Burning the Christmas	7.
8. In Chains	8.
9. In Sisterly Fashion	9.
10. The World Narrowed	10.
11. The Observer	11.
12. A Flowing River	12.
13. The Hounded Lovers	13.
14. The Cure	14.
15. To All Gentleness	15.
16. Three Sonets [*sic*]	16.
17. The Poem (It's all in)	New. St. Valentine
18. The Rose (The stillness)	New. Young Cat and the Chrysanthemums
19. Rumba! Rumba!	17.
20. A Plea for Mercy	19.
21. Figueras Castle	20.
22. Eternity	21.
23. The Hard Listener	22.
24. The Controversy	23.
25. Perfection	24.
26. These Purists	25.

The Wedge *(continued)*

The Wedge (1944) *(continued)* ⟶ in *CLP*	
27. A Vision of Labor: 1931	26.
28. The Last Turn	New. Fertile
29. The End of the Parade	27.
30. The A, B, & C of It	28.
31. The Thoughtful Lover	29.
32. The Aftermath	30.
33. The Semblables	31.
34. The Storm	32.
35. The Forgotten City	34.
36. The Yellow Chimney	35.
37. The Bare Tree	36.
38. Raleigh Was Right	37.
39. The Monstrous Marriage	38.
40. Sometimes It Turns Dry	39.
41. Sparrows Among Dry Leaves	40.
42. Prelude to Winter	41.
43. Silence	42.
44. Another Year	43.
45. The Clouds, I	44.
46. A Cold Front	46.
47. Against the Sky	47.
48. An Address	48.
49. The Gentle Negress (Wandering)	New. The Gentle Rejoinder
50. To Ford in Heaven	50.
*prose	18, 33: omitted accidentally and subsequently assigned to "The Rose"
	45: to "The Clouds"
	49: omitted

The Clouds

The Clouds (1948) ———————▶	in *CLP*

1. Aigeltinger
2. Franklin Square
3. Labrador
4. The Apparition
5. The Light Shall Not Enter
6. A Woman in Front of a Bank
7. The Night Rider
8. Chanson
9. The Birdsong
10. The Visit
11. The Quality of Heaven
12. To a Lovely Old Bitch
13. The Bitter World of Spring
14. Lament
15. A History of Love
16. Mists over the River
17. When Structure Fails
18. Education a Failure
19. The Banner Bearer
20. The Goat
21. Two Deliberate Exercises
    1. Lesson from a Pupil Recital
    2. Voyages
22. The Mirrors
23. His Daughter
24. Design for November
25. The Manoeuvre
26. The Horse
27. Hard Time
28. Dish of Fruit
29. The Motor Barge
30. Russia
31. The Act
32. The Savage Beast
33. The Well Disciplined Bargeman
34. Raindrops on a Briar
35. Ol' Bunk's Band
36. Suzanne
37. Navajo
38. Graph
39. The Testament of Perpetual Change
40. The Flower (This too I love)
41. For a Low Voice
42. The Words Lying Idle
43. Lear
44. Picture of a Nude
45. The Brilliance

Same as in 1948 original except for the accidental omissions noted below, the transfer of poem #16, and the addition of two new poems

The Clouds *(continued)*

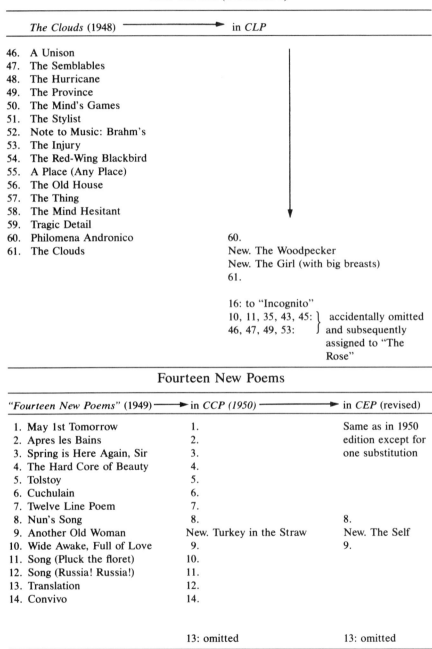

The Clouds (1948) ──────►	in *CLP*
46. A Unison	
47. The Semblables	
48. The Hurricane	
49. The Province	
50. The Mind's Games	
51. The Stylist	
52. Note to Music: Brahm's	
53. The Injury	
54. The Red-Wing Blackbird	
55. A Place (Any Place)	
56. The Old House	
57. The Thing	
58. The Mind Hesitant	
59. Tragic Detail	
60. Philomena Andronico	60.
61. The Clouds	New. The Woodpecker
	New. The Girl (with big breasts)
	61.
	16: to "Incognito"
	10, 11, 35, 43, 45: ⎫ accidentally omitted
	46, 47, 49, 53: ⎬ and subsequently
	assigned to "The
	Rose"

Fourteen New Poems

"Fourteen New Poems" (1949) ──►	in *CCP (1950)* ──────────►	in *CEP* (revised)
1. May 1st Tomorrow	1.	Same as in 1950
2. Apres les Bains	2.	edition except for
3. Spring is Here Again, Sir	3.	one substitution
4. The Hard Core of Beauty	4.	
5. Tolstoy	5.	
6. Cuchulain	6.	
7. Twelve Line Poem	7.	
8. Nun's Song	8.	8.
9. Another Old Woman	New. Turkey in the Straw	New. The Self
10. Wide Awake, Full of Love	9.	9.
11. Song (Pluck the floret)	10.	
12. Song (Russia! Russia!)	11.	
13. Translation	12.	
14. Convivo	14.	
	13: omitted	13: omitted

Notes

Preface

1. See Abrams, pages 258–63, for a further summary of these ideas and trends. And observe just how anti-aesthetic they are by considering the impossibility of applying them to the non-linguistic art of music.

Introduction: "To Gain 'Profundity'"

1. The particulars of Zukofsky's contributions to *Collected Poems 1921–1931* are impossible to determine. As Robert Bertholf, curator of the Poetry Collection at SUNY-Buffalo, has indicated after an exhaustive search of every likely archive, no manuscripts of any kind for the volume appear to have survived. Even more frustrating, according to Bertholf, is the Williams-Zukofsky correspondence: every time it approaches mentioning substantive editorial matters, it breaks off with a resolution to work things out in person over lunch in New York City.

2. See pages 233–68 of *The Modern Poetic Sequence* for a similarly evaluative treatment of *Paterson.*

Chapter 1. A New Textual Order, a New Lyrical Focus

1. A briefer version of "Primavera," one which concluded with "The Flower," was originally published in the 1930 *Imagist Anthology.* The "Spring and All" section comprises a selection and rearrangement of poems from Williams's 1923 prose/poetry volume of the same name. And "The Descent of Winter" is a similarly abridged version of the prose/poetry work as it originally appeared in a 1928 number of *The Exile.*

2. It should be noted here that throughout this study, passages cited from Williams's poetry will in general be taken from the actual volumes under study rather than from the recently published two-volume *Collected Poems of William Carlos Williams,* edited by A. Walton Litz and Christopher MacGowan. There are two primary reasons for doing so. First, in the interest of establishing truly final texts, Litz and MacGowan have sometimes incorporated changes in poems that Williams made only after the publication of a particular collection. Thus, for instance, texts from the 1951 *Collected Earlier Poems* supersede variant texts from the 1938 *Complete Collected Poems.* Second, it is only in *Collected Earlier Poems* that there is a significant corruption of the texts, and none of the poems from that volume cited herein is among those affected. Thus, with just a few exceptions (noted as they occur), Williams's real texts are allowed to stand in place of Litz's and MacGowan's ideal texts.

Mention should also be made here of the great extent to which passages from Williams's poetry will be cited. For all practical purposes, the first two of the four volumes under study here are very close to rare books, and the last two, while they are usually available in libraries, are nonetheless out of print. Moreover, the new Litz and MacGowan edition has entirely dismantled all of these volumes of collected poetry in favor of organizing Williams's work according to the contents of the separate individual volumes those collections incorporated; doing so renders the edition a useful companion to this study only with an inordinate amount of page-turning and cross-referencing to their title indexes and to their appended tables of contents for the original collections.

Thus, it is important to include throughout this discussion sizable extracts of the original texts themselves. These generous quotations substantively reconstruct the arrangements of the now dismantled books, and along with reference to the original tables of contents for the collections (included with this present study as Appendix A), they make it possible to corroborate the lyrical sense I make of the arrangements; the lyrical continuities I describe might otherwise appear as just so much perhaps unfounded assertion. Furthermore, such a discreditable appearance is a particular danger for any study of large-scale *poetic* continuity, for unlike most prose fiction, poetic sequences rarely employ the superficial linkage of plot, which allows at least the basic page-to-page continuity of a narrative work to be taken simply as self-evident. The proof for continuity in poetic sequences, in other words, needs (at least in our current time) to be far more explicit than it need be for other more familiar genres.

Finally, if the net effect of including so much illustrative quotation is to return the reader more fully to the actual body of Williams's poetry, then this study will have succeeded in at least one objective of good (non-deconstructive) scholarship: it will have avoided being autotelic.

3. In American English, "Sycamore" designates primarily *Platanus occidentalis* of eastern North America, not the Eurasian maple or the Middle Eastern fig.

4. Reference to the volume's table of contents, included in Appendix A of this study, will clarify the organization of the summary here.

CHAPTER 2. THE OPENING SEQUENCE OF "POEMS"

1. The word "brickish" is not in fact used in *Collected Poems 1921–1931*; "brackish" is. "Brickish" is used in both the original published version that appeared in the June, 1923, issue of *Contact* and the 1951 *Collected Earlier Poems.* Thus, "brackish" would appear to have been a proofreading error, and since "brickish" clearly makes better sense of the poem's other figures, I have adopted it here.

Another phrase from the original final versions—"lonely cock atop" rather than "lonely atop"—is adopted as well in the following citation and for similar reasons: the omission of "cock" in the *Collected Poems 1921–1931* version could have easily been a simple proofreading error and its inclusion is more faithful to the poem's sexual character.

CHAPTER 3. BROADENING THE SCOPE, EXTENDING THE FEELINGS: "PRIMAVERA," "SPRING AND ALL," AND "THE DESCENT OF WINTER"

1. The real title of the opening poem to "Primavera" is a confusing issue. The format of *Collected Poems 1921–1931*, which prints the titles of poems entirely in capitals, makes it appear that the opening poem is a *title* poem. It reads as follows:

Della PRIMAVERA Transportata al Morale
I.
April
the beginning—or . . .

The arrangement is especially strange since there would appear no reason to repeat the title of the entire section at all, the previous title page having already done so with a truncated version ("PRIMAVERA") of the full title given in the table of contents. The table of contents also lists "April" as the title of the first poem, and, as Litz and MacGowan point out (520–21), it is treated as such in all other printings of the poem. It would appear therefore that "April" is the title of the first poem, and that the anomalous "I." at the head of the poem designates not the first of a two-part poem but the first poem of the entire section. Indeed, there *is* no second part to the opening poem, and although none of the remaining poems in the section are numbered in this edition, they are so numbered in the other printings. "April," therefore, is adopted here as the actual title of the first poem. (Please note, incidentally, that within this study, "April" refers exclusively to this poem, while a briefer poem of the same title in "Sour Grapes" is always referenced to its own first line.)

   2. *Collected Poems 1921–1931* actually truncates the couplet to a single line: "to no end save—." But all other printings, including the original one of 1923, have the fuller version, which both preserves the otherwise uniform stanza format of the poem *and* makes for greater thematic clarity. Given that there is no real lyrical difference one way or another, the full version is included here as an expedient to the surrounding discussion. So too are the later lines "It/ lives" cited here as "It is beauty itself / that lives."

   3. The original and ultimately restored ending of the poem— "but aloof / as if from and truly from / another older world"— probably better accomplishes the closing effect here. Not only does the identification of the other "world" as an "older" one more clearly suggest a lost mythic age, but the suspension of the repeated "from" creates a greater sense of wonder at the spectacle of the hunters.

CHAPTER 4. RETRENCHING AMBITIONS, PACIFYING FEELINGS: "THE FLOWER" AND "(PRIOR TO 1921)"

   1. The omission of these poems from Williams's earlier volumes (*The Tempers, Al Que Quiere!,* and *Sour Grapes*) does not entirely explain their inclusion in *Collected Poems 1921–1931,* for many other poems of Williams's early period had suffered a similar fate, and they would have to await *The Complete Collected Poems 1906–1938* before seeing book publication. Moreover, each of the eight poems had originally appeared as entries in groups of their own, yet here they have been wrenched from those groups and assembled in a distinctly non-chronological order. Neither historically comprehensive nor representative, the new group locates its defining context only in all that has preceded it within *Collected Poems 1921–1931.*

CHAPTER 8. THE CRUDER COUNTERPARTS TO "LONGER POEMS": "THE TEMPERS," "TRANSITIONAL," AND "AL QUE QUIERE"

   1. Placed in the original volume just before rather than after "Crude Lament," "An After Song," with its sexual cast in the virile figure of Apollo, perhaps more

obviously complements the *theme* of cultural disjunction that is also at the heart of the sexually oriented "Immortal" and "Mezzo Forte." But placed as it is here after "Crude Lament," "An After Song" helps integrate with the section's earlier poems the "fire" poems that "Crude Lament" initiates.

CHAPTER 9. TOWARD A GREATER EQUIVALENCE WITH "LONGER POEMS": "SOUR GRAPES," "SPRING AND ALL," AND "THE DESCENT OF WINTER"

1. The poems of "Spring and All" are actually numbered rather than named in *The Complete Collected Poems 1906–1938*. Throughout this discussion, however, the titles assigned in the later *Collected Earlier Poems* are used in order to clarify reference.

2. To some extent, the lyrical reciprocity here is purely fortuitous since the "Spring and All" of *The Complete Collected Poems 1906–1938* is more of a *return* to the original arrangement of the 1923 *Spring and All* (sans the prose sections of course) rather than a revision of it. The later arrangement merely transposes two poems ("The Red Wheelbarrow" and "Quietness") and adds a single new poem ("The Hermaphroditic Telephones"). The essential return to the original arrangement also suggests just how specially tailored to the particular context of *Collected Poems 1921–1931* the radically shuffled and abbreviated 1934 "Spring and All" was.

3. Note in particular how in "11/2 (Dahlias—)" the pseudo parallelism of the second and seventh lines and the absence of capitalization effectively equate the lighter pastel colors of yellow and white with the chiaroscuro black and grey by suggesting a resumption of the question that declares itself in the sixth line.

CHAPTER 10. A BETTER RECORD THAN "LONGER POEMS:" "COLLECTED POEMS 1934," "AN EARLY MARTYR," "ADAM & EVE AND THE CITY," AND "RECENT VERSE"

1. In changing *An Early Martyr* for inclusion as a section in *The Complete Collected Poems 1906–1938,* Williams excised a great number of poems. Three poems--"The Sadness of the Sea," "Genesis," and "Solstice"—were presumably eliminated purely for a "lack of value," as Williams put it in his February 11, 1938, note to Laughlin, for they were to disappear from Williams's canon permanently thereafter. Another three—"Simplex Sigilum Veri," "To Be Hungry Is to Be Great," and "You Have Pissed Your Life"—were eliminated permanently from "An Early Martyr" but were assigned a few years later to new sections in either *The Collected Later Poems* or *The Collected Earlier Poems.* Most of the poems, however, were reassigned in *The Complete Collected Poems 1906–1938* to the two arrangements ("Spring and All" and "Della Primavera Transportata al Morale") from which they had originally been borrowed, no doubt in order to fatten the otherwise too slender 1935 volume.

In any event, although the excisions trimmed the bulk of the arrangement, they nonetheless left intact its essential lyrical and thematic movement, for all of the poems were either transitional pieces or, in some cases, even outright padding. "Young Romance" (an early title for "Young Love"), for instance— the brooding poem that conflates a cultural recrimination with a personal sexual regret in

"Spring and All"—was in 1935 placed quite transitionally right between the cultural denunciation of "The Yachts" and the aesthetic/sexual reconsideration of "Hymn to Love Ended." Similarly, "Auto Ride" (later entitled "The Right of Way") and "Simplex Sigilium Veri" settled the happy spirit of "The Catholic Bells" down into some incremental stages of aesthetic audacity—first in the proprietary rights a motorist feels in the passing beauty of a street scene, and second, in the even more proprietary evaluation of the aesthetic dimensions to some desk clutter. Both moments build to the bold aesthetic presumption over even human death in "The Dead Baby."

Four other poems followed "The Dead Baby" and brought its unnerving irreverence to a more assertive conclusion. "The Immemorial Wind" (later titled "The Black Winds") and "The Farmer" mixed some real ruthlessness with an explicitly self-justifying sense of aesthetic necessity. "The Wind Increases" and "To Be Hungry Is to Be Great" then translated the aesthetic vigor into a more genial sort of gusto, just before "A Poem for Norman Macleod" brought things to a fully friendly note. And finally, one last poem that originally followed the Macleod poem repeated and emphasized the sense of personal vindication in that poem, only perhaps more as a private score than as anything else. Opening and closing with chanted variations of Pound's nasty 1935 remark to Williams, "You Have Pissed Your Life" throws the taunt in the face of no doubt Pound himself (Mariani 371–72).

2. Recall especially the preoccupation with transience that laces both "Sour Grapes" and its counterpart longer poem, "The Crimson Cyclamen."

3. "Logged" both refers to an informational entry and recalls the aforementioned driftwood "washed / clean."

Chapter 11. "Much More to It Than I thought Would Be Involved": Some Problems With the Texts

1. Unfortunately, Hoagland herself, who died in February of 1984, has left no testimony on the matter. And the Williams-Hoagland correspondence for 1950 and 1951 (at the University of Virginia Library) is restricted primarily to travelogue letters and postcards sent by Williams during his various travels of those years.

2. Nearly all of October and November, for example, was spent lecturing at various colleges in Washington, Oregon, and California; December included radio and television interviews in New York (Mariani 622-29). Much of the New York activity was due to the promotional efforts of Williams's new Random House editor, David McDowell, and Williams in fact complained to him in late November about the hectic schedule (Mariani 635). Yet he had also complained as early as 15 September to Edward Dahlberg about being "timeless, without time, busted: too much on my tail, I am being driven to the wall or into a run rather by demands upon my energy" (quoted in Mariani 834).

3. Williams was actually rather forthright with Laughlin in this matter. As early as 9 February 1950, for example, he wrote Laughlin that by assigning his prose to Random House, "I shall gain a free hand to try myself out, to see just how far I can go with sales. For I tell you and you yourself confess it in the first paragraph of your letter, I'll never make any real cash through you. Nor have I wanted it until now when either I must go on with Medicine or somehow or other get me more income by writing, one or the other" (Williams and Laughlin 180).

4. Indeed, in Williams's 3 February letter to Laughlin outlining his publishing priorities, he lists the new collected poems as last and appears to acknowledge the impetus for it as more Laughlin's than his own: "Fifth should come the half century *Complete Collected Poems*—of which you have spoken or I should not now mention it; a big job" (Williams and Laughlin 177).

5. On 26 February, Williams also sent to Laughlin something like a tentative table of contents for "the Collected." "Here is what I want," he wrote in the accompanying letter; "give me your reaction. The 'books' of the Collected may be somewhat differently divided in the final version but this gives the setup in fair detail" (Letters). Unfortunately, the proposed scheme has not survived so it is impossible to say exactly what Williams's "hell of a good idea" was.

6. On 9 March, for instance, Williams announced to Laughlin his final decision to go with Random House for his prose, and then he immediately sought to soften the bad news by holding out as bait the flagrantly premature promise that he was "getting the new, two volume Collected in order for Kaplan [Laughlin's book designer]; it'll take me a few weeks to do it" (Williams and Laughlin 186).

7. Both this typescript as well as the final typescript for *The Collected Earlier Poems* were just recently discovered (April 1987) by Christopher MacGowan in the New Directions archives at Harvard's Houghton Library. They are catalogued respectively as 53M-179F and 51M-188F. The initial typescripts for the two volumes have also been preserved at Yale's Beinecke Library, but they only shed a confusing light on the formative stages of the final versions. Unlike 53M-179F, for instance, Za 47 (the initial typescript at Yale) lacks both consistent pagination throughout and section headings for everything but "The Clouds" and the single poem "All That Is Perfect in Woman"; the script is simply a folder of carbons for individual poems, one after another. And though the arrangement of those poems differs in a number of places from the final version, it is impossible to tell whether the differences are the product of some initial intent on Williams's (or Hoagland's) part or of some careless shuffling of the pages that has occured somewhere between Williams's attic and the last set of many hands that have since examined the script.

Both Za 49, identified by New Directions and Yale as the original typescript for *The Collected Earlier Poems,* and Za 50, identified as a carbon of an intermediate revision for the same book, differ from 51M-188F in that they match neither the contents nor the organization of the finally printed version but those of *The Complete Collected Poems 1906–1938* instead. It is possible that the typescripts have been misidentified, but if they have not been (as Litz and MacGowan believe), then it is clear that the final version of *The Collected Earlier Poems* was indeed a very late development, introduced perhaps only as late as Williams's actual post-stroke period. In this case, it would appear even stranger that Williams would have undertaken such a radical revision of his work during such an adverse time.

8. The final version actually omitted both the etceteras and Laughlin's alternative in favor of the lead poems' titles alone.

9. The numerals were ultimately blue-pencilled by a copy editor, who also added superscripts of A and B for some of the numerals that were repeated. The superscripts are included here to clarify the sequence that the page numbers otherwise confirm.

CHAPTER 12. *THE COLLECTED EARLIER POEMS:* AN INFERIOR SUCCESSOR

1. Williams also made additions to "Sour Grapes" and "Recent Verse," but they too were lyrically inconsequential. Two poems in "Sour Grapes"—"To Be Closely Written . . ." and "The Young Laundryman"—simply extend the movement of pity for some defeated fellows of an aroused life that formerly began with "Time the Hangman." And the addition of thirteen poems (including a bunch repeatedly entitled "Detail") just before the Paterson fragments in "Recent Verse" amount to little more than a simple multiplication of those fragments.

CHAPTER 13. *THE COLLECTED LATER POEMS:* A MORE UNIFORM RECORD

1. Compare, on the other hand, these lines from a similar "fire" poem in "The Tempers," the opening section of *The Complete Collected Poems 1906–1938:*

> The Ordeal
>
> O crimson salamander,
> Because of love's whim
>   sacred!
>
> Swim
>   the winding flame
>   Predestined to disman him
> And bring our fellow home to us again.

These lines are impossibly awkward and pretentious. The syntax and structure here seems driven by some convention of apostrophe rather than by genuine passion; by some inexplicable need to rhyme "whim" with "Swim" and even the ultimately insipid "him"; and by some affected taste for the pseudoheroic alliteration of "sacred" and "swim." The entire poem might be considered a classical problem in the "objective correlative:" the vehicle of feeling is simply insufficient to the ostensible strength of that feeling. It is a problem that demands a solution.

2. One hesitates to refer unequivocally to these units as sequences precisely because of their general lack of affective dynamics.

CONCLUSION: "THEY SAY I'M NOT PROFOUND"

1. See Donald Davie's nasty review of Litz and MacGowan's *Collected Poems of William Carlos Williams, Volume I,* in which Davie equates ranking the unprofound Williams as a major poet with a veritable threat to all standards of literature and culture. Then see M. L. Rosenthal's 1966 introduction to *The William Carlos Williams Reader* ("William Carlos Williams: More Than Meets The Eye") for an answer to Davie's diatribe.

Works Cited

Abrams, M. H. *A Glossary of Literary Terms*. 6th ed. New York: Harcourt Brace, 1993.

Arnold, Matthew. *Essays in Criticism: First and Second Series*. 1865, 1888. New York: Dutton, 1964.

Burke, Kenneth. "Heaven's First Law." *Dial* 72 (February, 1922): 197–200.

Bertholf, Robert. Telephone interview. 5 January 1994.

Bunting, Basil. "Carlos Williams's Recent Poetry." *Westminster Magazine* 23.2 (Summer 1934): 149–54.

Davie, Donald. "A Demurral." *The New Republic* 20 April 1987: 34–39.

Deutsch, Babette. "Heirs of the Imaginsts." *New York Herald Tribune Book Review* 1 April 1934: 16.

Kreymborg, Alfred. *Our Singing Strength: An Outline of American Poetry 1620–1930*. New York: Coward-McCann, 1929. New York: Tudor, 1934.

Laughlin, James. Letter to the author. 14 March 1985.

Mariani, Paul. *William Carlos Williams: The Poet and His Critics*. Chicago: American Library Assoc., 1975.

———. *William Carlos Williams: A New World Naked*. New York: McGraw, 1981.

Moore, Marianne. "'Things Others Never Notice.'" *Poetry* 44 (1934): 103–6.

Munson, Gorham. *Destinations: A Canvass of American Literature Since 1990*. New York: J. H. Sears, 1928. NY: AMS Press, 1970.

Pound, Ezra. "Dr. Williams' Position." *Dial* 85 (November, 1928): 395–404.

———. Rev. of *The Tempers*. *New Freewoman* 1 (1 December 1913): 227.

Rosenthal, M. L. and Sally Gall. *The Modern Poetic Sequence: The Genius of Modern Poetry*. New York: Oxford, 1983.

Wallace, Emily Mitchell. *A Bibliography of William Carlos Williams*. Middletown, Conn.: Wesleyan University Press, 1968.

Whittemore, Reed. *William Carlos Williams: Poet from Jersey*. Boston: Houghton, 1975.

Williams, Florence. Letter to James Laughlin. Za/Williams/295. Beinecke Library, Yale University.

Williams, William Carlos. *The Autobiography of William Carlos Williams*. 1951. New York: New Directions, 1967.

———. *The Collected Earlier Poems*. New York: New Directions, 1951.

———. *The Collected Earlier Poems*. Initial ts. Za 49. Beinecke Library, Yale University.

———. *The Collected Earlier Poems*. Carbon of initial ts. Za 50. Beinecke Library, Yale University.

——. *The Collected Earlier Poems*. Final ts. 51M-188F. Houghton Library, Harvard University.

——. *The Collected Later Poems*. New York: New Directions, 1950. Rev. ed. 1963.

——. *The Collected Later Poems*. Initial ts. Za 47. Beinecke Library, Yale University.

——. *The Collected Later Poems*. Final ts. 53M-179F. Houghton Library, Harvard University.

——. *Collected Poems 1921–1931*. New York: Objectivist Press, 1934.

——. *The Collected Poems of William Carlos Williams*. Volume 1: 1909–1939. Edited by A. Walton Litz and Christopher MacGowan. Volume 2: 1939–1962. Edited by Christopher MacGowan. New York: New Directions, 1986–88.

——. *The Complete Collected Poems of William Carlos Williams 1906–1938*. Norfolk, Conn.: New Directions, 1938.

——. *Imaginations*. Edited by Webster Schott. New York: New Directions, 1970.

——. Interview by Stanley Kohler. *Paris Review* 8 (Summer-Fall 1964): 111–51.

——. *I Wanted to Write a Poem*. With Edith Heal. Boston: Beacon, 1958.

——. Letters to James Laughlin and/or New Directions. Za/Williams/295. Beinecke Library, Yale University.

——. *Selected Essays*. New York: Random House, 1954.

——. *The Selected Letters of William Carlos Williams*. Edited by John C. Thirlwall. New York: McDowell, 1957.

Williams, William Carlos, and Kitty Hoagland. Correspondence. Accession 566. University of Virginia Library.

Williams, William Carlos, and James Laughlin. *Selected Letters*. Edited by Hugh Witemeyer. New York: Norton, 1989.

Winters, Yvor. "Poetry of Feeling." *Kenyon Review* 1.1 (Winter 1939): 104–7.

Index of Works by William Carlos Williams

General Index